PLUCKED *from the* BURNING

EMBRACING GOD'S PURPOSE

KEN & BETH
SPILGER

12001 Aragon Ave.
St. Louis, MO 63138
or kspilger@gmail.com
www.reflectionspublications.com
or pluckedfromtheburning.com

ISBN 978-0-9961441-0-0

Second Edition - 2017

All Scripture quotations are taken from the King James Version.

Printed in the United States of America

Dedication

To our children and grandchildren.

We love you all very much
and want you to live
in the great love
that comes
from our Heavenly Father.

"O God, thou hast taught me from my youth: and hitherto have I declared thy wondrous works. [18]Now also when I am old and grayheaded, O God, forsake me not; until I have shewed thy strength unto this generation, and thy power to every one that is to come."

~ Psalm 71: 17-18

Acknowledgments

Over the years, a multitude of folks have come alongside us. How can we ever truly express the deep gratitude in our hearts for their help as we walked through this difficult experience?

Thank you to the medical staff at St. John's Mercy Medical Center and Christian Hospital Northeast who compassionately and professionally cared for Ken's needs.

Thank you to our family, church family, neighbors, and friends who encouraged and helped us during that dark time of our life.

Thank you to all who have encouraged us to write this book.

Thank you to…

… those who have said to us over the years, "You've got to put your story in a book."

…our church family who has released us, encouraged us, prayed for us, and cheered us on to the finish line. Some have reminded us of stories they hoped would be included in the book.

… our children who have encouraged us by reading, critiquing, and sending us off to do our writing in a quiet place away from home. They have taken on some of our responsibilities to free us to write. They have reminded us of stories they've heard all these years and have supported our efforts in every way.

…our extended family who encouraged us and prayed daily for the completion of this book.

…the widows of the plane crash casualties who have

reminded us continually that this book is important to write and is long overdue.

Our hearts are also deeply grateful for all who came alongside us in this difficult task of writing. We had no idea what we were getting into! These, as well, have made our job easier and have cheered us on to the finish line.

Thank you to …

…our editors, Linda Stubblefield and Rachel Miller, who have asked the hard questions, made our feeble efforts at writing into a polished product, encouraged us along the way, and helped us in ways too numerous to mention.

… our graphic design artist, Nick Burns, who has used his God given talents to produce a beautiful cover— better than anything we could have imagined.

…our proofreaders, Debbie Guimon, Mildred Brush, and Lena Case, who have carefully polished the book.

…our "ghost readers" who read one of our later edits, giving us invaluable information for accuracy, tact, and readability.

…Bill Swinea and Jack Gray who helped us express a pilot's point of view.

…Naomi Walsh and Faith Hemingway who gave us invaluable medical advice, helping us express medical terms in layman's language.

Prologue

Beth looked out the front window of the living room and watched the sheets of rain slamming against the large plate glass window racing downward to the sill. The small plane carrying Ken and three other pastors was soon to leave Kansas City and fly home. She could tell the raging storm was not abating. *Can a small plane handle a storm of this intensity?* The ringing of the phone brought her back to reality. Ken was calling with a message that the flight would be delayed as they waited for the storm to pass through St. Louis.

Later...Ken looked out the window of the four passenger Grumman Tiger and spotted the runway lights of the Spirit of St. Louis Airport. Noticing a discussion taking place between the pilot and another pastor, he asked, "Is everything all right?"

"*It's a miracle* anyone survived — I've never seen an airplane so devastated." That is how one official "reacted to a light-plane crash that killed three area Baptist ministers and seriously injured another during an attempted landing early Wednesday... The Rev. Kenneth P. Spilger...was reported in serious but stable condition Thursday at the burn unit of St. John's Mercy Medical Center."

– *St. Louis Globe-Democrat*
September 18, 1980
used by permission

Table of Contents

Preface 13
Foreword by Gary Zimmerman 15

Ken & Beth ~ Embraced God's Purpose

Chapter 1 | Seeking God's Purpose 21
Chapter 2 | Snatched from the Fire 27
Chapter 3 | The Waiting Room 33
Chapter 4 | Communication 41
Chapter 5 | Damage 51
Chapter 6 | Healing 57
Chapter 7 | Home 67
Chapter 8 | Desire for God's Purpose 75

Fellowship

Chapter 9 | Salvation 91
Chapter 10 | Surrender 101
Chapter 11 | Priorities 115

Strength

Chapter 12 | Challenge 129
Chapter 13 | Exchanged Life 139
Chapter 14 | Waiting on the Lord 155

Trust

Chapter 15 - Prayer....171
Chapter 16 - Scripture....183
Chapter 17 - Focus....197

Ministry

Chapter 18 - Comfort....215
Chapter 19 - Love....229

The Widows ~ Embraced God's Purpose

Elaine Spurgeon Caskey (the pilot's wife)....241
Carolyn Lombard....249
Ruth Thompson Atkinson....257

Our Children ~ Embraced God's Purpose

Anna Spilger Huckabee....265
Esther Spilger....267
Naomi Spilger Walsh....269
Paul Spilger....271
Jonathan Spilger....273
Stephen Spilger....275
Joanna Spilger....277

Epilogue....279

Appendices

Appendix A — Glossary....283
Appendix B — Burn Information....287
Appendix C — Sequence of Events....289
Appendix D — Surgery Notes....295
Appendix E — Biographical Sketch....303

Preface

The short television news clip began with the plane crash and followed the progress of my lengthy hospital stay. Moments from the first sermon I preached after those months of recovery were captured. The camera followed as I descended the platform and walked slowly and stiffly to the back of the church. In those final seconds, the reporter did not speak. Instead, he allowed the chorus of a song our congregation had sung that morning to accompany me:

"This is my story, this is my song,
"Praising my Savior all the day long;
"This is my story, this is my song,
"Praising my Savior all the day long."

The words of *Blessed Assurance* captured the heart of his news clip: God was writing a story in my life, in my family, and in our church members. This single chapter of the overall story was an important one that would change the course of our lives and write His purpose for our service on our hearts. And as the song said, it was a story in which we could praise Him.

After years of prodding from friends and relatives, God impressed upon me that I was not being a good steward with the testimony He had given me. So my wife, Beth, and I began the writing process. Nearly 35 years after that horrific plane crash of which I am the sole survivor, we have now documented God's faithful work in us through the crash.

The book you hold in your hands details the struggles of our family's journey to embrace God's purpose for our life and ministry. We share how God worked to reveal our selfishness and to give us the desire to live in fellowship with Him, to exchange our weakness for His strength, and to trust in Him alone.

Foreword

by Gary Zimmerman

Gary & Artis Zimmerman

My friend, Pastor Ken Spilger, asked me to write a few words to be used as a foreword to his book *Plucked From the Burning*. During the time of his recovery from the crash, he entrusted me to serve as interim pastor, which I gladly accepted and served for many months. We had both graduated from Tennessee Temple Schools, and by the time of the accident, we were already on our paths in service to the Lord. Ken was a pastor, and I was a missionary working with the Jewish community in St. Louis.

This book, *Plucked From the Burning*, is for all who ask the questions: "How may I serve the Lord with a pure heart, knowing He is pleased with me?" and "What went wrong?" when suffering comes to our lives? We are not alone or sinful when we ask these questions. John the Baptist asked these same questions many years ago. By the time he met Jesus and pronounced Him to be *"the Lamb of God, which taketh away the sin of the world,"* (John 1:29) he had worked out the first question by serving the Lord with a pure heart. His service brought the second question to the main issue in his life:

"What went wrong?" He was serving with the King of all things, Jesus, and NOW he was in prison ready to have his head chopped off. "What went wrong?"

He sent two of his disciples to Jesus and asked, "*Art thou he that should come or should we look for another?*" (Luke 7:19) After Jesus answered his question, He added the following words: "*For I say unto you, Among those that are born of women there is not a greater prophet than John the Baptist: but he that is least in the kingdom of God is greater than he.*" (Luke 7:28)

My friend, Ken Spilger, did the right thing by praying and asking God to help him serve God in a way that was pleasing to Him and to do whatever was needed to make changes in his life. Only four hours later he found himself falling from the sky in a small airplane and crashing through the trees. In amazement, like in a slow-motion dream, fuel sprayed throughout the passenger cabin, and then the plane cut through electric wires which set the fuel ablaze.

When a disaster hits, it usually affects all within striking distance, such as the family. The book also reveals how Ken's wife, Beth, coped with the sudden changes not only in her husband's life but also in her personal walk with the Lord.

The tragedy which happened that rainy night did not grow bitterness. Rather, the heartbreak grew a fruitful and joyous life of many years in ministry and seven wonderful children who all love and serve the Lord.

As a personal final note, I would like to share how God used this time when we were helping the Spilgers and their ministry at Grace Baptist to also deepen and further our ministry to the Jewish community. God not only had His purpose for the Spilgers' ministry, but He had His purpose for ours as well. During the many months of serving as interim pastor to Grace Baptist Church, my wife and I questioned the Lord about *how this was doing Jewish mission work*, the ministry to which the Lord had called us.

Over the months, an elderly Jewish man named Mr. Weintraub started coming to Grace Baptist Church. He had accepted Jesus as his Savior but, for fear of his family, had never followed the Lord in believer's baptism. During the months at Grace Baptist Church, Mr. Weintraub grew in the Lord and helped us a great deal in our ministry to the Jews. He started Bible studies for me to teach in the Jewish retirement center where he lived, advised me on the Passover Seders we conducted, and finally was baptized. The Lord gave us many blessings as a result of Ken's prayer to the Lord.

God's purpose for us is to receive His grace in order to reflect His glory as we resemble His Son.

Ken & Beth

Embraced God's Purpose

"How precious also are thy thoughts unto me, O God! how great is the sum of them! [18]If I should count them, they are more in number than the sand: when I awake, I am still with thee."

– Psalm 139:17-18

CHAPTER ONE

Seeking God's Purpose

Beth and I were growing discouraged. We had experienced no doubts concerning God's call three years earlier for us to serve as the pastor and pastor's wife at Grace Baptist Church in St. Louis, Missouri. We confidently dreamed of reaching a multitude of souls for Christ, building the biggest church in the Midwest, and founding a ministry that would reach beyond the shores of the United States. We anticipated seeing these dreams fulfilled in a few short years. After all, we had been taught to have these goals in Bible college. However, though we had spent untold hours on outreach and other ministry responsibilities, these dreams and goals had not come to fruition.

Our focus moved from our personal walk with God to our performance for God. In our pride, we were disappointed in ourselves because we had focused on pleasing man—ourselves and others—not God. God had extended His grace to us, so we could please Him in the ministry; however, we couldn't receive His grace because we were offended with Him (Matthew 11:6). The ministry had grown—but not like we wanted and had dreamed it would grow. In seeking the growth we desired, we became totally focused on our agenda rather than God's will. Without meaning to, we had placed growing our ministry in a more prominent place than knowing our Lord—simply stated, our ministry had become our god.

Prior to our coming to St. Louis, the church leaders at Grace had expressed their desire that I, as their pastor, would give myself to prayer and the ministry of the Word. Still, my greater focus was on my personal ambitions. Rather than following the Biblical principles of delegation and simply giving leadership in tasks our people were willing and able to do, we were trying to do it all ourselves. This additional pressure left little time for prayer and ministry of the Word, let alone my personal walk with the Lord, my family, and God's real ministry for us. We were beginning to pay a price for skewed commitments and responsibilities. Beth found it increasingly difficult to keep up with her home responsibilities, to care for our children, and to find sufficient time to help me grow my ministry. In our exhaustion, the two of us had frequent conflicts.

At this low point in my life, God began to work. In the early spring of 1979, Beth and I attended a conference which addressed the Biblical aspects of marriage and family. As a result of that conference, we had begun to rebuild the special relationship we had enjoyed at the beginning of our marriage. I had also begun to reconcile with our children and to rebuild my relationship with them. However, none of these positives changed the fact that I was still deeply discouraged in my ministry ambitions.

In September of 1980, Beth and I made plans to attend a pastors conference in Kansas City. We had originally planned to drive together to the conference, leaving our two girls at home with a trusted missionary friend. As the time of our departure drew closer, needs within our family caused us to change our plans. Since we both strongly felt this conference would be a time of encouragement and possibly a needed boost from my discouragement, we began to look for another way for me to travel to the conference. When an area pastor unexpectedly called saying that room was available in a four-seater plane, we felt God had indeed provided a way for me to attend the conference and for Beth to remain home to care for our daughters' needs.

After spending a wonderful evening with my family Monday night, I left very early Tuesday morning, September 16, 1980, to meet three pastors I had never met. I left my car at the church pastored by Russell Spurgeon, our pilot. From there Pastor Spurgeon, Pastor Don Lombard, and I drove to Lambert Airport to pick up the rental plane—a single-engine Grumman Tiger. We then flew to Washington, Missouri, to pick up our final passenger, Pastor Lawrence Thompson. Our plans were for all of us to fly back to the Spirit of St. Louis Airport in west St. Louis County later that night.

A Grumman Tiger, the type of plane in which the pastors were flying

If you have ever flown in a small plane, you know the cabin is noisy. Because of that noise, I only had limited conversations with my fellow passengers. I remember one in particular when I yelled to Russ Spurgeon, "Are you related to Charles?"

"Yes," he replied.

"Do you believe the Bible like he did?"

He looked back smiling and said, "Almost." We all chuckled.

The flight to Kansas City was uneventful. We arrived at the convention center in time to find our places and get settled for the conference. My traveling companions went their way, and I went mine.

Many of my pastor friends were at that conference, but I kept to myself that day. My pride did not want them to sense my discouragement, nor to know I was harboring thoughts of giving up. So I sat in the back away from everyone I knew.

The conference went as expected, but my personal struggles were clouding my response to the speakers. I had learned the basics of surrendering myself to the Lord when I received Christ as my Saviour twelve years earlier, but surrendering was far from the forefront of my mind. As I listened to great speakers who sought to encourage and bolster the pastors attending, none of the messages I heard answered my heart's cry. At the end of the conference, the keynote speaker called for a prayer of dedication from all of the pastors attending. I had already prayed that prayer many times. So instead of praying the prayer he suggested, I expressed my heart's cry to God in a prayer that went something like this:

> *Lord, You know that I have made this commitment hundreds of times. I know something in my life is not right. I don't know what it is, so I ask You to deal with it and to do whatever You have to do to make whatever is wrong right.*

My prayer placed me right where the Lord wanted me. He once again had the pen after I surrendered to His being in charge of writing the book of my life. Because God heard the sincerity of my heart's cry, He would clarify His purpose for my life. He would answer my prayer and cause me to realize He wanted me—not my performance. He wanted to be my sufficiency. He didn't need me trying to impress Him with my abilities because apart from Him, I am nothing. He would also help me see that I had been wanting my Heavenly Father to conform to my plan instead of me conforming to His.

After my surrender, God had the freedom to begin shaping me through the fires of His refining. With my personal surrender in place, He would lead me, my wife, my family, and our church into a deeper surrender that would change us all as well as the direction of our ministry. What followed would challenge all of us and require us to be strong and very courageous, and to put away fear and depression. From the foundation of my surrender, God would deepen His message in us. Little did I know, I would soon learn more about surrender as God took me to a new level of commitment in my relationship with Him.

"Is not this a brand plucked out of the fire?"
– Zechariah 3:2

CHAPTER TWO

Snatched from the Fire

I *was eager* to return to St. Louis. As eager as I was to get home, I would have to wait. We had received word that a severe weather system was passing through St. Louis. Our pilot wanted to let the storm pass, so the four of us decided to delay our flight from Kansas City. Because of that unexpected delay, I was able to spend time with my nephew, Tim Jensen, who was attending Calvary Bible College in Kansas City. He drove me to the airport that night at 10:30, the time we had decided to leave. Thankfully, our delayed flight to St. Louis was uneventful. We had no issues with the weather and were glad we had waited.

Our airplane approached the Spirit of St. Louis Airport from the southwest over a high ridge along the bluffs that outline the Missouri River Valley. Because of the height of the ridge at the outer marker and the position of the airport, the pilot would make a descent to pattern landing altitude and then an abrupt left-hand turn to make his final approach for landing.

Although some rain and clouds still lingered, I looked down and saw the runway lights and looked up and saw stars. As I sat in that airplane, I was unaware of a storm outside. I could hear the mumble of voices as Russell Spurgeon and Don Lombard talked.

"Is everything all right?" I hollered over the rumbling noise of the small aircraft. The two men glanced back at me and nodded.

Assured they felt everything was fine, I checked my seatbelt, settled back into my seat, and prepared for the landing—fully expecting within the next few minutes to be soon reunited with my family.

Instead, the deafening crash, the blinding flash of lights, and the bone-jarring collision seemed like some indistinct nightmare. How could I know that our plane had struck the tallest tree on top of the ridge along Wild Horse Creek Road? The impact had created a sudden loss of airspeed and lift, forcing the plane to nosedive and hit the electrical utility wire running parallel to the edge of the road. Tree limbs tore open the plane's fuselage, causing the fuel line to split. Fuel sprayed everywhere, hitting me from left to right. As the plane struck the utility wire, the fuel ignited and the plane flipped, causing it to plunge into the wet, steep field. The plane's momentum sent it sliding down the sharp incline where it came to rest at the very tip of the v-shaped gully feeding into the sheer sides of the bluff's edge.

Wires are still spliced at the crash site.

By God's miraculous intervention, I had been ejected from that stricken plane before it reached the ground. The authorities believe I fell out of the plane when the tree limb opened up the fuselage. I surely would not have survived otherwise.

Even in my state of shock, I knew that somehow I had to get help for my three traveling companions.

The field is still very steep.

Though I have no memory of it, the investigators were certain I pulled the other men from the burning wreckage. I had no idea where I would go for help, but I knew they needed assistance. Because the field was so steep and the night so dark from the storm, I could not see the abrupt drop off on the side of the bluff where the plane had stopped. As I stumbled around, desperate to find my bearings, I fell 30 to 40 feet down the side of that steep bluff and landed on a small muddy shelf. Had I moved around much, I could have fallen farther down.

Remains of the stricken plane

A farmer heard what he thought was lightning striking a tree. When he saw fire down in the field, he called the fire department. As the firefighters worked to put out the blaze, they noticed another fire deeper in the field. One man was dispatched to make sure the second fire was extinguished. As he began to make the long trek down the steep slope, he tripped and almost fell over airplane parts. He immediately radioed for additional help after realizing they were dealing with more than fires caused by lightning strikes.

That firefighter had stumbled over the wreckage of our totally destroyed airplane. Parts of the aircraft were scattered the length of a city block down the width of the field to where the plane had finished burning at the edge of the ravine. There he found three men propped up against a large log and could hear a voice calling from somewhere.

"Someone help these men! They need help!"

My cries for help alerted the firefighter that a fourth person had been involved in the crash. He kept calling to me, asking me to answer until he found where I had fallen.

More of the plane wreckage

My first conscious memory of that night was the firefighter's yelling, "He's over here! He's over here!" He climbed down to where I was lying on the shelf where he did his best to assure me that help was coming until the paramedics arrived. Quite a few emergency workers were needed to get me out of the ravine. I was strapped into a specially designed stretcher for back support and carefully lifted from my muddy perch. I was carried out of the field, placed into an ambulance, and transported to an area hospital known to have one of the best burn centers in the world.

As we traveled in that ambulance, I knew without a doubt that God was answering the prayer I had prayed at the conference. I was also aware of the ease with which I breathed, and I had no doubt I would survive. The thought that I could die from the nightmare I had just survived never crossed my mind.

That stormy night changed lives, families, and ministries. Though medical workers tried to spare me from knowledge about the crash site, I knew my three traveling companions had unexpectedly finished their course. Each man's book was finished. Those of us left behind would be faced with difficult life questions. How would we survive the unbearable moments ahead of us? How could God use any of this for good? We were suddenly confronted with God's purpose for our life. Would we let fear and pride keep us from embracing it? Or would we humbly surrender our will to His and allow His grace to build a message in us that would glorify Him?

I never could have known when I prayed at the conference that within a few hours I would rapidly and unknowingly be approaching my death. When the plane crashed and I was still alive, I never doubted God was beginning a journey to show me what was wrong in my life and how to make the needed adjustments and corrections. My Heavenly Father stepped in and said to the evil one, "*The LORD rebuke thee, O Satan ... is not this a brand plucked out of the fire?*" (Zechariah 3:2) God spared me to meet and embrace a new challenge. He plucked me from the fires of death to be placed into the fires of His refining.[1]

---

[1] In context, this verse speaks of Israel's being brought out of the "fires" of the Babylonian captivity.

"In quietness and in confidence shall be your strength."

– Isaiah 30:15

CHAPTER THREE

The Waiting Room

I stood in my living room, watching sheets of rain pound against our large, plate-glass window. I knew Ken was discouraged, and I had prayed that the conference would be exactly what he needed. But now, as their scheduled departure time from Kansas City was drawing near and as I stood watching the storm, worry crept into my heart. Weather like this could mean trouble for a small plane.

"Please keep them safe," I prayed as flashes of lightning streaked across the sky.

The clamor of the phone broke into my reverie and pulled me away from the window.

"Hello."

"Is Ken home yet?" I heard the voice of my dad, Burton Brush, calling from his home in northeastern Nebraska. "I just wanted to check on you and Ken. When I saw the weather this evening, I was concerned for Ken's flight."

"Oh, Dad! I'm so worried! The weather here is horrible!" I knew my voice revealed my concern. "The wind is blowing so hard and with so much lightning, I'm not sure it's possible for a small plane to fly safely."

"God will protect him and watch over him," my dad reminded me. Though we didn't talk long, Dad's few words were comforting.

"I'll be praying," he promised as our call ended.

I returned to look out the window. As my two little girls played together, and a visiting missionary friend went about her own business, I simply watched the lightning illuminate the night sky and flash off of the deluge. The overwhelming uneasiness over the safety of my husband pervaded my heart. Again, the sound of the phone broke into my worried thoughts. I was relieved to hear Ken's voice.

"We're delaying our flight out of Kansas City because of the weather."

Instant relief flooded my soul. "Oh! I thought you might have left Kansas City by now."

"We want to wait until this front passes through St. Louis, so we now plan to leave around 10:30. I'll probably get home around 1:00 or 1:30."

"I'm so glad to know you're waiting! How was the conference?"

"Good. I'll tell you more when I get home. Go on to bed. Don't worry about me."

"Okay. I love you."

"I love you too."

Calling long distance was expensive, so we kept our call short. He simply wanted to let me know they were not taking any chances and to relieve my fear. It worked.

As the storm continued to howl, our phone continued to ring. Each call came from someone concerned about Ken's safety. Noel Foster, the chairman of our deacon board, was especially concerned. He shared that he and his wife had been prompted to pray for Ken that evening. Like the others who called, he was relieved to hear the men had delayed their flight.

Knowing that Ken was waiting for the weather to clear, I decided worry would not help the situation. I put the girls to bed and settled in for a quiet evening with my friend, Marcia Kittleson, a missionary appointee to England who was staying with us while visiting churches in the area. She was convinced I would love an old, black and white Sherlock Holmes mystery that was airing on our local PBS station. I have to admit I had an ulterior motive for joining her. Watching the late-night movie would give me an excuse to still be up when Ken arrived home.

One o'clock passed. When 1:30 came and went with nothing from Ken, I could no longer concentrate on the mystery. I was too concerned for Ken's safety. Though the weather had cleared some, I embraced the hope that perhaps the men had delayed their flight until later.

At 2:00 a.m., the phone rang, and this time I was not greeted by a concerned family member or a church member. I heard a voice I did not recognize.

"This is St. John's Mercy Medical Center. Mrs. Spilger, your husband has been in an accident. We need you to come to the hospital to sign papers before we can admit him."

"What kind of accident?" I responded.

"You need to come to the hospital to sign papers. We will talk with you when you arrive."

"Was it an automobile accident?" I asked, fishing for more information to ease my anxiety. "Did Ken break his arm? Why can't he sign the papers?" In my mind, a broken arm was the only sensible reason for my husband's inability to sign admittance papers. Though I pried for more information, the lady on the other end simply kept repeating her mantra.

"I cannot tell you anything until you come to the hospital. Please come to the emergency room as soon as possible, and we will answer all your questions when you arrive."

"I have two little girls in bed," I answered numbly, "but I'll come as quickly as I can."

My mind raced, trying to sort out the bewildering confusion. Anna and Esther were only three and one. I could not leave them alone. Marcia was adamant that I not go to the hospital by myself. In fact, Marcia's car was the only way for me even to get to the hospital.

Who could I call at 2:00 a.m. to watch my children? The only relative in the area was my Aunt Ramona who lived forty-five minutes away. I could not possibly wait that long.

"The easiest person to call," I thought to myself, "would be our neighbor Phyllis."

Bill and Phyllis Hoss and their three sons lived in the house next to ours. I dialed their number and waited for the sleepy answer I knew my call would produce. Phyllis answered, and I began a profuse string of apologies.

"Phyllis, I am so sorry to wake you, so sorry, but I don't know what to do. St. John's Mercy Medical Center called to say Ken has been in an accident, and I need to leave right now to sign papers for him to receive treatment. Marcia will take me, but I need someone to stay with the girls. Could you come stay with the girls until I get back?"

Phyllis was now wide-awake! She roused her family and came over with her son, Kevin, to spend the rest of the night with our girls. Bill insisted on driving Marcia and me to the hospital.

When we arrived, I continued asking the same questions I had been asking on the phone. I needed answers to squelch the fear and anxiety welling up from my soul. The hospital personnel would only give me one answer: "Your husband is alive." I was not told where he was, what had happened, or the extent of his injuries.

Someone finally escorted us to a small waiting room. The waiting seemed endless. Questions bombarded my mind. Will anyone come to tell me what has happened to Ken? Where is he? Why am I not being allowed to see him? Finally, the head of hospital security entered the room.

"You need to sign this paper so Ken's personal effects can be placed in the hospital safe."

Still confused and unsure of my husband's condition, I asked, "Why? Can't he sign this himself? Why do you have to store his things here? Why can't I take them home?"

This officer, I am sure, was rattled by all that was happening. He insisted that I had to sign the papers to keep Ken's items in the safe. I continued to ask my questions, and the man continued to resist.

"She's his wife," Bill interrupted. "Why can't she take his things home?"

As if someone had slapped him, the security officer suddenly realized who I was and that Ken's personal effects could be turned over to me. He then handed me the items, and as I looked through them, I noticed that my husband's wedding band was missing.

"Where is his wedding band?" I asked. "Was it lost at the accident or does he still have it with him?"

"This is everything that was in his possession. I wasn't given anything else."

An uneasiness crept over me. What kind of accident had Ken gone through to cause all of his personal effects to be removed and then given to me? Had the ring been stolen or was it lost at the accident site? Was the ring still on Ken's hand? How could I ever replace this precious token of my love for Ken?

Other hospital staff began filtering into the room. Instead of telling me about my husband, I was asked for information on the other men who were traveling with him. By this time I was even more confused, anxious, and afraid. Could they not ask Ken these questions? Why not? Nothing made sense. Suddenly, someone abruptly realized I still did not know what had happened because no one had informed me. The questioning stopped, and we were again left alone.

After another long wait, a doctor, several hospital officials, and other medical staff joined us. The doctor introduced himself as Dr. Ayvazian, the director of the Burn Unit. I noticed that he seemed to be a quiet, unassuming man with a calmness in his demeanor.

"The plane Ken was in crashed," he began. "The other men on board all died in the accident. Ken is alive, but he has been badly burned. You're lucky that I was here at this time of night. We happened to be filming a documentary for a local television station when Ken was brought in. As soon as you sign these papers, he will need my immediate attention."

Doctor Ayvazian took the time to explain what procedures my husband would need and how they would be performed. He kept reminding me how lucky we were that he was there, but I know his being there was God-ordained. God had exactly the right doctor in place at the moment of His child's need.

"We still don't know the full extent of his injuries," Doctor Ayvazian explained. "We don't know how he will respond to treatments or what complications will result. With three others dying in this crash, it is very possible that, in addition to the burns, your husband has other life-threatening injuries."

I sat motionless in a state of shock, my tired mind too numb to process everything into emotion. I listened and asked questions. I tried to control my tears because I knew I needed to be strong. Finally, I was given permission to see Ken for only a few minutes.

"Ken doesn't know the other men are dead," the doctor warned. "Be careful not to tell him. We don't need him upset. It could cause other issues."

However, as soon as I stepped into the room, my husband said, "I'm the only one who's alive; the others are gone."

God had already answered the fears of the physicians. The doctors didn't know that Ken already knew the truth in a way that would not cause further trauma.

I was shaken by my husband's appearance. Ken was still disheveled and muddy from the crash site. His body had already begun to swell from the burns, though not as much as would take place over the coming hours. He complained that his right hand hurt badly. I looked down to see that it had been wrapped in cool, wet cloths—like much of his body. He wanted me to check it, but the nurse intervened.

"No! Don't look!" she stated emphatically and then explained, "The pain is from second-degree burns he received on that hand. The other hand has third-degree burns, but he doesn't feel any pain because the nerve endings are dead from the burns." Ken's left hand was extremely burned as were his legs and buttocks.[2]

The attending physician only allowed me to stay for some brief minutes in the examining room. He knew time was of the essence in treating the deep burns Ken had sustained. Dr. Ayvazian had already explained that a procedure called an escharotomy needed to be performed immediately on the severe burns. When Ken was taken away to have these incisions made to release pressure and restore circulation in the injured areas, I was escorted to the family waiting room near the burn unit. And there Marcia, Bill, and I waited.

[2] Though he could not feel it at the time, the pain would intensify as the wounds began to heal.

“Fear thou not; for I am with thee: be not dismayed; for I am thy God: I will strengthen thee; yea, I will help thee; yea, I will uphold thee with the right hand of my righteousness.”

– Isaiah 41:10

CHAPTER FOUR

Communication

"*Mrs. Spilger, can* you give us the names of the men flying with your husband?"

"The only name I know is Russell Spurgeon, the pilot. He's the one who contacted Ken about flying with them to the seminar. I don't know who the other men are."

The investigators' questions seemed endless. Exhausted from the long night without sleep, my concerns centered on Ken. We were still waiting for the surgeons to finish Ken's escharotomies, and the police and air transportation board were still trying to analyze what had happened.

"Do you recognize any of these names your husband gave us: Ken Colman, Bob Winebarger, Wes Weiss?"

"Yes. They're all friends of ours, but I'm sure they weren't on the plane."

In his state of shock, Ken had mistakenly given the officials the names of some college friends.

"You're sure they weren't on the plane?"

"Yes."

"Who rented the plane?"

"Pastor Spurgeon. The others all shared in the cost."

"Why did they take those kinds of chances, flying in that weather?"

"They weren't taking chances. They had delayed the flight to wait for the weather system to pass."

"When did you last speak with your husband?"

"Last evening when he called to say they were delaying their flight due to the weather."

"Who was the last person to see him before their flight?"

"I don't know. His nephew Tim, I guess."

"Were the men drinking?"

"No. They are pastors. Ken doesn't drink, and I'm sure the others didn't either."

The questions went on and on. The anxiety inside of me was building. Already numb from exhaustion, I felt frustrated. Their interrogation only increased my confusion and frightened me. I was so grateful for Marcia and Bill—my God-appointed support team. How could I have managed without them? Time passed slowly; mere seconds seemed like hours. Bill had to slip out during the questioning to get ready for work. I will never forget how his presence and the knowledge that our girls were in his wife's good hands both blessed and comforted me during those harrowing hours.

Even though I knew the questions were important to solving the mystery of who was in the plane and what caused the horrendous accident, I had a thousand thoughts flying through my brain—the least of which involved the investigation.

Eventually the investigators began gathering their belongings.

"You've been very helpful, Mrs. Spilger," one of them said. "Russell Spurgeon's name matches other information we have. Thank you."

With their departure, my mind could finally turn to the questions that pressed most urgently on my own heart.

How will the girls handle the news? I wondered as I sat waiting to hear from the doctors. How will this accident affect our ministry? How can I possibly tell our parents, our families, our church members, and other friends—and still manage to hold it together emotionally? I need to call Ken's folks, but how can I wake them with this kind of news?

When I checked the clock, I saw it was now 4:00 a.m. Knowing his parents were early risers, I reached for the phone I had been given permission to use, even for long-distance calls. "They might be up," I thought to myself as I dialed their number. Unfortunately, I had misjudged their sleeping habits.

"Hello?" Ken's mother answered groggily.

"Ann, this is Beth. I'm so sorry to wake you." I felt the rush of my pent-up emotions push out the words, "Ken's been in a plane crash, and he's the only survivor. He's in the hospital." I began to sob.

In her sleep-foggy state of mind, Ann at first thought she was having a bad dream. She had received a letter the day before telling her that Ken and I would be driving to the conference in Kansas City, and now she was hearing me tell her that her son was the sole survivor of a plane crash. It didn't make sense. Finally, she woke Paul, and the two of them tried to figure out what was happening. Even with all of the confusion, they understood one thing: Ken was in trouble, and they were needed in St. Louis.

Soon after our conversation, my precious in-laws began calling Ken's siblings, taking an enormous weight of responsibility from my shoulders. The whole family pulled together and put things in motion so they could be ready to leave for St. Louis as soon as possible. We talked three more times in the next couple of hours, and from those conversations they realized the sooner they left the better.

Ann later shared that as they were leaving Nebraska, she told Paul to drive as fast as he could.

"If we were stopped," she reasoned, "we will simply explain that our son might be dead before we reached St. Louis and hope the excuse would get us off the hook."

"I never once thought we might die in a car accident," she told me later. "All I could think of was being there for my son."

I called my mother around 4:30. She listened as I sobbed out what had happened and what we knew. She wasn't surprised and explained.

"I woke up during the night burdened to pray for my children. I especially prayed for Ken's protection because I knew he was traveling. We will be praying, and we will come—if and when you need us."

The morning before the plane crash, Dad had been reading in Romans eight. The Lord specifically spoke to him from verses twenty-eight and twenty-nine. He was especially captured by the words in verse twenty-nine, *"He also did predestinate to be conformed to the image of his Son."*

When Mom got off the phone, she looked at Dad and said, "Ken's been in an accident."

"It's okay," Dad replied, the words from Romans eight coming instantly to mind.

"He's all right," he continued with confidence.

God gave both of my parents a perfect peace about the outcome of the situation.

I knew I needed to notify our church family about the accident. We needed their prayers. So my next call was to Noel and Lois Foster. I was certain they would be getting ready for work. As chairman of our deacon board, Noel would be the right person to let our people know about their pastor's situation.

As people rallied to help us, I realized in a new way that God does know our *way* and that He does indeed *try* us (Job 23:10). He moves in us with a purpose and a plan. We can trust Him. Not everyone will face a plane crash; God is much more creative than that. But we can know that, in whatever trial we face, God is perfecting us, maturing us, and conforming us to the image of His Son, the Lord Jesus Christ.

I am still amazed at how quickly the news traveled—even without our modern technology. Some of our friends heard of the crash on Christian radio, others by word of mouth, many by letter. Even in trying so hard to contact everyone, people were unintentionally missed. With accidents of this magnitude, an appropriate amount of time is needed for the information to disseminate properly. In those days before call waiting, when a call was made, the phone would be busy, and the call would need to be postponed to a later time. Added distractions and stress would sometimes divert the caller's focus from the situation at hand. As word would spread with one person calling another, eventually someone would learn the news in a disconcerting way. Hearing about the crash from a third or fourth party might lead them to believe they were intentionally missed. We found that Satan certainly loves to take advantage of trials to cause dissension in the body of Christ.

I was so confused and numb from all that had taken place the night of the crash that I simply did not have a clue as to who had and who had not been told. I felt as though I was walking in some kind of dream. I knew I simply could not take the responsibility of letting everyone know what was happening. It was too much. I had to let others help me.

After the escharotomies had been performed, Ken's doctors returned to the waiting room.

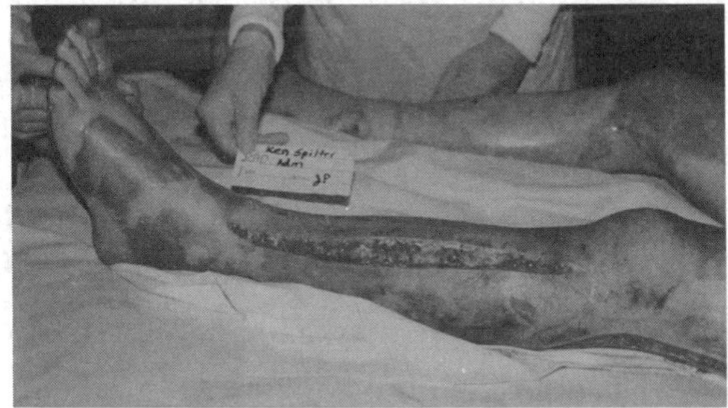

An escharotomy on Ken's left leg

"Your husband has experienced grave third-degree burns on a third of his body," one of them explained.

"Some of those burns are very deep into the muscle. We are still checking him for internal injuries and will be taking him

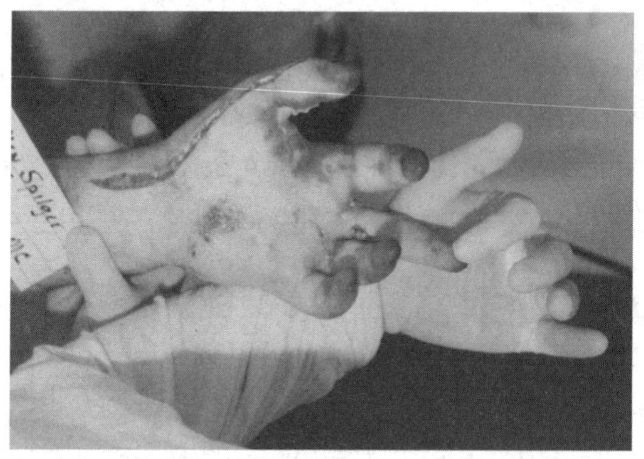

Ken's left hand after the escharotomies

for more x-rays." (Ken felt like he was constantly being x-rayed on a cold table. What he surmised was true, and whether or not he realized it, the need for x-rays was his fault! Every time he said something hurt, he was whisked off for another x-ray.)

"When do you think he'll be able to come home?"

"Your husband is in critical condition. We won't even know for 72 hours whether he will survive. It will be a miracle if he's home by Christmas."

My heart sank, and fear set in. Seventy-two hours?! I would have to wait 72 hours to know if Ken would live or die! And if he did live, which I certainly hoped would be the case, he would not be home until Christmas! It was now mid-September! Christmas was three months away!

"He won't be able to walk without a brace on his left leg," someone continued. "We're hoping he won't lose his left foot or hand. The timing of the escharotomies and the depth of the burns will determine how much loss he can expect. Do you have any more questions?"

Overwhelmed, frightened, emotional, and weary, I couldn't think. I had only one desire.

"May I see him?" I asked hopefully.

"No, not right now. You'll need to wait and come back during the regular visiting hours tomorrow. Here's the number for the burn unit. Feel free to call anytime—day or night. The receptionist will be able to tell you how Ken is doing. For now, go home and rest."

What seemed almost routine for them was the worst possible news for me to hear out of all of the news I had heard in the past hours. I simply wanted to be with my husband! I wanted to know for myself that he was okay—not to hear it from some third person.

In my exhaustion, I tried desperately to absorb everything that I had been told and to figure out how it fit together with our life, our ministry, and our family. Since I wasn't able to be with Ken, all I could do was go home and rest. The Kresses, one of our deacon families, graciously came to pick up Marcia and me around noon. They drove us to Pastor Spurgeon's church where Ken had left our car. Since I had not slept the previous night, Karen Kress drove our car home so I wouldn't have to drive.

By the time I arrived home, I realized I was bone-weary. The phone was ringing off the hook. Thankfully, Lois Foster was already at my house watching over things. I headed for the shower and privacy. I needed a place to be alone and cry. I knew I needed to cry out to my God for help and comfort.

While in the shower, I heard a rap on the bathroom door.

"Just want you to know I'm here to help." The familiar voice was music to my ears. Aunt Ramona, who worked with Child Evangelism Fellowship in Warrenton, Missouri, had heard the news about Ken, packed her bags without a moment's hesitation, and had arrived to help. She took immediate charge of Anna and Esther, allowing Mrs. Foster to return to her own responsibilities. Aunt Ramona's presence made it possible for me to rest, pray, and cry out to God. Marcia, who had been at my side the whole night, was as fatigued as I was and also needed to rest.

That night I attended church. Lonesome and afraid, I took my place at the piano for the singing and then retreated to the back of the church to listen to the rest of the service. Friends from Memphis who had come to see Ken shared a song, "Rejoice in the Lord" by Ron Hamilton, before the message. The words of that song bolstered my courage that night and became a constant source of encouragement throughout the grueling difficult months ahead.

Although several of us had tried to explain to our girls what had happened to their daddy, neither one could quite understand. When the girls asked where their daddy was, each time I explained.

"Daddy was hurt very badly and will have to stay in the hospital a long time. He can't come home right now."

Words cannot describe the depth of sorrow and agony of heart I felt as I tried to explain to our girls what their father had experienced and that he could not be home for a long time. How can a one-year-old and a three-year-old understand time—especially months? How could they understand the uncertainty of our predicament? How do you explain to a little child that her father might not survive? I could tell by the expressions on both of their faces that what we were saying did not make sense—until that late news broadcast on the television.

Our friends from Memphis could not go home that night because I-55 had been closed, so they were spending the night with us. When we arrived home from church, we turned on the news to find out why the interstate had been closed. Instead, we discovered the news media had somehow gained access to the burn unit, and we saw pictures of Ken—all over the news. That's when our girls first saw him.

Little Esther still could not make sense of what had happened, but I saw shock and horror in Anna's face. At the sight of her father's swollen face and the tubes and IVs hooked up to his body, everything we had been telling her became real. She began crying hysterically and ran to me for comfort. We cuddled and cried. The comfort I gained from comforting her was indescribable.

Ken's folks arrived late that night. Somehow we managed to find places for everyone to sleep. I am still not sure if I was alone in my bed as I cried myself to sleep.

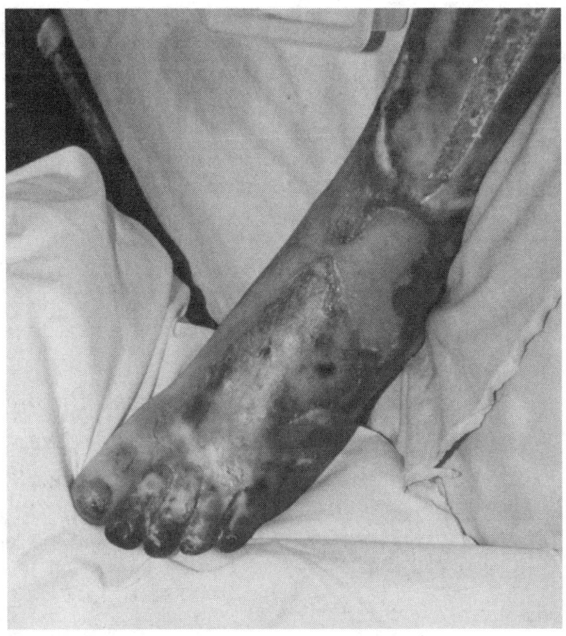

Ken's charred left foot

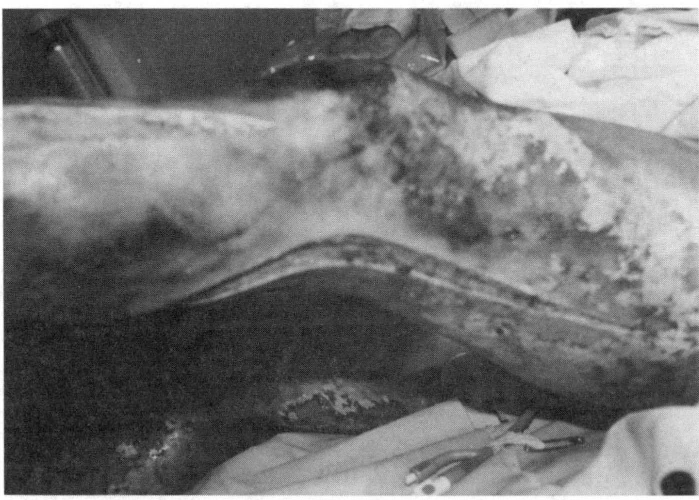

Another picture of the escharotomies on Ken's left leg

"When thou passest through the waters, I will be with thee; and through the rivers, they shall not overflow thee: when thou walkest through the fire, thou shalt not be burned; neither shall the flame kindle upon thee."

– Isaiah 43:2

CHAPTER FIVE

Damage

"*Okay, everything's arranged* with the sheriff's office." I placed the phone's receiver back on the hook and looked at my in-laws. "The girls will be taken care of; now we can go." Excitement rose within me. In just a couple hours I would be allowed to see Ken!

The day had quickly filled up. Paul and Ann, who had arrived late the previous night, had yet to see Ken. The sheriff had called and asked me to come by the precinct to answer more questions. Once again, I was grateful for those who were willing to care for my girls.

Paul & Ann Spilger

We went to the police station first. After answering the sheriff's questions, he suggested we go out to the crash site. A Christian officer volunteered to take us. As we rode along in his cruiser, he told us he had been involved in the cleanup after the crash. He filled us in on the details pulled together by the firefighters and investigators at the scene.

As we pulled up to the crash site, parked, and stepped out onto the road, that ever-present numbness surpassed every other emotion.

Even though I was not feeling strong, I needed to be strong for my in-laws. Ann had been in tears all morning, and I had spent much of the ride to the site comforting her. As I looked down over the steep terrain, I was shocked. The officer pointed out the damaged tree and fallen branch that had torn open the fuselage. He showed us the power lines that had snapped when the plane struck them. As I looked over the scene, all the bits and pieces of the story I had heard fit together. So much of the area had been charred that I finally understood how Ken had been so badly burned.

The officer said that the remnants of the plane had been hauled away in the back of a pickup truck. Only a few pieces of debris remained. The family members of the other three men had already picked over the site for their loved ones' belongings. Still, Paul, Ann, and I began searching the hillside in hopes of finding more of Ken's personal belongings—especially his wedding ring. I had already asked both the firefighters and the police officers about it the day before, but none of them had seen a gold wedding band in the debris. A great sense of loss swept over me as I realized the journal he had kept in college and still used, his Bible, and briefcase were gone—burned. Questions returned. Will Ken survive? Fear mixed with hope for Ken and our future together filled my heart.

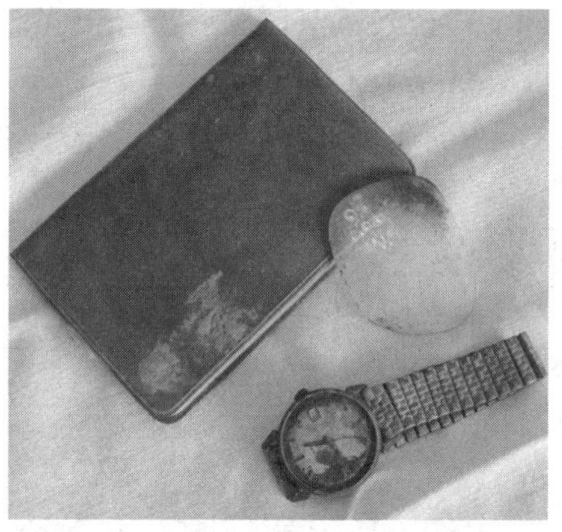

Ken's eyeglass lens, watch, and New Testament
A book and notes that were given at the conference were found but are not shown. They, too, were badly charred.

We did find a few items, which belonged to the other men. We would later exchange these items for some of Ken's belongings they had found. His wedding ring was never found.

Before we left, Ann and I stood at the edge of the ravine and watched as the policeman and Paul climbed down to the ledge where Ken had been found. Even though the climb was steep and they had to hang onto roots and branches to make their descent, my 75-year-old father-in-law was determined to go all the way to where his son's life had been miraculously spared.

One of the many washouts at the bottom of the field where the plane crashed

We returned to the police station with the officer and then headed to the hospital. I had not seen Ken since I had left him the morning of the crash. I could hardly wait! Ann, in particular, was especially eager to get to her son. While Paul and I struggled to don our isolation garments over our street clothes, Ann quickly finished and rushed into Ken's room alone, not knowing what she was about to face. The sight of her son's extremely swollen, pale face dotted with burns and the IVs, tubes, and machines all connected to his body overwhelmed her. She'd had no advance warning that the body of a burn patient swells in reaction to the burns.

St. John's Mercy Medical Center became Ken's temporary home away from home while he was healing and recuperating from the plane crash.

As I was about to enter the room, she rushed past me crying.

"Didn't you warn her about what to expect?" scolded a burn technician who was stationed near the door.

"No. How could I? I didn't know," I said in shocked surprise. "I haven't seen him since yesterday morning and the pictures we saw on the news last night. I didn't know he would look worse."

With my shocked explanation, the woman's scolding stopped.

I turned to see that one of our church members, Rich Crotser, had arrived just in time to see a stricken Ann flee from Ken's room. He caught her, put his arms around her, listened to her, comforted her, and simply let her cry. God had special-ordered the perfect solution to Ann's distress.

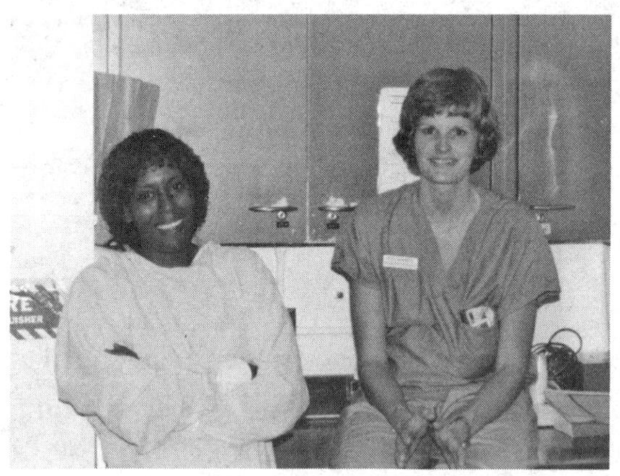

Two of the many Nurses and Technicians in the Burn Unit — excellent caring caregivers

When Ann had regained her composure and had listened to the technician's explanation that the swelling would go down in the days ahead, she was ready to try again. As she entered the room, Ken raised his bandaged hand and motioned for her to come close. He took her hand in his and kissed it. Then he asked, "Why have you come?"

Ann calmly replied, "Oh, we wouldn't miss seeing you for anything."

Paul's entrance into Ken's room was a bit different. Having seen and heard what had taken place with Ann, he was ready for about anything. Even in the face of all the medical equipment and Ken's appearance, he walked right up to his son's bedside and quipped, "I hope the other guy looks worse than you do! You look pretty rough."

That good humor would be a great help to Ken in the weeks ahead as he faced a multitude of difficulties. We learned that, in addition to the severe burns, Ken also had three broken ribs and a lung contusion. All these injuries would also take time to heal. Paul's strength, wisdom, and counsel would bolster me and encourage me in the decisions I would face not only then but throughout the coming months. That morning was the only time the three of us were allowed in Ken's room together. After that, no more than two people were allowed in the room at once. So began our long period of waiting for Ken's healing, and so began our new abnormal routine.

"But they that wait upon the LORD shall renew their strength; they shall mount up with wings as eagles; they shall run, and not be weary; and they shall walk, and not faint."

– Isaiah 40:31

CHAPTER SIX

Healing

Each day I worked at home in the morning, taking care of both home and church responsibilities. I seemed to be constantly answering the phone. At noon, I would prepare lunch, feed the girls, and put them down for their naps. Then I was able to leave home to drive the 45 minutes to the hospital. I always tried to arrive by 2:00 p.m. when visitation hours began. As I drove, I sang comforting songs like "He Giveth More Grace," "Rejoice in the Lord," and "I Must Tell Jesus." Once at the hospital, I usually stayed until around 4:00 p.m., which gave me time to make it home so Ken's parents could make the drive back and spend the evening with him. They usually stayed until visitation ended.

Ken seemed to sleep most of the time when I was in the room with him. He said, "I feel comforted in your presence."

Paul and Ann would read Scripture to Ken and pray with him when they visited. When the time came that Ken was able, they would walk up and down the hallway with him. For the most part, this schedule became our daily routine over the next two months, with the exception of surgery days, the days following the surgeries, or times when family or friends were visiting.

I felt like I was meeting myself coming and going. I was often relieved to have the 45-minute drive to the hospital because I simply needed time alone. I worried over the girls giving their grandparents a difficult time while I was gone in the afternoon. Sometimes I found it hard to come home in the evening because I would have to discipline them for disobeying their grandparents. In reality, I simply wanted to be with them and enjoy the precious time I had with them. I worried over finances, Ken's health, the church, and other matters. I spent time comforting others when I felt that I was the one needing comfort.

I spent my evenings answering the phone, responding to the questions of caring people who wondered first how Ken was progressing and then kindly asked how the girls and I were doing. Along with these calls, I took care of many other routine activities. People called from all around the United States simply to say, "We are praying."

Ken's condition was serious. The doctors were first concerned that the broken ribs and lung contusion would lead to pneumonia. Each surgery contained its share of risks.

I watched Ken endure extreme pain every day. No matter how hard he tried, he could not explain its intensity and duration. I sensed his pain, but I felt helpless because I could do nothing about it. The nurses and technicians begged him to scream or curse during the dressing changes because they understood the severity of the pain he had to endure.

"Encourage him to scream and curse," they urged me. "It will help him cope with the agony he is experiencing."

"Scream? Curse?" I asked. "He never screams or curses—even when he is in excruciating pain. He's learned to breathe through the pain. I'm sure he'll be okay without screaming or cursing. I also know he is trusting the Lord to help him get through this pain."

I was never again asked to encourage him to scream or curse. I think that their watching Ken's reactions to the pain over the next few days and weeks helped them realize he would get through the trauma without screaming or cursing. Even with the massive amounts of pain medications being administered to him, the pain was still beyond excruciating.

Ken simply knew he needed to trust the Lord to help him through this suffering. Even now, all these years later, Ken still finds it difficult to talk about those terrible months of pain without weeping. Never once did he scream or curse to endure the pain. God helped Ken to breathe through it by focusing on Him, His promises in the Bible, and the knowledge that each day brought him one step closer to healing.

At first our extended family refrained from visiting because of Ken's recovery and upcoming surgeries. The doctors did not know whether or not they could get enough skin from Ken for the grafts. His skin would be best and would heal faster, but they didn't know whether he would be in good enough physical shape to go through the grafting process, so if they were needed, his siblings all made plans to come as skin donors.

Ken's surgeries were scheduled about two weeks apart. His second surgery was scheduled for October 14, a week before Anna's fourth birthday. The third surgery was scheduled later that month on the day of Esther's second birthday. For that reason my Aunt Ramona planned to come to St. Louis to celebrate the girls' birthdays on Saturday, October 18. I talked to the doctors and the technicians about bringing cake and celebrating with all seven of us in Ken's room. The hospital staff told me we could, so we set our plans in motion. I was excited—excited that the girls would finally get to see their dad and excited that the staff had bent their policy to make the girls' birthdays special. I was especially excited to be together as a family again.

Aunt Ramona made two cakes—an elephant for Esther, and a giraffe for Anna. She brought them with her Friday night, all ready to take to the hospital on Saturday. The girls were excited. They had not seen their father since the day before he had left for Kansas City, a month earlier. We spent Saturday morning getting ready for our big birthday party at the hospital. Once the girls were ready and I had finished my preparations, I went to gather the other items we would need. The cakes had been sitting on the countertop in the kitchen, and I was shocked at what I found. A large chunk of cake was missing from the elephant. I did not have to look far to find the guilty culprit! One look at Esther's smiling face told me who had eaten that piece of cake. We had told her it was hers, so she had eaten it! We had been planning to leave the larger elephant cake with the hospital staff when we had finished our celebration, but our best-laid plans obviously changed.

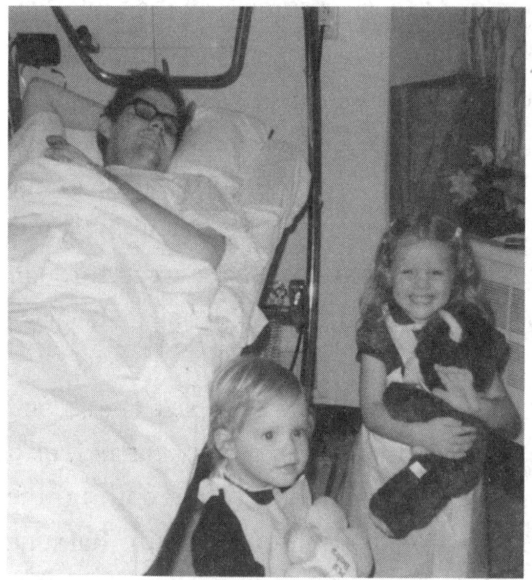

Two little girls excited to be with their daddy

When we arrived at the hospital, we discovered our other plans were going to change as well. Because of a misunderstanding, we found we would not all be able to be in the room at the same time. I was disappointed and confused as to what had changed since the day I had received permission from the doctors and the staff to have the party.

We regrouped, trying to make the best of the situation. Fortunately, we had driven three different cars. Paul and Ann decided to wait in the family waiting room since they would be staying until visiting hours were over. Aunt Ramona made a quick visit and left sooner than she had planned.

The girls and I went in next. I dressed Anna and Esther in their little, modified isolation robes and took them to see their daddy. The girls squealed as they came into the room and saw him. Ken was just as elated to see them. They ran to him, only to learn that Daddy could not hold them or play with them. Their disappointment quickly turned to joy because they could unwrap their gifts and eat cake with him. Not wanting Ken's parents to wait long, the girls and I left earlier than planned, leaving the cake behind for the doctors and nurses to enjoy. The girls were not disappointed with the shorter visit. They had seen their daddy with their own eyes. Now they knew where he was for themselves.

Anna in Ken's room during birthday celebration in her "modified isolation robe"

My heart was full of joy over the fact that the girls had seen Ken. On the other hand, my heart was heavy. I had been so excited over the plans for our party. I had wanted so much to have Ken's folks and Aunt Ramona in the room to see the girls unwrap their gifts. So with a somewhat saddened heart, I left the hospital with our girls so Ken's folks would have time with him. As the old cliché goes, "My parade had been rained on." I never did find out what happened to what should have been a happy time of celebration and reunion.

As Thanksgiving approached, Ken was looking forward to the possibility of seeing family and friends. For that to happen much had to be accomplished. He had already undergone three skin-grafting surgeries. For each surgery, the grafting specialists were able to use his own skin. Two of the grafts were a 100-percent success and the other a 97-percent success. God had worked miracles in Ken's body to bring about his healing. I have no doubt these miracles were the direct answer to the prayers of God's people. With the surgeries completed, we could now focus on reaching a point of recovery that would allow Ken to go home.

A high protein diet was vital to helping Ken's body *make* skin. When he was not taking in the needed amount of protein calories, the nurses once threatened him with a feeding tube. The memories of his first feeding tube were a strong motivator for him to take in the needed 8,000 calories every day. Ice cream shakes made with several raw eggs became a part of his daily diet. Even after he went home, I continued to make those shakes for him.

I watched the therapists and the technicians work with Ken by the hour, preparing him to walk and to function somewhat normally in the real world. I hurt to see the pain Ken experienced as they worked with him. A sizable portion of muscle from his left calf as well as the little toe and parts of the other toes on his left foot had been removed. Because the doctors had to remove much of the fingers on his left hand, his finger joints were permanently fixed at 90° angles to give him better functionality. The therapists taught Ken to walk again, to write, to pick up things, and to function as close to *normal* as possible with what muscle and movement he had remaining in his feet, legs, and hands.

Ken was ready to go home much earlier than expected because his healing and therapy had progressed so well. The majority of severely burn patients must stay in the hospital until the burned areas have closed and the fear of infection is past. However, with my being home to care for him, the doctors decided to release Ken early. Simply knowing I would soon have my husband home filled my heart with joy and expectation. I had no idea what the two of us would face with this *earlier-than-normal* release from the hospital.

For one full week before Ken was released, I was given careful instruction about the care Ken would need every day. I learned how to soak and debride his still open wounds, how to replace his bandages, how to keep the wounds clean, how to perform therapy on his legs, how to help him in and out of chairs and the bed, how to prepare the calories he needed, and a plethora of other tasks. As I took notes and paid close attention to my teachers, all I could think of was the excitement of having my husband home with us; we would finally be a family again. Even as I was taught how to care for him, I still had no concept of what we would face when he was home. My better judgment was clouded and colored by my simply wanting him to be home.

Ken's hands and legs were measured for JOBST garments, which exert a very strong, consistent pressure on the body. Without these pressure garments, the scar tissue would become grotesque and unmanageable. Ken would have to wear these pressure garments all of the time. Each day I would need to help Ken change them, then launder them by hand, and hang them to dry away from the sun. They were costly, but oh, so necessary. My job list was increasing, but I was still unaware of the huge load I would be carrying; my joy covered it all.

Finally the day arrived for Ken's return to *the outside world*. I was excited he was coming home. The thought that Ken's return could be a difficult transition still hadn't crossed my mind. To me, the long drives to the hospital had ended, the search for childcare was over, the huge hospital bills would stop growing, the long nights alone would no longer be alone, making decisions on my own was past, and much, much more of the overwhelming pressure I had felt was lifted.

The thought never occurred to me that Ken might be nervous and fearful about re-acclimating himself into society. The possibility of having difficult adjustments in our home and relationship was well beyond the realm of my reasonable thinking. Besides that, Ken's parents would be helping to get things on a more level plane at home before leaving for Nebraska.

How could I know that Ken, on the other hand, was not at all sure what being at home would mean for him. He knew the staff in the burn unit understood his handicaps, but those outside of the hospital probably would not.

"Will I still be able to care for my responsibilities with all the changes that have taken place in my body?" Ken wondered.

Like me, Ken would soon find out—whether or not he was ready.

We had decided that Ken's dad would take me in their car to get Ken. Their four-door vehicle would be more conducive to getting Ken home comfortably. When we arrived, I saw members of the press were there to see us off, but I didn't care about them. My beloved husband was coming home! Excitement reigned in my heart.

The nurses helped Ken dress in the sweat-suit we had purchased for the trip home. They helped us gather his belongings, and then Paul and I loaded him into the car. On November 14, after 59 days in the hospital, we took him home to two excited little girls and his mother. God had shown Himself to be the Lord who heals. He had indeed worked a miracle, and my husband arrived home not after Christmas as the doctors had predicted—but before Thanksgiving!

When we arrived, Ann had lunch waiting for us. We helped Ken sit at the table and eat. Ours was a joyous meal full of happy banter as the girls chattered away with their father. I simply listened and watched my family, happy and relieved to have Ken home.

When lunch was finished, I helped Ken to the couch for some needed rest. He was weak, and the merest effort exhausted him. As I was getting him settled, I suddenly became aware that his parents were carrying their things out to load their car. Fear seized my heart. How can I handle all I will be facing without their help?

When I voiced my thoughts, Ann wisely said, "You have much to work through, and we don't want to have to referee. You need to work through these things without our interference."

Both Ken and I were shocked at her words. We wanted them to stay, but they knew they needed to go.

We prayed for their safety since they were eager to make it home before a forecasted storm, and we were relieved the next day to know they had arrived safely. We cried as they left, wishing they would stay. The Ken Spilger family was officially on their own—with no other human hands to help us. Feelings of helplessness suddenly overwhelmed me as I realized it was only the four of us: two little girls, a weak and needy husband, and me.

"And though the Lord give you the bread of adversity, and the water of affliction, yet shall not thy teachers be removed into a corner any more, but thine eyes shall see thy teachers: [21]And thine ears shall hear a word behind thee, saying, This is the way, walk ye in it, when ye turn to the right hand, and when ye turn to the left."

– Isaiah 30:20-21

CHAPTER SEVEN

Home

Life became a busy ritual of caring for Ken's wounds, going to therapy, and doing therapy at home. He did not have much time to worry about his fears of the *outside world*. Not only was his participation required for these activities, but so was mine. The arrival of his JOBST garments added two new elements to our routine because they had to be changed and laundered every day. What a happy day it was when I discovered they could be laundered in the washing machine on the gentle cycle!

The JOBST arrived the day before Thanksgiving. My parents and extended family were with us for the holiday. As I started taking Ken through his daily routine, I realized I was unprepared for this new task of helping him into the JOBST garments. I had no idea of the massive strength of these pressure garments or how to put them on over the fragile skin so as not to cause additional damage as well as extra pain for Ken.

Burton & Mildred Brush

As I began to slip on Ken's gloves, he quickly sucked in his breath to

JOBST for Ken's left hand *JOBST for Ken's right hand*

fight the pain. I jerked back, not wanting to hurt him. I tried again, but the result was the same. Time after time I tried to put the gloves on him, and with each try he reacted to the pain. Seeing him in pain broke my heart.

Finally, I was too overwhelmed. Fighting back tears, I left the room, and ran to my mother.

"Mom," I wept, "will you please do this for me? I can't do it!"

"No," she replied, "I won't always be here to help you. You must put those gloves on Ken because his healing depends on them. Go in there, and do it!"

To this day, I thank God for my mother's answer and for her strength of character to make me do right by my husband. We soon discovered that the leggings Ken had to don were even more difficult than the gloves, but we finally got everything on. Every day this task was a daunting challenge until another burns caregiver showed us how he put them on his wife. His technique worked beautifully! Both Ken and I marveled how once again God had brought the right person at just the right time.

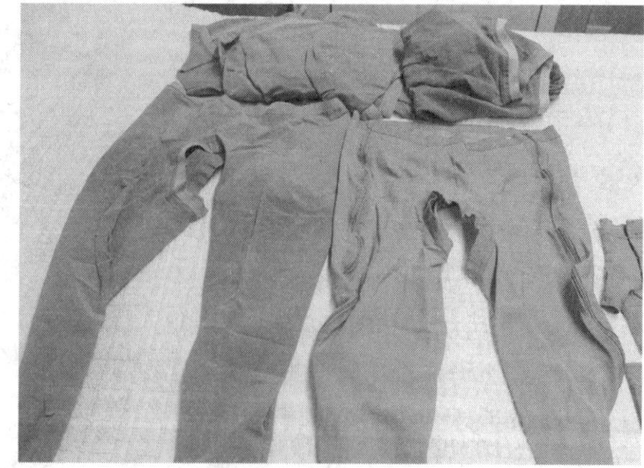

JOBST leggings – worn day and night

After Thanksgiving celebrations concluded, we got down to the nitty-gritty of daily life. With our extended family gone, we were alone to settle into this new chapter of life. The soaking, debriding, and wrapping process took hours each day—sometimes three or four. Our routine was exhausting. Anna and Esther were often left to themselves as I tended to their daddy's needs. We quickly learned we needed to put the girls in separate rooms to keep them out of mischief, but even that separation did not always work.

One day, as I was helping Ken through our usual routine, I realized that the house was strangely quiet. I left my husband and went in search of my daughters. I stepped into the living room where Esther, our two-year old, had been left to play. To my horror, every houseplant in the room had been turned upside down. A dozen little mounds of dirt were carefully placed all over the carpeted floor. Esther brightly smiled at me. What a discovery she had made: every plant had a root system!

Esther - Age two

"Esther, what did you do?" I asked in a frustrated mom voice.

She shrugged at me and then looked back at one of the many piles of dirt.

I burst into tears, scooped her up, and set her on the couch. "Wait here until I am finished with Daddy," I ordered.

In addition to finishing up with Ken and all of my other normal duties, I now had several additional messes to clean up. To this day, I do not remember what I did with the plants, but those piles of dirt are indelibly impressed in my mind.

I believe that being the wife of a man who has gone through the extreme trauma my husband endured has given me a greater understanding and empathy toward caregivers in similar situations. I always want to be positive about what God allowed us to experience, but I would be less than honest if I did not admit that I often felt alone. I also learned that people can be so caught up in the needs of the one going through the trauma that they miss the detail of other family members' experiencing a trauma of their own. Their worlds have also been turned upside down—like my world was turned upside down. The uncertainty of life, the disruption of schedules, the financial pressures, the needs of other family members, my own needs, the lack of down time—all added to the stress I felt. Though I was hurting emotionally, I felt the need to comfort our family and our hurting church family. I felt I had to be strong for everyone.

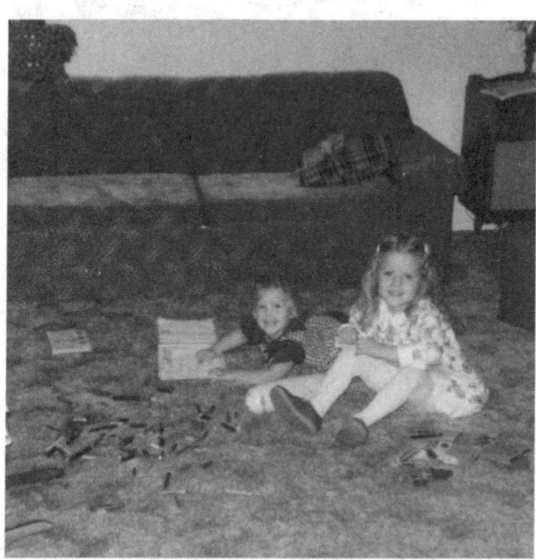

Staying busy so Mom could take care of Daddy

Often others do not understand the altered behavior of the children in the family. Even children experience stress. Hundreds of questions are running through their little minds. Adults misunderstand their behavior, pass judgment that the behavior stems from disobedience, and someone (child or parent) is invariably hurt. In those moments, I determined to be like Christ and to do as He did in Luke 23:34 when He said, *"Father, forgive them; for they know not what they do."* Understanding that not everyone can comprehend what is happening is a real part of life. In knowing this truth, we can walk on and leave the offenses behind. Psalm 119:165 says, *"Great peace have they which love thy law: and nothing shall offend them.*" I praise God for the few people who really do understand and come alongside those suffering to encourage, love, and help.

For several months after Ken arrived home, he reported to the burn clinic for regular checkups. At first, he went every other week, then finally once a month. The doctors checked his progress and continued to offer additional helpful advice.

Ken's therapy continued for seven months after he came home. In the beginning, I loaded up the girls five days a week and drove the forty-five minutes to St. John's Mercy Medical Center, the same hospital where Ken had been in the burn unit. After a few weeks, he was transferred to Christian Hospital Northeast (CHN), only ten minutes from our house, to complete his therapy.

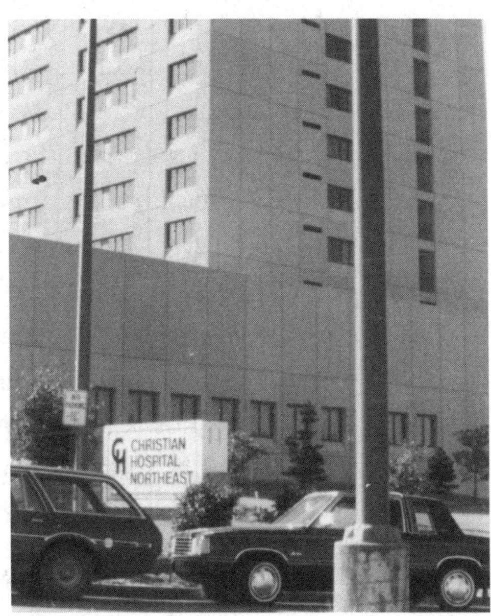

Christian Hospital Northeast

At CHN, his therapist, Mary, began with an overall evaluation of Ken's health and progress. She checked the range of motion in his hands, legs, and feet to help her know how to guide the other therapists as they worked to help Ken's body function as normally as possible. He wore a pair of shorts so the therapists could see the extent of the burns and how his body worked in relation to them. The calf of his left leg was merely skin and bone since most of the muscle had to be removed. The full circumference of the ankle had been burned, and the little toe and tips of the other small toes on that foot also had to be removed. To Mary's surprise, Ken was able to move his ankle in a full circle. We knew this ability was another miracle and another "I love you" from God to Ken.

Going shopping together proved to be quite an experience for Ken and me that first Christmas after he arrived home. In his weakness, walking was difficult since he was still adjusting to wearing shoes. Long walks had to be broken up with frequent rest time, and then he did not find it easy to let himself down into a seat or to get back up. While sitting and rising was becoming less difficult, he still needed help.

We found someone to care for the girls and headed out to do our Christmas shopping. We had been given money for special gifts for the girls: a wagon and a tricycle. However, when we found them in the store, Ken did not have the strength to lift them into the cart. When we went to the checkout, I had to lift them onto the counter and then carry them out to the car. Ken hated seeing me walking through the store carrying our packages, but I was basking in my happiness of having him with me. He felt like some of the other shoppers were looking at him strangely, but I couldn't have cared less. How could they possibly know my husband had miraculously arrived home from the hospital and had little to no strength?

Shortly before Christmas, a friend came by and assembled the wagon and the tricycle. What a blessing to have someone else assume the job of attaching part A to part B—successfully! We were jubilant. Ken was home with his family, he was able to be at church, and, contrary to the doctor's predictions, it was not yet Christmas! God had indeed been very good to us! What a wonderful Christmas!

Pictures of Anna and Esther at age four and two

Esther was in a wedding the summer of 1981 and Anna is holding a 3 pound Snicker bar that was a gift to Ken from some friends.

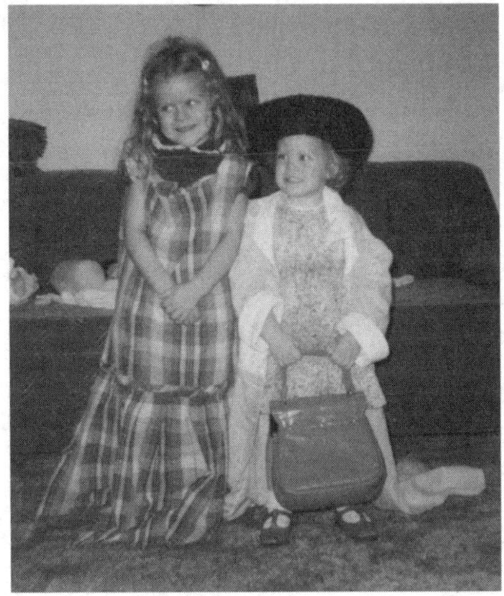

Dress-up time!

"How amiable are thy tabernacles, O LORD of hosts! [2]My soul longeth, yea, even fainteth for the courts of the LORD: my heart and my flesh crieth out for the living God. [3]Yea, the sparrow hath found an house, and the swallow a nest for herself, where she may lay her young, even thine altars, O LORD of hosts, my King, and my God. [4] Blessed are they that dwell in thy house: they will be still praising thee. Selah.

[5]Blessed is the man whose strength is in thee; in whose heart are the ways of them. [6]Who passing through the valley of Baca make it a well; the rain also filleth the pools. [7]They go from strength to strength, every one of them in Zion appeareth before God. [8]O LORD God of hosts, hear my prayer: give ear, O God of Jacob. Selah.

[9]Behold, O God our shield, and look upon the face of thine anointed. [10]For a day in thy courts is better than a thousand. I had rather be a doorkeeper in the house of my God, than to dwell in the tents of wickedness. [11]For the LORD God is a sun and shield: the LORD will give grace and glory: no good thing will he withhold from them that walk uprightly. [12]O LORD of hosts, blessed is the man that trusteth in thee."

– Psalm 84

CHAPTER EIGHT

Desire for God's Purpose

I *was extremely* thirsty. Three days had passed since the plane crash, and I hadn't been allowed even a sip of water. My desire for a glass of water was intense. As I looked around, I spotted a sink on the other side of my intensive care room. Beside the sink was a paper cup dispenser. My desire for one small drink became even more overpowering. For the first time, I believe I could understand how a man lost in the desert without a canteen must feel. I had asked for a drink many times, but none of my caregivers would give me one. "The danger of hypovolemic shock is too great," I was told countless times. That explanation meant nothing to me. I didn't understand why I had to be restricted to carefully doled out ice chips. I simply wanted a drink.

I decided to take matters into my own bandaged hands. I realized the feeding tube and IVs would be my biggest hindrance to getting out of bed and across the room to the sink. I began by removing the feeding tube. Then I would have to deal with the IVs, pulling them along on their rolling stand. I worked as quietly and quickly as I could to make sure that nothing would keep me from getting that drink—even a sip—of the water I so desperately craved.

I started toward the sink, but crossing the room was going too slow.

Suddenly I heard a voice exclaim, "Mr. Spilger! What. Are. You. Doing?!"

I'm caught! The drink I so desperately desired once again became an elusive dream. The hospital staff escorted me back to my bed and my encumbrances. Little did I know that if I had taken the little drink I so desired I could possibly have caused my death. What I had thought was best for me, in reality, was not.

Similarly, the devil easily dupes us into believing that our happiness depends on getting what we want in the way we want it. In the same way I craved that drink of water, my selfish desire to build a ministry simply to impress people was so strong before the crash that I had been systematically removing everything which I thought hindered me from fulfilling that desire. My basic desires, which were good and Biblical on the surface, all revolved around my plan—not God's. Feelings of inadequacy and insecurity overwhelmed me because I was focusing on my own selfish desires. I could not see that achieving my dream in my way could be my undoing.

My Heavenly Father lovingly brought my selfishness to a grinding halt. The plane crash, my resulting weakness, and my long recovery became God's way of *catching* me. If nothing else, the plane crash kept me from the damage and possible destruction of my life, marriage, and ministry. God turned my focus onto His Word, so His Spirit could shape my wrong desire into having a desire for His purpose. I realize today that even if I had succeeded in attaining my desires, I would not have enjoyed a sense of fulfillment.

How do we find God's blessing or happiness? Every person expresses that search in different ways. The *Our Daily Bread* devotional booklet for October 13, 1989, quotes Clarence Macartney regarding that quest for happiness:

> *It is not found* in pleasure. The English poet, Lord Byron, who lived a life devoted to seeking pleasures, later wrote, "The worm, the canker, and the grief are mine alone."
>
> Happiness is not found in money. Jay Gould, the American millionaire, had ample wealth, but when dying he said, "I suppose I am the most miserable man on earth."
>
> It is not found in position and fame. The British politician, author, and former prime minister, Lord Beaconsfield, enjoyed more than his share of both position and fame. Yet he wrote, "Youth is a mistake, manhood a struggle, and old age a regret."
>
> Happiness is not found in military glory. Alexander the Great, upon conquering the known world in his day, wept in his tent because he said, "There are no more worlds to conquer."

If happiness cannot be found in pleasures, money, position, fame, or military distinction, how can a person truly be happy? Where is God's blessing to be found?

This was the very question I was facing at the pastors conference. As the ambulance was transporting me to the hospital, I knew God was beginning to answer my prayer. He was clarifying His purpose in my life. He was purging the wrong desires I had allowed to control my life. In fact, He would use the events of the next several years—not days or weeks or months—to further illuminate His purpose and desire for my life and ministry. He was beginning a refining work in me that has continued to this day. Doing His work His way has taught me that His purpose and desire bring the happiness and blessing I sought.

Our desires determine our blessings because our desires (what we want) will determine whether or not we choose God's blessings. Over the course of more than forty years of ministry, I have worked with many people and have found that people usually do what they want. They work to acquire what they want, regardless of whether or not their acquisitions are good for them.

Our desires also determine our temptations. Even though having that simple drink of water was not good for me, I still desired it—desperately. I wanted it enough to harm my body. When we are tempted, we are tempted in the very area of our desires. We cannot blame God or the devil for our temptations. They stem from our own desires, as God teaches us in James 1:13 and14, which says, *"Let no man say when he is tempted, I am tempted of God: for God cannot be tempted with evil, neither tempteth he any man: [14]But every man is tempted, when he is drawn away of his own lust* [desires], *and enticed."*

Grace is the dynamic influence of the Holy Spirit upon the heart.

So then, how can a Christian have God's desires? Simple! We must allow God's grace to work in our hearts.

Grace is the dynamic influence of the Holy Spirit upon the heart, and is reflected in our life by gratitude in our salvation, sanctification [growth in Christ], and service. This *influence* of the Holy Spirit gives us the desire for God's purposes in our life. Grace comes only as we humble ourselves to God, according to James 4:6, *"But he giveth more grace. Wherefore he saith, God resisteth the proud, but giveth grace unto the humble."* God is incredibly faithful to lead us to receive His grace, which allows us to reflect His glory and molds us into the image of His Son; therein is His purpose for our life.

We receive God's grace by our humility before God.

Through my intense desire for a drink of water in those first few days in the burn unit, God was teaching me to want His desires with a similar thirst. In Psalm 84, God identifies three desires that lead to our happiness. The Hebrew word for *blessed* in verses 4, 5, and 12 also means *happy*. God promises to bless those who desire His fellowship, strength, and trust. These three desires motivate us to receive God's grace in order to seek His purpose. Holding fast to these desires will also work to strengthen our relationship with God. As we see Who He is through fellowship, learn to trust Him, and are strengthened by Him, His purpose for us is clarified. That intense thirst to reflect His glory and image to others then comes.

Desire His Fellowship

God placed in my heart the desire to live in fellowship with Him when I was saved. However, through the years I allowed lies like, "I need more!" and "What I want is better!" to take root in my life. God continues to use the trials of the plane crash, the recovery, and the ongoing limitations I face to remove these lies.

While I was in the hospital, I was unable to go to church or to read my Bible and pray effectively. Many visitors came to my hospital room. Some prayed with me and for me when they visited. Others read the Bible to me. I had all of the essential elements of fellowship, but I lacked

Grace Baptist Church – 1980

the ability to fully participate with them because of the severity of my injuries.

We receive God's grace by our knowledge of Christ.

My responsibility during this time of pain, weakness, and uncertainty about my future was to know my Lord in the fellowship of His sufferings as the Apostle Paul stated in Philippians 3:10,11, *"That I may know him, and the power of his resurrection, and the fellowship of his sufferings, being made conformable unto his death; [11]If by any means I might attain unto the resurrection of the dead."* In 2 Peter 1:2 God promises that through my knowledge of Him, His grace will be multiplied unto me. *"Grace and peace be multiplied unto you through the knowledge of God, and of Jesus our Lord."* Knowing Him enabled me to live in the power of His strength and opened the door for me to live in fellowship with Him—especially during this time of great suffering as I had to wait patiently for my health and strength to return.

Psalm 84:4 says, *"Blessed are they that dwell in thy house: they will be still praising thee."* Dwelling in God's house is the Old Testament equivalent of the concept of fellowship with God found in the New Testament. Fellowship is "a partnership and participation with God." Living in fellowship with God gives every Christian a great sense of security and fulfillment. God designed mankind to live in fellowship with Him. Man will never be satisfied in this life until he is living in fellowship with God as his Creator and Redeemer.

I find it amazing that in Psalm 84 God describes the fellowship we can have with Him in ways to which we can easily relate—a home that we love (v. 1), a person who is starving (v. 2), and a nesting bird (v. 3).

My desire for personal fellowship with my Lord grew as I came to know Him better and grow in His grace. My desire for His fellowship increased more and more. My increased fellowship with my Lord also increased my knowledge of Him, making His grace to be multiplied in me.

My time away from church while in the hospital also taught me the importance of consistent fellowship and corporate worship with other believers. How I longed to be in church! I missed the time spent together with other Christians, learning the Bible, praying, singing praises to God, and sharing the blessings God had given us each week. In Hebrews 10:24, 25, God tells us that we are to stimulate one another to love and good works: *"Not forsaking the assembling of ourselves together, as the manner of some is; but exhorting one another."* As a result of my absence from church, I gained a better sense of why God was so emphatic on this point.

Shortly before I was released from the hospital, I was finally able to have some of the fellowship I so intensely desired. The doctors agreed to allow me to attend church to see how I would do outside the hospital walls. The anticipation of that day was a huge motivator to achieve certain goals established by my caregivers. While I worked hard in therapy, God's people prayed. Finally the day came when the doctors awarded me with that coveted pass to leave the hospital for only a few hours. Like David of old, *"I was glad when they said unto me, Let us go into the house of the Lord"* (Psalm 122:1).

I wasn't allowed to wear regular street clothes. Thankfully, I didn't have to wear my hospital gown—but I did have to wear pajamas. Knowing this prerequisite beforehand, my parents purchased a brand-new pair of light-blue, double-breasted, pin-striped pajamas to wear in honor of the speaker at the conference our church was holding. The

Part of the Spilger family with Dr. Roberson in early 1994

late Dr. Lee Roberson, the president of my alma mater, was the keynote speaker. He was known for wearing double-breasted, navy-blue, pin-striped suits. Dad and Beth patiently waited for me as I put on my improvised adaptation of the speaker's attire and a new brown robe over the many bulky bandages. Then we were on our way.

Some men from our church met me at the car, helped me into a waiting wheelchair, rolled me into the church building, and assisted me into a brand-new, soft recliner strategically placed at the front of the church. How I looked or what I wore made no difference to me. I was in church for the first time in two months! The thought that I was able to participate with my church in this special service was foremost in my mind.

The church building was packed, and the extra chairs placed in the aisles were filled. Many people came from area churches. We rejoiced greatly together over the goodness of the Lord and His answer to prayer. As I sat in this service, I knew God was working out His purpose in my life. My, oh, my! The fellowship in that service was sweet! Those precious memories still flood over me like that event happened yesterday!

Desire His Strength

The plane crash brought me to a place of incredible weakness. After weeks in bed, I had little to no physical strength of my own. I couldn't walk, stand up by myself, roll over in bed, or feed myself. Nearly everything had to be done for me. At this point in my life, I came face-to-face with the question: Would I continue to rely on my own strength, or would I draw my strength from the Lord? Psalm 84:5 says, "*Blessed is the man whose strength is in thee; in whose heart are the ways of them.*" The blessing offered in this verse can only take place if the Christian humbles himself to God to seek his strength from God. My Heavenly Father used this trial to place in my heart a desire for His strength. I had to learn to depend on Christ in the same way I had to depend on others to help me do everything. Though my greatest strength is always very weak, His might is always very strong.

God used this trial to create a desire in my heart for His strength. Fulfilling that desire in my life can only be accomplished when I find His grace sufficient as I take pleasure in my weakness. I had to learn this same lesson just as the Apostle Paul testifies of learning it in 2 Corinthians 12:9, 10, *"And he said unto me, My grace is sufficient for thee: for my strength is made perfect in weakness. Most gladly therefore will I rather glory in my infirmities, that the power of Christ may rest upon me.* [10]*Therefore I take pleasure in infirmities, in reproaches, in necessities, in persecutions, in distresses for Christ's sake: for when I am weak, then am I strong."*

We receive God's grace by rejoicing in our weakness.

My family and I were going through a time of weeping as we walked through this particular valley. God places promises in His Word for His children's benefit. We lived from promise to promise, which became a source of strength and refreshment for each of our trials and needs. Psalm 84:6, 7 says, *"Who passing through the valley of Baca* [weeping] *make it a well; the rain also filleth the pools.* [7]*They go from strength to strength, every one of them in Zion appeareth before God."* As we pass through our *valley of Baca* (weeping), God wants us to make "wells" for other travelers passing through their own valleys of weeping. Because of the valley we passed through, I have often been able to share God's precious source of strength with other burn patients and their families as well as those facing different difficulties.

God used the plane crash to teach us that prayer is the key to victory in our trials. My church went to God to find a *well of refreshment* for me during many times of need. Those prayers were also *wells* for others going through trials. Psalm 84:8 says, *"O Lord God of hosts, hear my prayer: give ear, O God of Jacob."* As believers, we are often broken by the sorrows of life, but we are promised victory in each trial. We are *more than conquerors* through our Lord Jesus Christ (Romans 8:37). Our prayers are heard and answered only through Him. Every Christian has access right into the presence of God because of our relationship with Christ. There we can draw strength directly from our Heavenly Father. Like the bird nesting in God's house, there are no restraints in His presence—only freedom and access to everything we need.

Little did I know that eight years after the crash, God would deepen the *well of refreshment* that had been dug during those days. Early in the morning of December 24, 1988, my mother called to let me know my father's medical tests verified that he had cancer. We wept together as we talked on the phone. My dad, who was a believer, was not frightened by death, but he was not excited about going through the extreme suffering involved with cancer—even though the path would ultimately end in the presence of His Savior.

After talking with my mother, I read my Bible. My reading that day included Psalm 84. Through that Psalm, God spoke to my heart and said, "Ken, as you walk through this valley with your dad, make it a well with which to refresh others. Do with it as you have done with the plane crash."

When I was with my father, I watched his face glow as I read Bible passages about dying, Heaven, the resurrection, and Christ's victory over death. I watched how sharing these verses ministered to him. Dad battled the cancer valiantly, but in November 1989, he lost his battle and met His Saviour face-to-face.

I had faced death in the plane crash. I faced it once again as my dad battled his cancer. That time with my dad gave me the boldness to speak the truth of God's Word to others also fighting cancer. God, by His grace, began a well that has helped refresh others on their individualized journeys through their trials.

God used the events of the plane crash to show both Beth and me that our hope rests in Him. He makes no mistakes. He is always good. He keeps His promises. He is faithful. These are only a few of the *wells of refreshment* we began digging in those days of weeping.

Trust Him

My need for physical care continued after I was released from the hospital. This necessity gave my family many opportunities to grow in our trust of God. Each need required us to humble ourselves to God as we set aside our own plans, expectations, or agenda. God poured out His grace, giving us the desire to trust Him and not to lean on our own understanding (Proverbs 3:5, 6). Responding to God in humility moved Him to give us His grace as He promised in James 4:6, *"But he giveth more grace. Wherefore he saith, God resisteth the proud, but giveth grace unto the humble."*

The morning after I arrived home from the hospital, Beth's week-long training was immediately put to the test. She disinfected the tub, ran the water, and helped me into the bathroom to prepare to soak in the tub. The same thought hit both of us at the same time: Beth had been taught how to help me into the tub without a lift, but no instructions had been given on getting me out! We knew gravity would help me into the tub, and we both decided that somehow God would help get me out when the time came.

I got into the tub and soaked off the dressings. Beth did the necessary debriding of my burn wounds. It was nearing the time when I would be getting out of the tub. As Beth slipped out of the bathroom to check on our daughters one more time, the phone rang. She paused in her ministrations long enough to take a quick message. Noel Foster, who was running some errands, called wondering if there was anything he could do to help. When Beth explained our dilemma, Noel had a ready answer.

"I helped a disabled friend learn how to get out of the tub," he said. "I think I could help Pastor get out of the tub and teach you how to do it in the future."

By the time Beth had toweled me off, wrapped my legs, and had prepared me to get out of the tub, Noel had arrived. God's timing was perfect. We realized we could always trust God—even in the little things.

In Psalm 84:11, 12, God has promised to bless those who trust in Him: *"For the LORD God is a sun and shield: the LORD will give grace and glory: no good thing will he withhold from them that walk uprightly. [12]O LORD of hosts, blessed is the man that trusteth thee."* Trust is "having confidence in God, being secure in Him, and depending on Him as our refuge in times of trouble." Mrs. Charles E. (Lettie) Cowman, a faithful missionary in the Orient, goes on to write the following about trust as a part of the December 15 entry of her devotional book, *Streams in the Desert*:

> The word trust is the heart word of faith. It is the Old Testament word, the word given to the early and infant stage of faith. The word faith expresses more the act of the will, the word belief is the act of the mind or intellect, but trust is the language of the heart. The other [faith] has reference more to a truth believed or a thing expected.

In Proverbs 3:5, 6, the Christian is commanded to *"Trust in the LORD with all* [his] *heart."* We can trust God because He is our *Shield*—that protection which we need in our days of trials. He is a *Sun*—giving life to those who believe, lighting the path on which we are to walk, and providing warmth against the cold, cruel hardships of life. He helps us to see the beauty around us through the difficulties. He gives grace and glory that can only come from Him. This grace moves us to desire His blessing above all else. Best of all, God will not withhold any good thing from His children. He has given promise after promise of His faithfulness in Scripture. By simply trusting Him, we can claim every promise and know that God's blessing will follow.

God gave our family many opportunities to grow in our ability to trust Him. He has been there with us throughout the journey. He walked with us through the trial of the plane crash and is still walking with us through each and every subsequent trial we encounter.

God graciously protected me from my selfish desires. He gave me the desire for His fellowship, His strength, and to trust Him. Seeking to fulfill these desires has enabled me to focus on God's purpose for my life. Through them, He has blessed me in my pain, my salvation, my surrender, my walk, and my ministry. Truly, God does give good through every trial. We know. We have experienced it.

Fellowship

We receive God's grace as we live in fellowship with Him.

"Blessed are they that dwell in thy house: they will be still praising thee. Selah."
– Psalm 84:4

God's blessing—true happiness—comes to those who desire fellowship with God. This fellowship begins with salvation through faith in Jesus Christ, is based on surrender to Him, and is maintained with Biblical priorities.

"Jesus saith unto him, I am the way, the truth, and the life: no man cometh unto the Father, but by me."

– John 14:6

CHAPTER NINE

Salvation

Pain became my constant companion. As I lay healing in the hospital, I often thought, "How could somebody not only live eternally without Christ but also experience this kind of pain forever? How could anyone endure this?" I knew that the excruciating pain I was experiencing wasn't anything compared to the fires of Hell. I found comfort in the truth that God did not make Hell for people but for the devil and his angels. Jesus stated this truth in Matthew 25:41, which says, *"Depart from me, ye cursed, into everlasting fire, prepared for the devil and his angels."* Though God's original purpose for Hell has changed, the suffering of Hell's fire has not changed one whit.

After hearing the news of the plane crash, an associate pastor-friend of mine asked his church to pray for me. A nurse who attended his church later told him, "The only pain worse than dying from burns is to be burned and live." When he shared that comment with me, I could only attest that this nurse's words truly expressed my experience.

I daresay nearly everyone knows how painful even the slightest burn can be. A child who inadvertently touches a stove suddenly understands in a new way the meaning of the word *hot*. As I languished in my hospital bed, I began to learn some facts about burns I did not know. Burns can be caused by heat, electricity, chemicals, light, radiation, or friction. All burns remain painful in various stages of their progress—especially those that affect the first and second layers of the skin (epidermal tissue and dermis). Rarely do burns affect anything deeper than the skin, but occasionally the burns are deeper. Burns can also affect the muscle, bone and blood vessels.

The majority of my burns were third-degree burns which also affected the muscle, bones, and tissue under the skin. [See Appendix B for more information about burns.] These third-degree burns covered over 30 percent of my body. I was overwhelmed by the excruciating pain when I first arrived at the hospital because my right arm and hand had suffered a great deal of second-degree burns, which are the most painful initially.

My body swelled with water. As a result, the medical staff had to closely regulate and limit my fluid intake. I have since learned that a child with a mere 10 percent of his body burned, or an adult with 15 percent of his body burned is in life-threatening danger from what medical professionals call hypovolemic shock. Fluid leaking out of the bloodstream causes a low blood volume, which in turn causes low blood pressure and can potentially lead to the failure of vital organs. To give more fluids to a person in hypovolemic shock would only cause additional problems. At the same time, not being able to drink water creates intense thirst—that same desperate thirst I felt which drove me to do what could have led to my harm or even my death.

Burton Brush

The pain went on and on. Ten days after the crash, my father-in-law came to visit and later shared how helpless he felt as he watched the bed shake because of the raw pain I was experiencing.

My brother, Gib, and his family came before the last surgery. From the moment he heard of my accident, Gib had felt a deep, personal pain for me. When they came to visit, he wanted to spend as much time with me as possible, so after a quick, early morning trip to the crash site with Dad, he made sure to be ready to ride along with Beth to the hospital. When they came into the room that day, Beth could clearly see that I was struggling.

"Ken, is something wrong?" she questioned.

"My arm is hurting." I tried to downplay the intensity of my pain so Beth wouldn't be concerned, but somehow she knew. As the hours of their visit passed, it was all I could do to keep my composure. Finally, I asked Beth to check my arm.

"Something's wrong," I told her. "Maybe you can see what it is."

Beth stepped up to the bed and examined my arm.

"I think it's the IV from the blood infusion."

Beth was getting ready to leave, so she could take over caring for our girls, and then my sister-in-law and parents could come for their evening shift.

"I'll see if I can find someone to help you," she promised as she left the room.

By this point the pain level had driven tears to my eyes.

"You've got to stop crying," Gib pleaded.

"I'm going to cry," I told him. "It hurts!"

"You've got to stop crying because if you don't, I'll cry," Gib confessed as I saw the tears begin to well up in his eyes.

Dr. Ayvazian stepped into the room.

"Ken, I just spoke with your wife," he greeted us. "She said you're in a lot of pain from the IV. Let's see if we can find out what's wrong."

The doctor walked to the side of the bed where the IV was attached to my arm and took a hard look at it.

"I see the problem. The IV has dislodged from the vein, and it's infusing the blood into the muscle." The doctor was already removing it as he spoke. He left the room and called a nurse to reinsert the IV. When the nurse attempted to replace the IV, her attempt failed. She tried again, but with the same result. Each effort sent a wave of nausea over me, until finally I couldn't take it anymore.

"Could we please wait a while before trying again? I can't handle any more pain right now."

"Yes. We certainly can."

I was delighted by her response. I needed that respite. Thankfully, an anesthesiologist came later to reinsert the IV successfully without pain and on his first try. The stiffness in my arm remained for months until the infused blood dissipated from the muscle.

As I lay in the hospital bed enduring pain that could not even be quenched by all of the pain medication the medical personnel could give me, I thought of what Scripture says about the fires of hell. I thought of Jesus' story of the rich man and Lazarus in Luke 16. The man had lived an abundant life, but he would spend an eternity in hell. As the rich man looked up from the torments of hell, he saw Lazarus who had lived on crumbs from his table. The rich man begged for Lazarus to dip his finger in water and to touch his tongue because he was in torment. Even a drop of water would have felt cooling to him. However, nothing could be done for the rich man. A gulf had been fixed between the two that no one could cross. I can honestly say that during those weeks of painful convalescence, I understood the rich man's desire. But the desire of those in hell will never be met.

During those weeks of pain, I also thought of the size of hell. I thought of all those who still did not know Christ as their personal Savior. I wept easily and often, because I was experiencing many of the attributes of hell, but my experience was only for a time, whereas theirs would be for all eternity. I thought back to the time nearly twelve years earlier when I received Christ as my personal Savior.

I had grown up on a farm in the Midwest as the youngest of five children. The first nine years of my schooling were in a little, one-room country schoolhouse. My twin sister was my only classmate.

My life on the farm and my education were simple. On the outside, I did not appear to have some of the problems often found in other people. Yet, I knew something was absent in my life. That missing ingredient made even my simple life very complex. I became more involved in church activities, hoping to fill the void. However, because my church did not accurately teach the Bible, this religious influence only worked to cause me more frustration.

I remember driving around our family farm after a tornado had passed through a portion of it. The tornado had traveled low enough to take down treetops and topple haystacks. Though very localized, a horrible mess remained in the wake of the storm's destructive path. Along with all of the other cleanup, we had fences to repair. My brother, Gib, had come with me to help fix the fences. I was driving the tractor at the time, which was a privilege little brothers didn't always have. Gib was standing behind me on the draw bar where I usually stood.

The storm brought my brother's conversation to a question. "Ken, where would you spend eternity if you were killed in a storm like this?" The question challenged my sincere, but superficial, understanding of Christianity

I said, "You were in the church service when I went forward the time we had that visiting preacher. I'm a Christian!"

"Well, buddy," Gib responded, "all I can tell you is that if you die without Christ, you are going straight to hell."

I was angry at Gib for challenging me. Repentance and salvation were the furthest thing from my mind at that point. I wanted to turn in my seat and push him off the tractor.

I have found that most of us do not like to be faced with our eternal destiny. We all have *stuff* in our life with which we are dealing. We tend to become so focused on our *stuff* that we forget to see the bigger picture—our eternal destiny. We fail to see how that bigger picture will affect us for good or bad.

I clearly saw my frustration, but I saw no remedy. I only sensed more pressure to do something. The question was, "What?" Seemingly, the harder I tried, the more frustrated I became. During this time, my brother, Gary, led me and several others in my family in a Bible study to find these answers.

As I studied the Bible, I realized my problem was disobedience against God. I had sinned against Him. In Romans 3:23, God makes it clear that each person has this problem: *"For all have sinned, and come short of the glory of God."*

I also began to realize that sin has a penalty—death—eternal death. In Romans 5:12, God confirms this truth: *"as by one man sin entered into the world, and death by sin; and so death passed upon all men, for that all have sinned."*

I came to understand that God has appointed a time for each person to die and after that would come the judgment (Hebrews 9:27). As I read in Revelation, the truth of God's judgment and Hell both became real to me:

> *"And I saw a great white throne, and him that sat on it, from whose face the earth and the heaven fled away; and there was found no place for them. [12]And I saw the dead, small and great, stand before God; and the books were opened: and another book was opened, which is the book of life: and the dead were judged out of those things which were written in the books, according to their works. [13]And the sea gave up the dead which were in it; and death and hell delivered up the dead which were in them: and they were judged every man according to their works. [14]And death and hell were cast into*

the lake of fire. This is the second death. [15]And whosoever was not found written in the book of life was cast into the lake of fire." (Revelation 20:11-15)

As a young man, I had little comprehension of the pain and suffering of Hell; however, many years later as I lay in the hospital convalescing from my burns, the pain of Hell became very real to me. But I knew the excruciating pain I was experiencing was nothing compared to the fires of Hell.

The discussions that I had with my brothers many years before had helped me to understand that neither my church activity nor anything else would be enough to fix that empty place in my life. In Ephesians 2:8, 9 God, instructs us that religion and good works cannot pay the price for sin: *"For by grace are ye saved through faith; and that not of yourselves: it is the gift of God: [9]Not of works, lest any man should boast."*

Right along with this, I learned that Christ had already paid the penalty for my sin by His death on the cross. In Romans 5:8, God teaches that Christ made this payment for me even though in my pride I was refusing Him: *"But God commendeth* [demonstrates, shows] *his love toward us, in that, while we were yet sinners, Christ died for us."*

This study in the Bible helped me understand that I had to receive Christ's payment for the penalty of death on my life. In John 1:12, God simply states that we receive Christ's payment by believing on His name: *"But as many as received him, to them gave he power to become the sons of God, even to them that believe on his name."* Romans 10:10, 13 explains that our belief must come from our heart—our inner being—and can be expressed in prayer: *"For with the heart man believeth unto righteousness; and with the mouth confession is made unto salvation…For whosoever shall call upon the name of the Lord shall be saved."*

Finally, as a young man of seventeen, I made that pivotal decision to receive Christ and His payment for my sin. I came to realize that I had found the ingredient I was missing. Since then, I have experienced peace, fulfillment, and real satisfaction. The greatest benefit is that I know I have eternal life. Only by true salvation in Jesus Christ do we establish our fellowship with God, who then enables us to walk in fellowship with Him each day of our life.

Several years after I was burned, Aunt Ramona called and asked me to visit a man in the burn unit who had been burned in a garage fire. He had inhaled both flames and smoke. This same fire had also taken the life of his son.

When I went to visit this man, I found him resting under an oxygen tent; he could not speak. I began to share my experience, and I explained why I had been called to visit him. In the course of conversing with him, I found out that he was not a Christian. He acknowledged the fact by nodding his head.

"Would you like me to share with you how you can know you won't have to experience the pain you are experiencing now for all eternity?" I asked.

When he nodded, I shared the Gospel of Jesus Christ as I heard it many years earlier, and asked him if he believed the truth of the Gospel and wanted to receive the Savior.

He nodded.

Since he could not speak, I asked him to pray in his heart, acknowledging his sin to God, admitting his need for forgiveness, and confessing his belief in Jesus Christ alone for salvation. "God will hear you," I assured him.

We were silent for a while, he with his eyes closed.

"Did you receive Christ by believing in your heart?" I asked when he opened his eyes.

He nodded again.

Knowing how quickly having visitors had tired me in the early days of my stay in the burn unit, I prayed for him and his healing one more time. Then, after promising to return to see him again in a few days, I excused myself.

About a week later, I went back to see him again. He was no longer under a tent, and by now he was able to barely whisper. The first words out of his mouth testified of his assurance of salvation, "I've come as close to Hell as I will ever have to come!"

What about you?

Have you come as close to Hell as you'll ever have to come? Have you received the Savior's payment for your sin and His gift of eternal salvation? You, too, can receive the gift of eternal salvation and never have to experience any of the painful attributes of Hell. Will you be careless with the Gospel message of our Lord Jesus Christ, or will you receive Him? You don't have to be one of the people in Hell.

If you are already a Christian, do you understand the importance of sharing the Gospel with others and leading them to salvation, so they never experience the pain and suffering of Hell's fires? Will you be careless with the Gospel message of our Lord Jesus Christ, or will you be a faithful witness? Let the truth of Hell's painful fires and its separation from fellowship with God motivate you to share the Gospel with others, so they do not have to suffer Hell's never-ending pain.

"For the which cause I also suffer these things: nevertheless I am not ashamed: for I know whom I have believed, and am persuaded that he is able to keep that which I have committed unto him against that day."

– 2 Timothy 1:12

CHAPTER TEN

Surrender

The pain that sought to overwhelm me became worse when the grafting process started. With my second graft, an acute psuedomonas infection threatened to destroy the graft. The treatment included applying an antibiotic cream to the grafted skin and the donor site. When applied, this ointment seemed to burn these already wounded surfaces. Each application in the morning and again at night also brought an increase of pain.

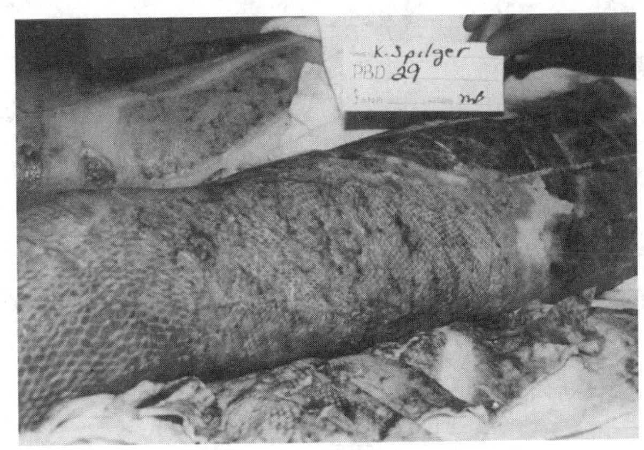

A close up of the psuedomonas infection
The bandages and grafts are green.

On Sunday morning the doctor announced that I would no longer need this pain-causing cream. This additional pain will finally be over! However, when my evening dressing change was to take place, I saw the antibiotic cream. I even shuddered at the sight and said, "The doctor said I did not need it anymore."

The staff looked at their orders again. "This order still calls for the cream," one of them explained.

"Can you call the doctor and double-check with him?"

They did as I requested and attempted to call him; however, being Sunday they could not reach him.

"Please, trust me," I begged the nurse, "I don't need the cream."

"I still have to follow the written orders," she said. As she applied the cream, the pain was excruciating. In that moment, I chose to surrender myself to God, to His care, and to the care of the medical staff. This choice of surrender, being based in humility, activated God's grace in my life, and I was able to bear the unnecessary pain.

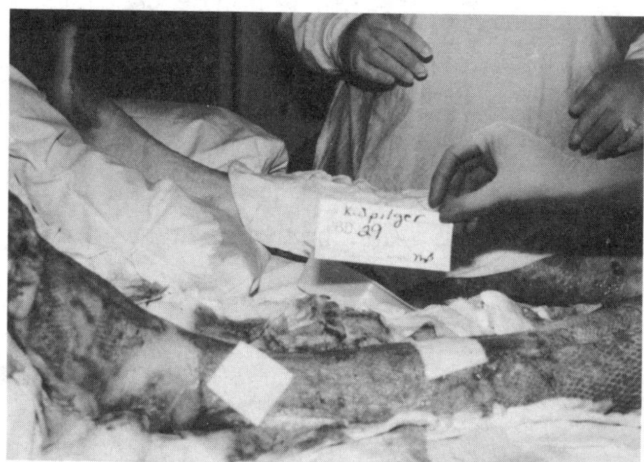

Another picture of the pseudomonas infection

The next morning the doctor apologized for his negligence. The nurse also spoke to me conveying her understanding of why I would want them to refrain using the cream.

"I hope you understand why I had to go ahead and use it," she added.

Through this situation, I found God to be faithful to me—even though I didn't get what I desired. My surrender was possible because of a truth God had taught me early in my Christian life. I knew God was always true to His Word even though man sometimes fails.

A couple of weeks after my salvation, in June of 1968, while attending a church service we sang the hymn, "I Know Whom I Have Believed" by Daniel Whittle. As we were singing, I noticed a Bible reference to 2 Timothy 1:12 at the bottom of the page. When we finished singing, I turned to the passage in my Bible and read, *"For the which cause I also suffer these things: nevertheless I am not ashamed: for I know whom I have believed, and am persuaded that he is able to keep that which I have committed unto him against that day."*

As I read that verse for the first time, God whispered to my heart, "Ken, whatever you keep for yourself, you will mess up; but if you will give it to Me, I will keep it, bless it, and give you rewards for eternity."

I Know Whom I Have Believed

STANZA ONE:

"I know not why God's wondrous grace
To me He hath made known,
Nor why, unworthy, Christ in love
Redeemed me for His own."

CHORUS:

"But 'I know whom I have believed,
And am persuaded that He is able
To keep that which I've committed
Unto Him against that day.'"

~ Daniel W. Whittle

The best I could, I dedicated my life to Him. I had no idea at the time what all God would bring into my life. Neither did I realize that dedicating my life to Him was simply the beginning of a process that God would work in me for the rest of my life. All I knew was that I did not want to keep my life and mess it up! God had promised that whatever I gave to Him, He would bless, guard, and keep for eternity. I was eager to allow Him to do what He had promised. From that day forward, I began a lifelong process of giving myself to the Lord. He has never failed me!

Through the years that followed, God would give me many opportunities to choose whether to surrender to His will and strengthen that fellowship or to walk in my own way and damage it. God used the stresses of day-to-day life leading up to the pastors' conference to bring me to a new point of surrender—willingness to let Him take complete control. He used the plane crash to place me in a position which would deepen my fellowship with Him; but that fellowship would include much suffering. He used the negligence of the doctor causing another more painful dressing change to remind me once again that I must surrender to His will.

Know Christ

Second Timothy 1:12 is all about the One in whom I place my trust. The verse says, *"I know whom I have believed."* Fellowship gives us a greater understanding of who God is. The Apostle Paul yearned for this type of knowledge. In Philippians 3:10 he wrote, *"That I may know him, and the power of His resurrection, and the fellowship of his sufferings, being made conformable unto his death."* We cannot know the *"fellowship of his sufferings"* until we ourselves have walked through suffering. Suffering gives us a new opportunity to surrender to His work in us—so that we might better know Him and His power.

As I convalesced in that hospital bed, I was being forced to return to the truth of surrender He had begun teaching me shortly after I was saved.

My life took on a new routine: IVs, reports, regular checks of my vital signs, therapy, blood draws, a daily tub soak, and painful dressing changes twice each day. In the process, I came to know those who were caring for me. In fact, I trusted them and surrendered myself to their care.

In much the same way, we get to know our Lord. The daily routines—the work, the pain, the joy, the defeats, the victories—are all necessary to our truly knowing Christ. Before the crash, I had been getting to know Christ in my daily routines, but I had also been advancing my own agenda and was being haunted by my selfish expectations. For a number of years, this selfishness hindered my fellowship with Christ. Now, in the Burn Unit, God was renewing our fellowship. I was again in a place to know Christ—to really know Him.

Through the years of walking with God, He has taught me that there are four key ways the Christian can truly know Him. These four ways build on the foundation of our personal salvation. They also work with the foundation of our surrender to Him.

- The first way is the *Bible*. In His written Word, God has revealed Himself to us (John 14:21).
- The second way is *prayer*. Hebrews 4:16 says prayer brings us into the very presence of God.
- The third way is *church attendance*. In church we fellowship with God's people, and Jesus promised to meet with us when we meet in His name (Matthew 18:20).
- The fourth way is *soul winning*. Finally, we know Him as we tell others about Jesus Christ and His great salvation, because He promised to be with us in our outreach (Matthew 28:18–20).

Yes, being in the hospital was a new experience for me, let alone being in the Burn Unit. My awareness of others and my concern for them in the midst of a personal catastrophe and suffering was clearly an evidence of God's working in my heart, teaching me more about what it means to fellowship with Him.

A couple of days after the accident, a young nursing student was assigned to my care. Her program included rotation to various wards in the hospital to acquaint her with the possibilities for specializing her training. I could tell my extreme injuries were somewhat unnerving to this nervous, young nursing student. I sensed her uneasiness and tried to ease her tension

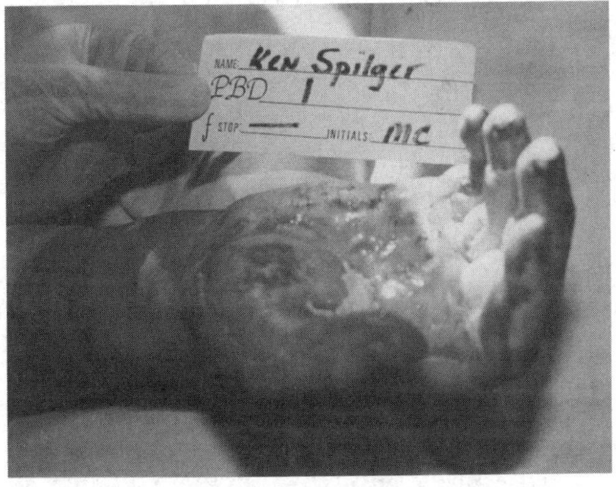

Ken's right hand

by making conversation, but I found conversation was difficult. Then I noticed a pin on her lapel and commented on it, after reading the words "Christian Nurse of the Year Award" out loud.

I asked, "If you died today, do you know you would go to Heaven?" Even though my question was sincere, I was unable to ease her tension.

She smiled nervously. *This man who was near death was asking her if she was ready to die?* She merely shrugged her shoulders and quietly went on with her work. Though she was not unkind in her response, I felt she was evasive in her answer.

About a year later, Beth spoke at a ladies' meeting at a church in a nearby city. After the meeting, a young lady approached her and shared the following story:

> *I was a nursing student at St. John's when your husband was brought to the hospital. A couple days after the accident, a fellow student and I were assigned to the Burn Unit as part of our training rotations. She was assigned to care for your husband. I happened to have lunch with her on our break, and she told me what happened while she was in his room.*
>
> *She asked, "You know that pastor who was burned in that plane crash? He asked me the strangest question: 'If you died today, do you know you would go to Heaven?'" Because of your husband's question, I was able to share the Gospel with her.*

God was helping me to understand that I was not to be ashamed of the suffering I was passing through; rather, I was to live in constant communion with Christ. By so doing, I was able to be aware of the spiritual needs of those around me.

All four of these disciplines—fellowship with God through His Word, through prayer, through church attendance, and through witnessing—had already been a part of my life for years. However, God used the new routines resulting from the plane crash, the burns, the therapy, and the pain to take me out of the rut I had formed through my personal struggles. God was now able to lead me to a fresh knowledge of Jesus Christ.

Trust Christ

"Ken, I know you're a minister, but it's okay to scream when you feel the pain."

The dressing change routine, which happened twice a day, was very difficult for me to endure. It was also difficult for the medical staff to perform.

"It's okay to curse if it helps you deal with the stress," one of my caregivers said, "We won't tell anybody."

"I'm trusting in the Lord." I sought to find the words I needed to explain. "He helps me to focus on Him as I work with my breathing and work through the pain."

God was faithful, and this daily routine of trusting my Lord through the pain built my confidence in Him.

Once a person knows Christ, he can confidently trust his Heavenly Father. This trust further establishes the foundation of surrender for a child of God. Second Timothy 1:12 continues, *"I... am persuaded that he is able to keep."* Our confidence has to be in Christ and in His ability to keep us—no matter what the circumstances may be.

My salvation was secured twelve years before the plane crash when I had received Jesus Christ as my personal Savior. God gave me His peace that He gives freely to all who call upon Him for salvation because of Christ's death on the cross. Romans 5:1 says, *"Therefore being justified by faith, we have peace with God through our Lord Jesus Christ."* Because of this gift of salvation, we can have the peace of God that passes all understanding: *"Be careful for nothing; but in every-thing by prayer and supplication with thanksgiving let your requests be made known unto God. [7]And the peace of God, which passeth all understanding, shall keep your hearts and minds through Christ Jesus."* (Philippians 4:6, 7)

As I pondered the fact that even a plane crash could be God's *good pleasure* (Philippians 2:13), I experienced a peace that did indeed pass all understanding. I knew God does nothing wrong. I understood He has a purpose in everything. One of His purposes is to mold me into the image of His Son, the Lord Jesus Christ. God wants me to bring glory to Himself, and He wants me to show others His power and majesty.

When we realize that He is working out His purposes, we are enabled to trust Him more fully and to enjoy fellowship with Him more deeply. Christ is not who we sometimes make Him out to be; rather, He is who He has revealed Himself to be. Ask yourself these questions about how you view Christ and your relationship to Him:

- Am I allowing Him to be God, or am I making Him into an image that I want Him to be (Psalm 135:15-18)?
- Do I believe that He has made me in His image (Genesis 1:26, 27)?
- Do I believe that I am blessed beyond measure in Christ (Ephesians 1:3)?
- Do I believe that I am chosen in Christ, accepted, redeemed, forgiven, made part of His purpose (Ephesians 1:6 –12)?
- Do I recognize that I am dead to sin because I am in Christ (Romans 6:11)?
- Do I understand that I no longer have to obey the old *boss* who led me into sin because now I have a new *Boss* who will bring good into my life—if I will obey His orders and yield myself to Him (Romans 6:16-22)?

As I am caught up in the routines of life, I find it becomes easy to forget who God really is and how He works on our behalf. I have found that writing down what God has done in my life—His answers to prayer, His victories, etc.—and then going back over it during times of trial helps me not to forget His goodness. The children of Israel often forgot who God was because they simply failed to pass on the truths about the goodness of God to succeeding generations. The Bible is a book of principles to be passed from one generation to the next. The testimonies contained within the pages of God's Word surely make wise the simple or the naive (Psalm 19:7). God's desire is for the next generation to see life from His perspective. One way to see God's perspective is by sharing what He has done not only in my own life and the lives of others but also in the lives of people recorded in Scripture (Psalm 78:1-8).

One of my greatest personal losses in the plane crash continues to be a journal that I began in college. Its pages held my thoughts and struggles about some of the biggest and most difficult decisions I have had to make in my life. In that journal, I wrote down Scriptures God gave me in answer to those needs. Those answers helped me walk through the struggles I faced. I wrote about experiences, blessings, and how I was *persuaded that he is able to keep* me in every experience I had during those years. Once I could write after the plane crash, I again began a journal. I still take time to record what God is doing in me through His Word and life experiences. For the benefit of the generation coming after me—my children and grandchildren—this recording is worth my effort.

Commit to Christ

Not long after the plane crash, Elaine Spurgeon, the pilot's widow, called to talk to Beth.

"Beth," she said, "I want to encourage you to take whatever legal action is necessary to make the liability insurance pay what the policy specifies. The company has a history of not paying. Russell and I discussed the possibility of something like this happening back when he started flying. We discussed what steps I would need to take to initiate payment from this company. Please, I beg you to do whatever you need to do."

Sure enough, the insurance company sued us and all three of the widows. God was leading all of us on another part of His journey. His purpose was to lead us into greater surrender and deeper into His grace. The declaratory judgment stated that there was no coverage for any of us. The law demanded that a countersuit be initiated. Those being sued, however, cannot countersue the insurance company; the law required that we personally sue the policy holder, Mrs. Spurgeon. Taking this step was very difficult for us. We agreed with the lawyer representing three of us (Mrs. Spurgeon, of course, was represented separately) that we would not take any more than the policy stated.

One evening, we turned on the local news and were shocked to see a report misrepresenting us as dreadful people who were suing the pilot's widow for a huge amount of money—far beyond the policy limits. We were all the more shocked because the reporter had covered our story several times. He had been to the hospital, our home, and the church while reporting on my progress. He had been very gracious and sensitive to our pain in each report. We could not understand why he would report such false information, so I called the television station to clarify the situation.

"I want to thank you for trying to help us," I began the conversation.

"I'm not trying to help you," he replied dogmatically. "I'm reporting the news as I see it."

"Well," I replied, "I wondered if you are aware that the other two widows also sued the pilot's widow. The pilot's insurance company filed the first suit in the form of a declaratory judgment, which stated we were not covered by their policy."

"No. I was not aware of that."

"Are you aware of the agreement we have with our attorney not to take anything more than the policy limits?"

"No," he admitted.

"I think it would be good to include all of the facts before the report is aired again," I suggested calmly.

"Your attorney was the one who gave me the information I reported."

This bit of news shocked me. When the call ended, I immediately called our lawyer to find out why he had put out such a story to the news media.

Our lawyer was doing a great job, but I didn't understand all the requirements in these legal matters. I had never before traveled through this territory, and at this point, I was well behind the learning curve.

"Please," I implored, "check with us first before doing something like this again."

"Ken," he patiently responded, "believe me. I know the mental gymnastics you have gone through to handle the plane crash, the pain of the burns, and the therapy."

Again, I was shocked. "You do?" I asked. "Could you tell me what they are?"

"I know what they are."

"What are they?"

He stuttered a bit but made no answer.

This public embarrassment on the news pushed me to a selfish, defensive reaction, but God once again prompted me to refocus on my surrender to Christ. God also helped me to see this confrontation as an opportunity to share my faith in Christ.

"Yes, I do go through mental gymnastics. Let me tell you what they are," I continued. "When I was seventeen-years old, I received Christ as my personal Savior. I knew from that moment on I could trust God with my life. Just like I gave myself to God then, I have given myself to Him each day of my life. This was true the day the plane crashed. It was true for the pain of the burns. It is true for each day of my therapy. Each day, I simply give myself to God and trust Him to do with me what He wants. God is faithful to take care of what I give Him. He gives me peace."

This thought process helps me to exercise my faith in God and to maintain my focus on Him and His purpose. These *mental gymnastics* were possible only because of the work God had done in my life.

God used our lawyer to give us the best outcome for the insurance settlement. We were able to pay off all of our bills, and we would not be strapped with crippling debt.

Not one of us can possibly know what our future holds, but we can know who holds our future. Therefore, we must totally surrender ourselves to Jesus Christ as the Lord of our life. He alone is able to fill our days with His peace that passes all understanding—no matter what trials are ahead.

Living in fellowship with God requires not only knowing Christ and being persuaded that He is able to keep me, but also committing every part of life to Him. Why? Because Christ *"is able to keep that which I have committed unto him against that day."*

The foundation for working out God's purpose in your life is your surrender to Christ. This surrender produces true fellowship with God and activates God's grace in your life. You may be saying, "But why surrender? Do I really want to experience a plane crash like you did or another traumatic event of some sort?" I really don't think any one of us wants to experience pain and suffering, but every person knows that life contains its share of these. Since no one is exempt, why not commit your life to God for His keeping? Why not receive His grace for these trials? I can promise you from my own experience that God is faithful to guard anything we give to Him. Not only will He bless your willingness, but He will also bring good out of the experience.

My ability to live with God's peace ruling my heart in the midst of all the pain, suffering, and uncertainty from the plane crash was literally based on my salvation through Jesus Christ and my total surrender to Him based on 2 Timothy 1:12. God was preparing me to embrace His purpose for my life—my whole life—through total surrender.

"But seek ye first the kingdom of God, and his righteousness; and all these things shall be added unto you."

– Matthew 6:33

CHAPTER ELEVEN

Priorities

Plaque Beth gave Ken

On my study wall is a small plaque, which reads, "Along the way take time to smell the flowers." My wife gave it to me shortly after the plane crash because of the drastic changes we had to make in determining our priorities. God taught us that time is life. How we choose to use our time determines our fellowship with Him. Time became of much greater value. My time on earth should have ended at the plane crash, so how would I use the additional time God had given me?

Before our marriage, God blessed Beth and me with a wonderful, godly courtship. We were best friends. We served God together. We dreamed together. We enjoyed every moment we had together. We were truly in love with each other. But I realized we had lost that joyful togetherness due to my selfishness.

When we were married, Beth knew Christ held first place in my life. As we began our ministry following college, however, I began a slow process of replacing my focus on the Lord with an egotistical focus. Beth had been reared in a missionary/pastor's family. She had experienced firsthand the sacrifices families in full-time ministry had

Ken & Beth's wedding

to make. Because of her rearing, I figured she should understand my purposeful focus on ministry—even though I basically neglected her in the process. As a result of my attitude, Beth felt very insecure. Sometimes, she even felt she had no place in my priorities at all. My focus was entirely selfish as I became more concerned about making a name for myself than bringing glory to my Lord.

During those days of misplaced priorities, Beth struggled to maintain a quiet time. She was under so much pressure to perform, that those *invisible* areas tended to be neglected. The day simply did not have enough hours to keep a clean house, care for little children, go on visitation with me, teach a Sunday School class, play the piano for services, make meals, and have time to spend with God in His Word.

I went through the motions of my fellowship with God. I read His word faithfully, but carelessly. I prayed, but very little and selfishly. I went to church faithfully, but mechanically. I witnessed, but without power and out of duty. My relationship with Beth, our girls, and others was also becoming careless, selfish, mechanical, and out of duty. My problem with priorities became very evident before our second daughter's birth and resulted in Beth's being hurt deeply. With Esther's birth, Beth was overwhelmed. Instead of taking my place as Beth's husband and the father of our children, I was unwittingly, yet very successfully, destroying our marriage and neglecting our children—especially Esther.

By the time Esther was a year old, I barely knew her. One night, as I held her on my lap in the rocking chair, she cried and cried, simply because she wanted her mother. Beth could not come because she was tied up with other responsibilities. I knew in my heart that Esther would not be comforted by me because she barely knew me. My heart broke. God convicted me that I was wrong in my relationship with my baby girl.

As I held her close, I said, "Esther, I've been so wrong. When you were born, I was too busy to take time for you. I've asked God's forgiveness for doing this. Would you please forgive me?"

In her little girl voice, she answered, "Uh-huh." She hugged me back, laid her head on my shoulder, and promptly went to sleep. I don't know how much of what I said she understood, but she certainly responded to my broken spirit.

Both Beth and I had a great desire to rear children who would love the Lord and carry on serving Him with their own families. In fact, when I came as a candidate to pastor Grace Baptist Church in 1977, I preached a message in the evening service that reflected this desire of rearing up the foundations for godly generations. In my mind and practice, however, I had twisted the concept and convinced myself that I was doing what was necessary for our children to grow into responsible Christian adults who would pass on their faith to the next generation. Though my words declared my priorities, my life did not demonstrate them.

With my priorities out of order, I was unable to fulfill God's design for my life. I was carrying the weight and burden of my expectations. I was about to splinter and break from the weight of discouragement, disillusionment, and depression. I was also destroying my family and ministry in the same manner. But Jesus Christ was faithful to call me to Himself as He said in Matthew 11:28–30, *"Come unto me, all ye that labour and are heavy laden, and I will give you rest* [this is salvation]. [29]*Take my yoke upon you, and learn of me; for I am meek and lowly in heart: and ye shall find rest unto your souls* [this is service]. [30]*For my yoke is easy, and my burden is light."*

About a year before the plane crash, I answered Christ's invitation to take His yoke upon me for His service—not mine. My life was still busy, but Christ shared the burden with me. Truly His yoke is easy and His burden is light especially when compared to the burden of my own expectations.

The impact of this decision was seen in the days just prior to the plane crash. Sunday, September 14, 1980, was the church's Heritage Day celebration. We had an old-fashioned dinner on the grounds. We dressed in old-fashioned period pieces. I even rode a horse to church that Sunday. The celebration was a very busy day, but the attendees had a great time.

On Monday, September 15, I returned the old-fashioned suit I had rented for the church service, tied up some other loose ends from the weekend, prepared for my trip to Kansas City the next day, and spent as much of the rest of the day as I could with my family. We laughed, played games, went to the park, and enjoyed a special dinner. We had a truly wonderful time. That last day was not spent in pride, anger, and arguing. I loved and held my little girls. I loved and cherished my wife.

*Photographer said, "Don't smile" due to his **old** camera —thus the sober faces*

Little did we know that this was the last day that we would have together at home for two months. In fact, that day could have been the last day I would have with my family on this earth, but God chose to spare my life. I thank God for every day He has given me. I have become very conscious of time. In fact, I have discovered that I can live my life for God only as I use each moment for His purpose.

Seek Christ First

When Christ holds first place in a man's life and he is following God's leadership concerning priorities, a wife feels very secure. When I moved Christ out of first place in my life, every other relationship was up for grabs, left to the whims of my desires and the pressures of my expectations. But God in His mercy chastened me and led me to make the necessary corrections. God had Beth and me back to that place of the freedom, love and joy that we had during our courtship.

Living out my decision to take Christ's yoke upon me pushed me to study the Bible. Five times in Ephesians chapters four and five, God commands us to walk with Him in very specific ways. We are to…

- *walk worthy of the vocation wherewith ye are called.* (4:1)
- *walk not as other Gentiles walk.* (4:17)
- *walk in love, as Christ also hath loved us.* (5:2)
- *walk as children of light.* (5:8)
- *walk circumspectly, not as fools, but as wise* (5:15)

In short, God wants us to walk wisely.

Walking wisely means *incorporating God's order of priorities*. In the opening chapters of Ephesians, God states that He has saved us for His praise and glory. Chapter six tells us to stand in God's whole armor. Walking wisely and standing in God's armor requires us to live in the truth of our place in Christ as God teaches us in the first three chapters of Ephesians.

After the plane crash, God used the truths of this passage to help me understand that He had put His hand of blessing on my life and had a definite purpose for my living. The Apostle Paul prayed that the Ephesian Christians would have the spirit of wisdom and revelation (Ephesians 1:17). He wanted them to see life from Jesus Christ's perspective, to understand His truth in Scripture, and to be at peace with what He was doing in them. God wanted the same for me. I needed to see my life from Jesus Christ's perspective. I needed to grasp a clearer understanding of His Word—in my head and in my heart. I also needed to be at peace with what He was choosing to do in my life.

While in the hospital, I lived in continual, extreme pain, which left me feeling hopeless, helpless, and very worthless. I needed God's hope, a sense of value, and His power to make it through all I was facing both in the Burn Unit and especially after I arrived home. God wanted me to see that He had given me all of these the day I received Christ as my Savior (Ephesians 1:18, 19). He had given me life—real life—in His Son. Now, as I passed through this trial, He was teaching me to grow in the confidence I needed to live for Him. I knew I was still alive for a purpose. I am His *poem* created in Christ Jesus, and He has some *good works* for me to accomplish in my life (Ephesians 2:10).

Walking wisely also means that *our relationship with Christ must have first place*. This new life in Christ requires a fellowship with Him that is real. We cannot simply go through the motions of Bible reading, prayer, church attendance, and witnessing. We must seek Christ in all of these avenues. This relationship must come first, then God will lead us and bless us in our relationship with our spouse, our children, our work responsibilities, and our ministry responsibilities.

Redeem the Time

Time is one of life's most precious commodities. As we only have one life to live, we only have one opportunity to live each moment. As time slips past us, it is gone forever. God tells us in Ephesians 5:16 that we are to be *"Redeeming the time, because the days are evil."* In essence, we are to buy back each moment and use it for God-intended purposes.

Jesus Christ, our Example, demonstrated the need to make the most of every moment. He said in John 9:4, *"I must work the works of him that sent me, while it is day: the night cometh, when no man can work."* In John 12:35 He also instructed believers to do the same: *"Yet a little while is the light with you. Walk while ye have the light, lest darkness come upon you: for he that walketh in darkness knoweth not whither he goeth."*

I have now lived nearly thirty-five years fully aware that I should not have lived each of these precious moments. I should have died in the plane crash, but God gave me many more moments. I have become very aware that, when *redeeming the time*, we must make the most of every opportunity and be obedient to God's will. Because life is measured by time, how we prioritize our time demonstrates whether or not we are seeking Christ first. If we allow it, the *evil* of each day will easily rob and waste our life.

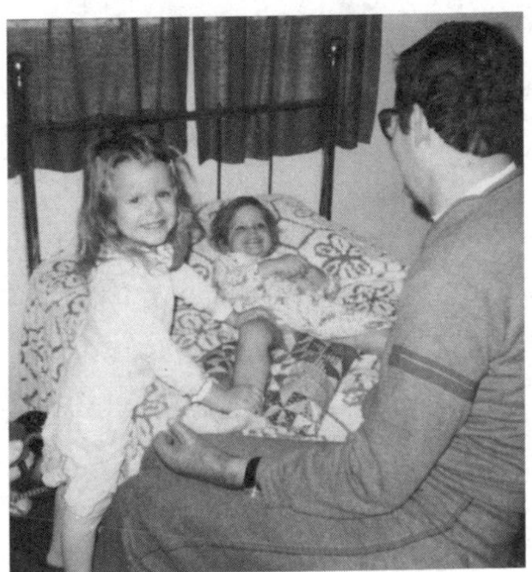

Anna playing doctor with Esther and Ken

Through a study of God's qualifications for a pastor (1 Timothy 3; Titus 1), I realized He placed my relationship with my wife and children very high on the priority list. Without them, I could not successfully carry out the ministry to which He had called me. I found I was only able to keep all of my priorities in their proper order as my Heavenly Father held first place in my life. I began taking definite steps of correction. Beth and I began to have a weekly date night. I began making our family Bible reading time more meaningful. I began planning and giving quality time to my family as well as to each of our children. God used Ephesians 5:15-21 in my life to help me make those corrections.

As a result, God was accomplishing a marvelous healing of my relationship with Beth. As we worked through our difficulties, we once again began communicating. God was teaching us to walk wisely.

In Ephesians 5:17 God commands, "*Wherefore be ye not unwise, but understanding what the will of the Lord is.*" When my focus became seeking God and His desires for the use of my time, I was able to do God's will for my life. Doing His will gave energy and enthusiasm to all Beth and I did. We were once again serving God—not ourselves.

Walking wisely does not mean doing only that which involves ministry. God's will for each believer is to honor and glorify Him in all we do. 1 Corinthians 10:31 says, "*Whether therefore ye eat, or drink, or whatsoever ye do, do all to the glory of God.*" In the process of glorifying Him, He wants us to have wisdom and understanding of what His will is for us. We must, therefore, spend time reading, memorizing, studying, and meditating on the Word of God in order to live it. He will help us bring the details of our lives together, and see them in relationship to each other. As He gives us wisdom—the ability to see life as He sees it—we'll be able to think clearly.

We are not in control of our lives as we so often think we are. We must give God His proper place and redeem the time so we can follow His Word to correctly order our priorities.

Be Spirit-Filled

Ephesians 5:18 commands us to be filled with His Spirit. God says, "*And be not drunk with wine, wherein is excess; but be filled with the Spirit.*" When we have surrendered to God, allowing His Spirit to continually fill us, we are able to seek Christ first and redeem the time. Having true fellowship with God enables us to walk wisely and do His will.

This truth was one of the greatest lessons I learned. In my selfishness, God's Spirit was not in control. After all, whether or not I was willing to admit it, I was doing my own thing—making my own plans. Instead of being filled with the Holy Spirit, I was grieving Him as God warned us in Ephesians 4:30, *"And grieve not the holy Spirit of God, whereby ye are sealed unto the day of redemption."* My relationships were all wrong. I lacked the fruit of the Spirit—love, joy, and peace, etc. (Galatians 5:22–23).

As I began surrendering myself to God and allowing the Spirit of God to control my life, my walk and my talk began to take on the distinct characteristics of the One who was in control. That's why God likens being Spirit-filled to a drunkard. We know a person is drunk—even without conducting sobriety tests—because of his characteristic walk and talk. The Scripture says that our walk and our talk will evidence the Spirit's control when we are singing psalms, hymns, and spiritual songs; making melody in our hearts to the Lord; and being grateful. Ephesians 5:21 also lists this evidence of a Spirit-controlled life: *"Submitting ourselves one to another in the fear of God."* Submitting ourselves to one another will definitely impact our family relationships: husband and wife, parent and child, married children and parents, etc. Being submitted to one another will affect our relationships at work and in our life, in general. Being submissive and Spirit-filled to one another will enhance our ability to live a victorious life in Christ by standing in His full armor.

Ken taking time with Anna and Esther shortly after getting home from the hospital

The added stress of the responsibilities from the hospital stay, therapy, and recovery tested us in new ways. By God's grace, we continued seeking to walk wisely, putting Christ first, and redeeming the time one step after another. Now the very precious nature of our family relationships held a proper Biblical place of priority. I sometimes wonder, "Where would we have been if I had not listened to God's working in my life before the crash?"

Once we decided to make our relationship with God come first and whatever fit in after that was acceptable, our fellowship with God changed. We worked to encourage each other to have a personal quiet time. We knew this fellowship with God was vital to our spiritual health, and necessary to be Spirit-filled and have a healthy relationship with each other as a family. This decision also had a significant impact in our church services in how we were—and are—able to fellowship with and encourage other believers.

Many people erroneously think, "My quiet time with God takes the place of church time." When Paul (Saul) persecuted the church, Christ stopped him on the road to Damascus and asked, *"Saul, Saul, why persecutest thou ME?"* In God's eyes, our behavior toward the body of Christ, the church, is the same as if we were carrying out our actions toward Christ Himself. When Christians neglect the fellowship of the local church, they are literally neglecting Christ!

I have learned so much about time management since the plane crash. In fact, at that time God gave me a *crash* course in this subject. God has helped me learn to use my time more wisely through the use of checkup sheets, to-do lists, calendars, and other helps. God has taught me that He, His Word, people, love, and praise are eternal; and everything else will burn someday. He has taught me that to be foolish with the time He has given me is a sinful waste. By prioritizing my time, I am able to live in fellowship with God and live every moment for Christ.

No earthly explanation exists as to why I survived and the other three men did not. I have to believe that, while their work was

Ken and girls

completed, God had more for me to accomplish on this earth. The fact that I lived through the plane crash got my attention and helped me focus on the importance of following God's guidelines for choosing—and living out—His priorities.

Not only should I not have survived the plane crash, but I also should not have lived through some of the challenges I faced during the hospital stay. So much of what happened could have had a different outcome. I believe God was using these experiences to help move my focus off myself and onto Him to deepen my fellowship with Him in every area of my life.

My friend, even though it may not seem like it, God is not wasting anything in your life. God desires true fellowship with you, and true fellowship with Him requires that we seek Him first, redeem the time, and be Spirit-filled. He is working to help focus your time on His purpose. He wants your priorities to be in line with His. He wants you—all of you. Time is life: live it ALL for Christ.

God's blessing—true happiness—comes to those who desire fellowship with God. This fellowship begins with salvation through faith in Jesus Christ, is based on surrender to Him, and is maintained with Biblical priorities. When our fellowship with God is in place, we are able to receive God's strength.

Strength

We reflect God's Glory
as we reflect His strength.

"Blessed is the man whose strength is in thee; in whose heart are the ways of them."
– Psalm 84:5

God's blessing—true happiness—comes to those who desire God's strength. This strength comes as we receive God's challenge, exchange our weakness for His strength, and wait on the Lord.

"Now after the death of Moses the servant of the LORD it came to pass, that the LORD spake unto Joshua the son of Nun, Moses' minister, saying, [2]Moses my servant is dead; now therefore arise, go over this Jordan, thou, and all this people, unto the land which I do give to them, even to the children of Israel. [3]Every place that the sole of your foot shall tread upon, that have I given unto you, as I said unto Moses. [4]From the wilderness and this Lebanon even unto the great river, the river Euphrates, all the land of the Hittites, and unto the great sea toward the going down of the sun, shall be your coast. [5]There shall not any man be able to stand before thee all the days of thy life: as I was with Moses, so I will be with thee: I will not fail thee, nor forsake thee. [6]Be strong and of a good courage: for unto this people shalt thou divide for an inheritance the land, which I sware unto their fathers to give them. [7]Only be thou strong and very courageous, that thou mayest observe to do according to all the law, which Moses my servant commanded thee: turn not from it to the right hand or to the left, that thou mayest prosper whithersoever thou goest. [8]This book of the law shall not depart out of thy mouth; but thou shalt meditate therein day and night, that thou mayest observe to do according to all that is written therein: for then thou shalt make thy way prosperous, and then thou shalt have good success. [9]Have not I commanded thee? Be strong and of a good courage; be not afraid, neither be thou dismayed: for the LORD thy God is with thee whithersoever thou goest."

– Joshua 1:1-9

CHAPTER TWELVE

Challenge

The thought of getting up to walk after a full week of lying only on my stomach was beyond overwhelming. I walked little between each graft. In order for the grafts to take, I had not been allowed to move after my third and final grafting surgery. I had even been medically constipated to avoid having a colostomy. Now even that waiting was soon coming to an end.

Dr. Copeland, Ken, Dr. Ayvazian, & Linda Brooks

I knew the doctors, nurses, technicians, and therapists would all be in my room Monday morning. Everyone who had helped me over the weeks would be there to cheer me on as the Stryker frame circle bed was turned so my feet were relatively close to the floor.

"Okay, Ken," one of the staff members would say with enthusiasm. "It's time to walk. Now, on the count of three..."

And all of them would count: "One...two...three..."

And I would be expected to take a step. I knew my caregivers expected me to take a step, but I was afraid.

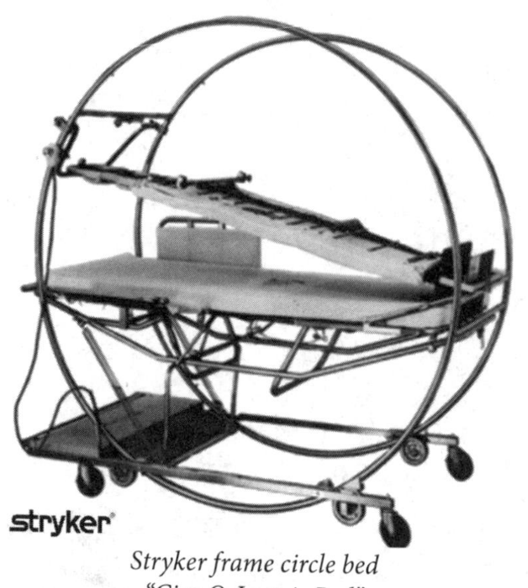

Stryker frame circle bed
"Circ-O-Lectric Bed"
- use by permission from Stryker

The last time I had tried to walk, I had fainted. My equilibrium wasn't right. I would have to try to find my center of balance without all of my toes. My legs were weak from a lack of use and from the removal of so much of the muscle in my left calf. On top of these issues, I was extremely weak.

I also knew that step was the first of many *first steps* toward my going home. What I would have to relearn was overwhelming. I could not roll over in bed. I could not dress myself. I could not feed myself. I could not pick up my Bible. I had not done any of these activities for most of the two months I had been in the hospital. I knew intense work would be required not only to relearn all of these things but also to readjust to society. I would have to learn to live in my new situation in the world outside of the hospital.

I also dreaded another battle I was facing. Without knowing it, I had become dependent upon the pain medications the medical staff had prescribed for me during my convalescence. The pain had been so intense that even those extreme doses of painkillers could not *quench the fires* that seemed to envelop my body. I had come to the point where I was dealing fairly well with the pain, but I was quickly approaching the point of being weaned off of the medications. I was both frightened and besieged by doubts.

These negative thoughts weighed down on me the Sunday before I was to take my first step. The more I focused on the negative realities ahead of me, the more fearful I became. I was afraid of walking. I dreaded therapy because it forced me out of my comfort zone. I feared leaving the Burn Unit where my weakness was received with understanding from the employees. I was afraid people would focus on my weaknesses and see me as weak. I was afraid I would be handicapped not only because of my physical limitations but also because of the stereotypical mold forced on me by others. I wanted to go home, but I was plagued with questions. Can I really handle being at home? What if I fail? How will I be able to handle the embarrassment? Will I ever be able to pastor again? How can I be the husband my wife needs? Will I be able to be the dad Anna and Esther need?

I doubted people's love for me. I felt I would be a burden to my family and church. I doubted God's love and care for me because I had allowed the evil one to bring fear and doubt into my life. I entertained Satan's lie: "If God loved me and cared for me, why would He let this happen to me?" These fears haunted me, because I wasn't walking with God to receive His strength.

I knew from the past that God had been faithful through every trial I had ever faced. I knew that my healing from the effects of the plane crash was a greater demonstration of His faithfulness than anything I had ever experienced. But when I took my eyes off of God's faithfulness and focused on my weakness, I lost all hope, courage, and the confidence I so desperately needed to take that first step. As I began to focus on myself and my inabilities, I became discouraged. I then lost my trust in God, and I began putting trust in my own understanding. By the time Beth came to see me Sunday afternoon, I was in deep despair. I tried to put on a good front for my wife, but I could not hide the truth.

All of us are weak, but only in our weakness is God's strength made perfect (2 Corinthians 12:9).

As I vacillated in my fear, God set His challenge before me. He commanded me to be strong, very courageous, to be unafraid, and not dismayed. I knew I was failing in following all four commands. In my weakness, God began working on my behalf by showing His faithfulness. My church family prayed for me all night that Sunday night. God heard their prayers and gave me hope. When I awoke the next morning, I realized I could be strong in Him. I could have courage because He was faithful, He was with me, and His Word was still true.

God's Faithfulness

In Joshua 1:1-5 God reminded Joshua of His faithfulness to Moses and the children of Israel. Moses had died, leaving Joshua to take the leadership of the people. God made His constant commitment to him very clear: *"As I was with Moses, so I will be with thee: I will not fail thee, nor forsake thee."* In the same way, God was faithful to me. Because He is always faithful to who He is, He will always be faithful to His children.

Dr. Lee Roberson

God restored my focus because of the prayers of His saints at Grace Baptist Church, who prayed that I would be able to walk the next day. They prayed that I would be able to attend a meeting at our church one week later with the late Dr. Lee Roberson from Highland Park Baptist Church and Tennessee Temple University. God answered. I was able to walk, and I was able to attend the conference. God gave me courage and made me strong.

As long as I kept my focus on Him, my fears were dispelled. God's strength and faithfulness had not changed. I had changed because I had removed my focus from Him and His promises. When I kept my eyes on Him, I could face the unknown. I could face the hard therapy, the withdrawal from the pain medication, and the responsibilities I feared. God had called me to this station of my life, and He would be faithful to me in all that I faced. He would give me grace for every trial. His strength would be made complete in my weakness.

God's Presence

Christianity is not a game believers are invited to play; it is a life they are called to live. Shortly after I was saved, several of my friends abandoned me because I had chosen to follow my Lord Jesus. One day during this difficult time, I was working on our family farm, driving a tractor pulling a large trip rake across a field of prairie hay. As I raked, I began singing a song we had learned in church:

> *"Walking in sunlight all of my journey;*
> *Over the mountains, through the deep vale:*
> *Jesus has said, 'I'll never forsake thee,'*
> *Promise divine that never can fail."*
>
> **Chorus:**
> *"Heavenly sunlight, heavenly sunlight.*
> *Flooding my soul with glory divine:*
> *Hallelujah, I am rejoicing,*
> *Singing His praises, Jesus is mine."*
>
> ("Heavenly Sunlight" by Henry J. Zelley)

When I came to the words, "Jesus has said, 'I'll never forsake thee,' Promise divine that never can fail," I broke down and wept. I was overwhelmed with the wonderful truth that, though my friends might leave me, Jesus would not. Like God promised Joshua, *"As I was with Moses, so I will be with thee: I will not fail thee, nor forsake thee,"* God will be with every believer through every trial.

That old hymn became even more endeared to me after the plane crash. He was with me the night of the plane crash. He was with me through each surgery. He was with me through the long months of therapy. In the middle of all that was unpleasant and painful to me, God assured me it was okay because He was with me. He gave me courage and strength. He is still with me each step of my journey. He is enough.

God's Word

The truth of God's faithfulness and the truth of His presence comes out of His Word. In Joshua 1:8, God says, "*This book of the law shall not depart out of thy mouth; but thou shalt meditate therein day and night, that thou mayest observe to do according to all that is written therein: for then thou shalt make thy way prosperous, and then thou shalt have good success."* God's promised success comes only from God's Word becoming such a part of our life that we *"observe to do according to all that is written therein."* Very simply, this verse means that the application of God's Word must come from our heart and be made a part of us—every day.

About a week before I was dismissed from the hospital, a lady from the JOBST Company came to measure me for my personal JOBST pressure garments. She had to measure my hands, legs, and feet.

When she saw my burns, she exclaimed, "Oh, you poor thing!"

"Excuse me!" A technician assigned to my room stepped up to the lady. "He is no 'poor thing.' His wife loves him. His church cares for him. He can walk. He is no poor thing!"

The staff in the burn unit understood how easily a burn survivor can grow discouraged. They worked very hard to keep me in a positive mindset. And though they were not quoting Scripture,

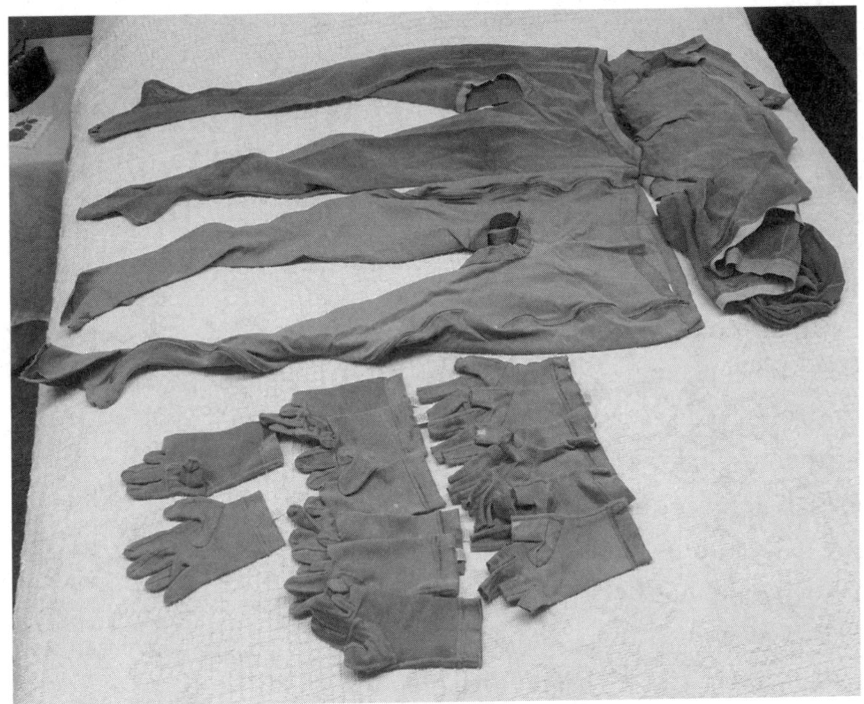

The assortment of JOBST needed for Ken's recovery

that mindset was right in line with godly thinking. You see, the real battle is in our mind. God says, "*For as he thinketh in his heart, so is he*" (Proverbs 23:7). Focusing on His truth gave me courage and strength.

When I was tempted to be fearful or dismayed, I had to choose what thoughts I would entertain. I faced many opportunities to become negative. How grateful I am that I had committed many verses to memory throughout my life. At exactly the right times, God would bring those truths that I had hidden in my heart to my mind. I often quoted Hebrews 13:5, which says, "*for he hath said, I will never leave thee, nor forsake thee.*" Philippians 4:13 was another passage which helped me deal with those negative thoughts. "*I can do all things through Christ which strengtheneth me.*"

In addition to the staff in the burn unit, God used other key people in my life to help me keep my focus on Him. They influenced me by living the truth of the Scriptures, even though they weren't actually quoting them. One such person was my father. I know he truly loved me. He even told my mother, "I wish I had been the one in the crash. I'm 75. Ken has his whole life to live." At the same time, he knew I had to face this trial. Dad accompanied Beth to the hospital the day I was released. I fully expected to have my folks with us for a while after I was home, but two hours after I arrived home, Mom and Dad loaded their car to begin their journey back to central Nebraska. They told us we would have to work through our struggles without their refereeing. I was lying on the couch too weak to sit up or stand. As Dad stood in the doorway looking at me, he said, "Ken, you have a very important decision to make. You can lie there and feel sorry for yourself, or you can get up and do something about it."

Paul Spilger

At the time, I could do very little for myself. I could barely roll over in bed on my own. I couldn't get out of a chair without help. But his was the most important counsel I received for my therapy and recovery. I realized that counsel from my father was given in love and deep concern. Quite possibly, it hurt him to say it. God used Dad's words to motivate me in the days ahead to try to do my best in therapy, to work hard to regain my strength, and, in general, to work at keeping a good, positive attitude.

I have since verbalized my dad's counsel in a more positive light: "I cannot focus on the things I cannot do, but I must focus on things

I can do. I cannot focus on the sole-survivor guilt, but on God's purpose for my life. I cannot focus on my weakness, but on God's strength."

Claiming God's promise that *"I can do all things through Christ which strengtheneth me"* (Philippians 4:13) helped me be strong in the face of my fears and to be courageous in the face of discouragement. Embracing God's challenge to be strong and courageous enabled us to embrace His purpose both for this trial and for every trial of our life. As He was there to help me be strong and courageous then, He will give me strength to face the tomorrows and their tough times. He never changes. His Word is always true. He fills us with hope. All we have to do is keep our focus on Him.

"Let this mind be in you, which was also in Christ Jesus:
6 Who, being in the form of God, thought it not robbery to be
equal with God: 7 But made himself of no reputation, and took
upon him the form of a servant, and was made in the likeness
of men: 8 And being found in fashion as a man, he humbled
himself, and became obedient unto death, even the death of
the cross. 9 Wherefore God also hath highly exalted him, and
given him a name which is above every name: 10 That at the
name of Jesus every knee should bow, of things in heaven, and
things in earth, and things under the earth; 11 And that every
tongue should confess that Jesus Christ is Lord, to the glory of
God the Father."

– Philippians 2:5-11

CHAPTER THIRTEEN

Exchanged Life

"*Haven't you learned* your lesson?! You could drive. You don't have to fly."

I had not flown anywhere since the plane crash. The Lord had provided for me to fly to another pastors conference. Seven years had passed since the accident, but still my mom worried at the thought.

"Dad, what do you think of my flying?"

The other end of the line was silent for a moment as Dad formulated his answer. "I was out walking the other day," he began. "I tripped and fell, but I haven't quit walking."

"Oh, you would say that!" Mom retorted.

I realized as a young Christian that God was working to build His character and likeness into my life. Complete Christ-likeness will not take place until we arrive in Glory. Our weaknesses express themselves in different ways, but strength grows out of our walk with Christ. While on earth, our walk should be about obedience to His commands and submission to His leadership, allowing Him to work in us and to conform us to His image. This key process is a part of our entire life—daily, weekly, monthly, and yearly. One event is not the finale. The work God started the day I was saved was deepened through the events surrounding the plane crash, but God wanted to take that work deeper still. And I wanted Him to have the freedom to do that work in my life—even if it meant getting back on a plane.

Despite her initial negative response, Mom assured me that she and my dad would be praying. According to statistics, flying is actually safer than driving. We have flown many times in the years since the crash, and God has always kept us safe.

During this second conference, God led me to memorize Philippians chapter two. God has used the lessons contained in this chapter to work marvelously in my life. In particular, God used five truths from verses 5-11 which enabled me to lay hold of the victory God has given me in Christ over my selfish desires. I want to walk with Him in His strength and victory, and these truths have since carried me through many difficult trials. I have been able, by God's grace, to exchange my expectations and plans for God's purpose.

Embrace Christ's Meekness

Before I attended that 1987 conference and came face to face with myself, I again struggled with the old feelings of inadequacy, which were now exhibited in anger. I did not choose to be angry on purpose, nor was I consciously aware of my anger. Nonetheless, my countenance and my tone of voice demonstrated my inward anger. Our children would ask Beth, "Why is Daddy angry?"

"I don't know," she would reply. "Go ask your daddy."

My daughters would come to me and ask, "Daddy, why are you angry?"

"I'm not angry!" I would answer sharply.

Each time this scenario took place, as I looked into my family members' stricken faces, I began to realize something was amiss in my life. I asked them to be patient with me and to help me. I knew I needed to recall what I had been thinking when I appeared to be so angry. I didn't have an outburst of anger, but what had caused the harshness and sharpness in my tone of voice?

In this time of searching my heart, God helped me understand that I was offended at Him. I realized I wanted Him to work in my life the way I thought He would or should—rather than accepting the work He had chosen.

Jesus warned believers about this problem after the disciples of John the Baptist questioned Him on John's behalf. John, the forerunner of the Messiah, found himself in prison, and soon he would be executed. He sent his disciples to ask Jesus, *"Art thou he that should come, or do we look for another?"* (Matthew 11:3) Life simply wasn't going as John had expected, and the Scripture seems to indicate that he was beginning to doubt. Jesus told John's disciples to carry word back to their master of the things which they had seen him do. He then addressed the root of their question in Matthew 11:6, which says, *"And blessed is he, whosoever shall not be offended in me."* Jesus was warning them not to look at Him from a perspective grounded in their circumstances and expectations; rather, they were to focus on the work He was doing, lest they be offended—literally scandalized.

I asked God to change my focus. I began to thank God for His work in my life rather than questioning or accusing Him. Only then could He begin to pour out His grace in my life. God has continued to help me understand that I need His strength and His grace. Grace is "the dynamic influence of the Holy Spirit upon my heart" (adapted from Strong's Lexicon). We are able to demonstrate God's grace in our lives through a grateful attitude as we serve Him.

I wanted to serve God with my life in such a way that He would be pleased and glorified, but I struggled with letting Him choose how my service would look. My plans were not sinful or wrong, but my plans were still my plans. I realized I was making my plans an idol. My plans were desires that I wanted whether or not God wanted them for me. God was calling me to take on Christ's yoke, to submit to Him, and to enter into His rest. Instead, I was struggling to get my own way, which brought anger, added stress, conflict, and more discouragement.

Philippians 2:5 says, *"Let this mind be in you, which was also in Christ Jesus."* This verse means we are to have the same thinking process—the same thoughts, opinions and attitudes—as Christ. In Matthew 11:28 and 29, Christ described Himself as *"meek and lowly."* In order to be like Christ, I must choose to embrace Christ's meekness. This is not weakness, as some would suppose, rather it is power under God's control.

I discovered that when I yield to the Lord what I feel are my rights, the things I am expecting or feel I have coming, then I am demonstrating the same meekness Christ displayed. Jesus Christ had the right to be the sovereign ruler and not only sit on Israel's throne but also the world's throne. He humbled Himself (became lowly) by yielding His right to rule, so that He might fulfill the purposes of God the Father. His humbling meant giving His life to purchase man's redemption. His sacrificial death was all a part of the Trinity's original plan. Jesus willingly submitted Himself to this plan and voluntarily gave Himself to die in our place.

God blessed me so much throughout the plane crash and recovery. He also blessed our ministry in a mighty way since the crash, but I was still struggling with seeking my own agenda. During the second conference, God revealed my need to humble myself and to embrace the thought process of Christ if I was to overcome these inner struggles. My prayer at the end of this conference was almost exactly the same as the one I prayed at the conference in 1980. Thankfully, this time the plane did not crash when I returned!

Embrace Christ's Faithfulness

Meekness is *strength or power under God's control*, but it is not without action. Jesus practiced the action quality of meekness as He faithfully carried out the responsibilities God the Father had given Him to accomplish. Christ knew exactly who He was; He was God, yet He became man. Philippians 2:6 says, *"Who, being in the form of God, thought it not robbery to be equal with God."* Christ also knew He was the only One who could purchase redemption for mankind.

God wanted me to be faithful with my ministry responsibilities as Christ was faithful in His. This decision included allocating leadership responsibilities. I did not need to take on all of the work at church; after all, God had given us people who wanted to serve faithfully. God used my time of recovery after the plane crash to help me discern what my boundaries should have been. Through this process, I began to learn to separate my responsibilities from God's responsibilities.

Working through this area of leadership helped me keep my focus on the Lord as I worked on my therapy. I worked hard every day—not only at the hospital but even more so at home. Right away, the doctors and therapists recommended that we purchase an Exercycle. God immediately provided the money for that expenditure. I worked hard on that stationary bike. We adjusted the seat so that my legs would bend tight as I rode. My cheerleaders, Beth, Anna, and Esther, cheered me on as I worked to rebuild the function in my legs. That exercise not only worked to stretch and strengthen my legs, but it also exercised them so well that the physical therapy on my legs at the hospital was discontinued. God provided for the Exercycle, gave me the desire to work hard, and even healed me; but He never rode that stationary bike for me. He never worked the therapy for me. That part of the healing process was my responsibility.

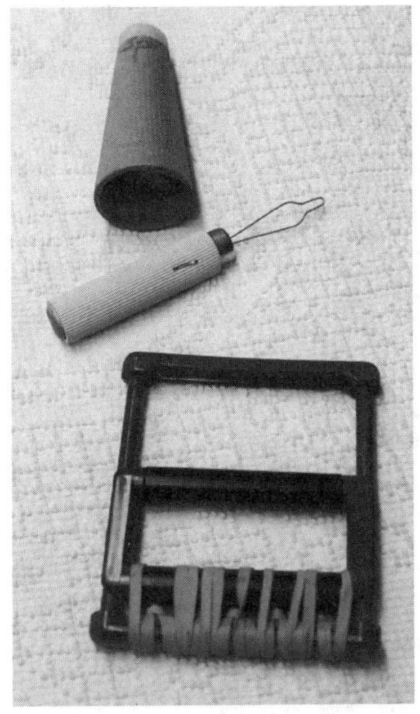

Items used for therapy

Because of the work I was doing on my legs at home, the therapists were able to focus solely on my hands, performing both physical and occupational therapy on them five days a week. My hands bled every day as the therapists worked with them to help them function properly. One responsibility, which was mine alone, included wearing special splints on my left hand to help correct problems and maintain function in spite of the developing scar tissue. I wore these splints during all of my waking hours. At times, I even had to wear some of the splints during the night.

One of the splints was made with two long, neck-like prongs rising off of a piece that fit around my hand. Head-like shapes at the top of each prong were designed to hold a long rubber band. A pad in the palm of my hand was attached to the rubber band so it would pull back my thumb. Beth painted the necks and heads of the prongs to look like green dinosaurs. She added eyes and a smile on each head. We named the dinosaurs Arnie and Agnes. When I wore these *decorative* splints to the burn clinic, the doctors dubbed them "The Serpents."

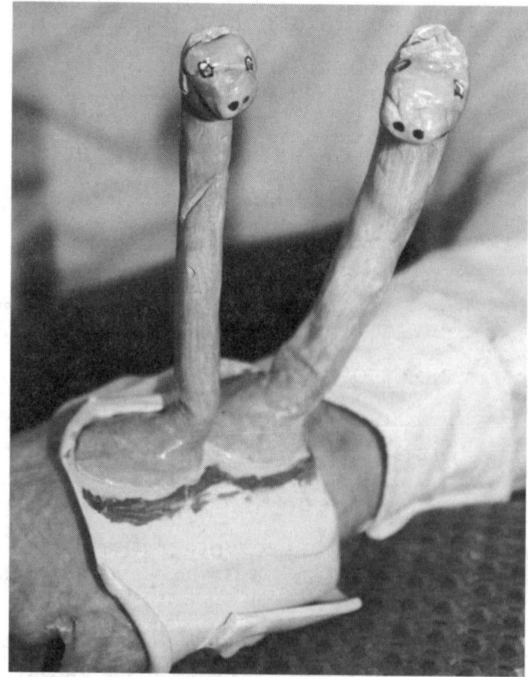

Arnie & Agnes, lovingly called "The Serpents" by Ken's doctors

Little did we know that Arnie and Agnes would become a great help with training our children. Two-year-old Esther occasionally had trouble eating her food.

"Now, Esther," I would say in a high-pitched voice as though Arnie and/or Agnes were speaking, "Take that bite!"

"Okay," she would reply, as her little eyes focused completely on the dinosaur splint.

She loved having Arnie and Agnes talk to her. Not only did Arnie and Agnes help with training our children, but they actually helped make part of the healing process fun and amusing for all of us.

Soon after I arrived home from the hospital, I had to wear a splint to bed at night. I was having trouble sleeping at night because I was still facing withdrawal symptoms from ceasing the pain medications. One night, I simply could not sleep. I was afraid I would move my hands and accidentally hit Beth with the splint. With much effort, I finally got out of bed and slowly walked to our guest room.

As soon as I sat down on the bed, I heard a loud hissing noise. I

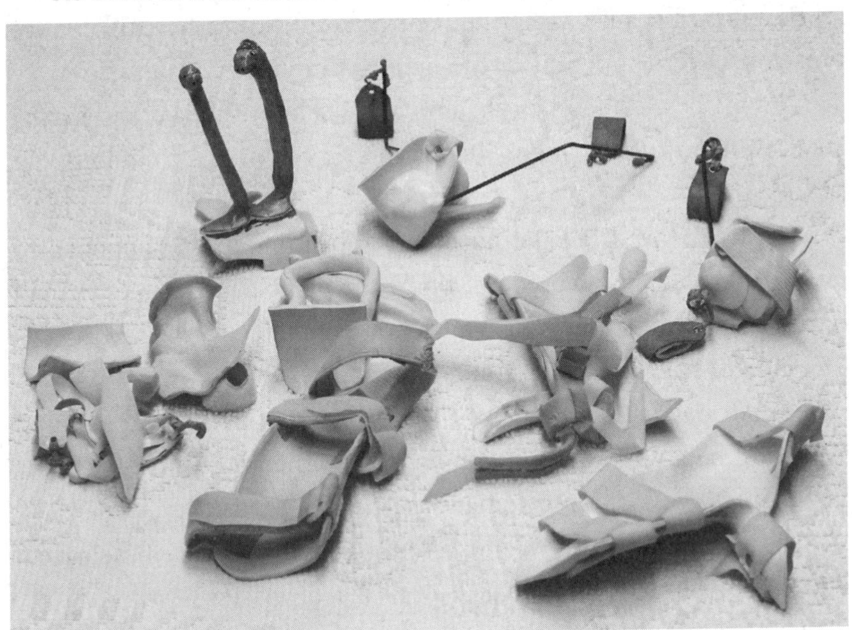

The many varied kinds of splints worn by Ken to aid in the function of his hands

jumped up as quickly as I could and looked around, but I could not find the source of the noise. Then I remembered that shortly before the plane crash, we had purchased a water softener. It was set to recharge on a regular basis in the middle of the night, but I had been in the hospital and had not heard that particular noise. I laughed at myself. I hadn't moved that fast in months! To know that I could still move that fast was gratifying—I was healing! I realized that I had been faithfully wearing those splints because that was my responsibility, and God was faithful with His responsibility to heal my body.

This lesson has helped me to stay faithful in my walk with Christ. God has given me a ministry. He will continue to give me direction, strength, and peace as I submit to Him. He is always faithful in His responsibilities, and He expects me to be faithful with mine.

Embrace Christ's Surrender

The body's reaction to something the mind cannot process is called shock. Because I went into shock after the crash, I still cannot consciously remember all of the details. Only three impressions remain in my mind: a loud crash, a big flash of light, and a bone-jarring impact similar to the concussion felt in every joint of a child jumping out of a tree.

Shortly before I left the hospital to go home, Beth happened to see the sheriff from the precinct where the plane had crashed. He had stopped by the hospital to visit a friend, and he recognized Beth.

"How is your husband doing?" he asked.

"Much better," Beth replied. "All of his surgeries are done, and he'll soon be going home. If you have the time and want to, I know Ken would love for you to stop by his room for a visit."

The sheriff did stop by, and, after introducing himself, he asked, "Do you remember how you got out of that airplane?"

I smiled. "God reached down and took me out."

"That's as good an answer as you could give. You certainly didn't ride the plane to the ground because you wouldn't have survived. That plane was so broken in pieces that we hauled it off in a pickup truck."

He paused for a moment and then dove into a string of speculations. "Do you think when the plane hit that treetop you might have fallen out of the plane still strapped in your seat? We know you were sprayed with fuel because the fuel line came in under your seat, between your legs, and under the pilot's seat to the engine. When the plane hit the tree, the fuel line was ruptured. When the plane hit the power lines, the sparks ignited the fuel. I believe you were on fire in your seat."

The sheriff stopped reminiscing as he contemplated my hands. "You know, you may have burned your left hand when you had to reach into the fire to release the seat belt after you hit the ground."

"I honestly don't know," I replied. "I still can't remember those kinds of details. I don't think I ever want to."

As I think back to that conversation, I am still not sure any value would come from remembering those details. I do know that my left hand and side suffered more burns than the rest of my body. We really don't know the whole story, but the sheriff's theory made perfect sense. The impressions I had at the time of the crash coincide with what he shared with us. One fact is clear. I can trust God with all the details as I surrender myself to Him and His will for my life. God has everything under control. He had everything under control that stormy day in September. I know He does not need my help because He knows what is best for His children.

Meekness requires surrender. It requires the Christian to die to self. Christ certainly modeled the surrender aspect of meekness! He "*made himself of no reputation, and took upon him the form of a servant, and was made in the likeness of men*" (Philippians 2:7). Jesus Christ laid aside all of His rights to divine glory and dignity to become a mere bondservant—a man. A union of divinity and humanity took place in the body of Jesus Christ. Charles Wesley's Christmas hymn, "Hark the Herald Angels Sing," says it best: "Veiled in flesh the God-head see, Hail the incarnate Deity!" Through the mindset of meekness, Christ willingly surrendered Himself to die on the cross, giving His life so that man could have God's great salvation.

As Christ had surrendered Himself to His Father, He also wanted my full surrender to Himself. I wanted complete surrender in my life, but my confusion had caused me not to trust God's perfect will. God used the trials of the plane crash and the burns I sustained to help me follow Christ's example—to teach me that surrender comes moment by moment.

Practice Christ's Humility

As He embraced His crucifixion, Jesus was practicing the humility aspect of meekness. He became obedient unto a death reserved for slaves, rebels, and the lowest of criminals: *"And being found in fashion as a man, he humbled himself, and became obedient unto death, even the death of the cross"* (Philippians 2:8).

The key in this level of obedience is humility. Earlier in this chapter, I defined meekness as *strength or power under God's control.* God's power—not our own—has the control. When we seek to take control, we step into pride and all of its destruction. In James 4:6, God makes a very clear distinction between humility and pride: *"But he giveth more grace. Wherefore he saith, God resisteth the proud, but giveth grace unto the humble."* This level of humility, which allows us to meekly submit ourselves to God's control, is demonstrated by our obedience—even unto death.

How do we walk in the humility demonstrated by Christ? We must choose to identify with Him in His crucifixion by dying to self and to our desire to control our own life's destiny.

In Luke 22, the Bible shares a glimpse of the anguish of this decision. The night before His crucifixion, Jesus sweat great drops of blood as He agonized in prayer. *"Father, if thou be willing, remove this cup from me: nevertheless not my will, but thine, be done."* (Luke 22:42)

Through the plane crash itself, the intense pain, and the ongoing struggle to heal, God was teaching me to humble myself. I had to surrender to the doctors' best plans for my water intake, for enduring the excruciating pain of the grafting procedures, and for completing the long, painful therapy. I had to surrender to God's best plans, which included living with the difficulties of permanent handicaps. God has greatly helped me to humble myself to His plan. He has truly blessed me and used my handicaps to help others.

Several years after the plane crash, Beth's father spoke with one of the students attending Pioneer Bible Institute. This student, who was majoring in Biblical Ministry, also happened to have cerebral palsy. He looked at his handicap through a lens of self-pity, consistently making excuses for himself and the things he didn't want to do.

"Is Pastor Spilger handicapped?" Burton asked him.

"No," replied the student, "he's not handicapped."

"Think again about that answer. Is Pastor Spilger handicapped? He is missing fingers, toes, and muscle. Does that not mean he is handicapped?"

A look of understanding crossed the young man's face. "Yes, he IS handicapped!" A positive change occurred in the attitude of that young man during the rest of that school year.

Because I have accepted my handicaps, our children have accepted my handicaps. When our children were growing up, they fought over who would hold my left hand. They have lovingly mimicked my use of that hand because they were so intrigued by it.

Epictetus, a Greek sage, once said, "It's not what happens to you, but how you react to it that matters." When I read this quote, I was reminded of my father's admonition when he was leaving the day I came home from the hospital. "Ken, you have a very important decision to make. You can lie there and feel sorry for yourself, or you can get up and do something about it." Rather than focusing on what I cannot do, my focus has been on giving thanks for what I can do and pushing myself to do my best.

God is still teaching me to follow Christ's example of meekness through humble obedience.

Live in Christ's Confidence

We were on vacation with our extended family at a cabin owned by Beth's grandparents near Dubois, Wyoming. Granddad loved *his* Wyoming and always wanted us to see everything we could while we were vacationing there. This particular morning near the end of our stay, we were making plans to see the Tetons. Granddad was encouraging us to see a number of sights between the cabin and Jackson Hole. Seemingly, if anything could happen to change our plans, it did. In fact, plans for the day changed several times that morning. I had to purpose in my heart not to get irritated. I had to believe that God had our sightseeing all under control, and all I needed to do was enjoy each moment with both my family and our extended family.

Once we as Christians choose to have the mind of Christ in our life, we can also take on His confidence. In His resurrection, Jesus was demonstrating the victory aspect of meekness. Death and the grave were conquered, and Christ took His rightful place at the right hand of God the Father. "*Wherefore God also hath highly exalted him, and given him a name which is above every name: [10]That at the name of Jesus every knee should bow, of things in heaven, and things in earth, and thing under the earth; [11]And that every tongue should confess that Jesus Christ is Lord, to the glory of God the Father*" (Philippians 2:9-11). Christ won the ultimate victory, giving us the confidence to have victory in every avenue of our life. A Christian's confidence comes only by meekness demonstrated through faithfulness, surrender, and humility.

That morning in Wyoming, my meekness and understanding of the confidence we have in Christ was being tested dramatically. We finally started for the Tetons later than we had planned. I knew we needed to stop for gas, and the nearest service station was at Togwotee Pass, several miles northwest of the cabin. As we pulled into the lodge, a ranger came out to pump our gas. Believe me, rangers simply don't pump gas, especially not at a self-service station.

"Where do I pay?" I asked as he finished pumping the gas.

He pointed to a small cabin near the gas pumps, and said, "I can help you over here." We walked inside. As I signed my name to the traveler's check, I placed my left hand on the check where the ranger could easily see it. When I finished the transaction, I handed him one of my Gospel tracts about the plane crash. He took the tract and glanced at it.

"I placed my left hand on the check."

"I had a dream about you last night," he said. "What do you think about dreams?"

I hesitated to answer because I could not believe what he was saying. I'm a Bible-believing Baptist! Why do these strange questions come to me?

"Well," I said, "you can eat too much pizza before you go to bed and have a dream. Or the devil can give you a dream. In the tract I gave you about the plane crash, I share how I was trusting in my good works to get me to Heaven. Like I couldn't trust my good works, you can't trust in dreams. We must go to God's Word in order to get our direction for life." I continued to talk, carefully explaining the Gospel.

"Well, actually," he interrupted, "I saw your hand in my dream last night. When I saw your hand today as you drove up, I knew you were going to talk with me like this."

We talked further about salvation and the importance of getting our direction from the Word of God—not dreams. He responded well, but he did not receive Christ.

I am certain that if I had reacted to all the irritations of the morning, I would not have had the opportunity to give the Gospel in the power of the Spirit. I may have been totally unaware of the opportunity altogether. God obviously coordinated the timing of our meeting. As I thought about it later, I realized a powerful truth: God had helped me exchange my flesh for His strength. He helped me to put aside irritations and humbly give myself to Him that morning. The reward was an opportunity to share the wonderful Gospel with a needy soul whom He had prepared to listen.

I can testify that the transformation process is still going on in my life. I can receive the strength of God when I choose to exchange my mindset for Christ's. These truths have transformed the way I look at ministry. I take my orders from the Lord through His Word. My view of success is now governed by the Word of God—not by man's standards. I can serve Him free of guilt, condemnation, and pressure as I rest in these simple truths. When I feel agitated or weighed down by cares and anxiety, I ask myself some simple questions, including the following:

- Am I yielding to God those things I feel I have a right to or expect to happen?
- Am I being faithful to what God has called me to do?
- Am I surrendering to God's will by fulfilling the responsibilities He has given me?
- Am I humbling myself or forcing my own way?
- Have I found God's directives for me in the issue at hand?
- Am I walking in the confidence that only God can give?

Strength is a result of choosing the mind of Christ and allowing God to mold me into His image. If I can answer these questions properly, then I am becoming more like Christ. Instead of being defeated, I can exchange my prideful, selfish mindset of defeat for Christ's mindset of victory.

"Truly my soul waiteth upon God: from him
cometh my salvation. 2He only is my rock and my
salvation; he is my defence; I shall not be greatly
moved. 3How long will ye imagine mischief against
a man? ye shall be slain all of you: as a bowing wall
shall ye be, and as a tottering fence. 4They only con-
sult to cast him down from his excellency: they de-
light in lies: they bless with their mouth, but they
curse inwardly. Selah.

5My soul, wait thou only upon God; for my ex-
pectation is from him. 6He only is my rock and my
salvation: he is my defence; I shall not be moved. 7In
God is my salvation and my glory: the rock of my
strength, and my refuge, is in God. 8Trust in him at
all times; ye people, pour out your heart before him:
God is a refuge for us. Selah.

9Surely men of low degree are vanity, and men of
high degree are a lie: to be laid in the balance, they
are altogether lighter than vanity. 10Trust not in op-
pression, and become not vain in robbery: if riches
increase, set not your heart upon them. 11God hath
spoken once; twice have I heard this; that power be-
longeth unto God. 12Also unto thee, O Lord, belon-
geth mercy: for thou renderest to every man accord-
ing to his work."

– Psalm 62

CHAPTER FOURTEEN

Waiting on The Lord

My foot was vibrating again. I stretched my leg and rotated my foot in circles. The vibration traveling up my leg stopped—for a while. I knew the annoyance would be back. As the scar tissue healed it formed a strange bubble, for lack of a better name, on the top of my left foot just behind my toes. Though the bubble had the look of a blister, I could tell the bubble ballooned deeper into the scar tissue. With the appearance of the bubble, an annoying vibration started traveling through my foot and leg in sync with my pulse rate. Stretching my foot and rotating it was the only means of relief I had found.

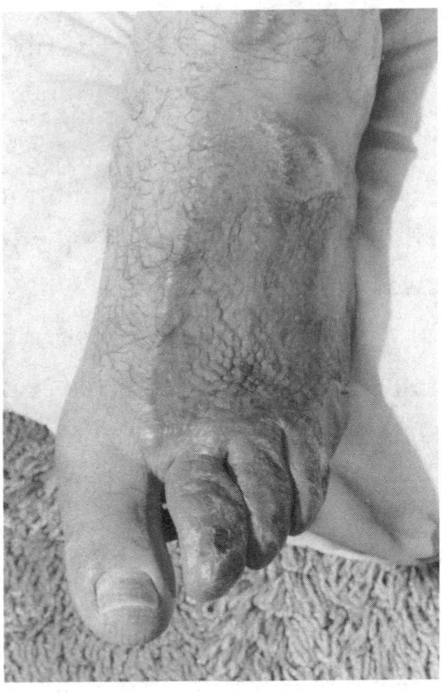

The scar where the bubble formed on the top of Ken's left foot

"Is there anything we can do about this bubble and vibration?" I asked my doctor one day.

"Ken," he replied, "everything is fine. I believe it's simply the scar tissue healing in an unusual way."

His answer meant one thing: I would have to keep working with it and simply wait for relief.

In the same way that God was using the disturbing vibration in my foot to bring about His healing, He was using some disturbing questions in my soul to bring about His healing work in my life. What do you do when you've believed God and obeyed Him in a matter, and He isn't doing what you thought He would do? Even worse, what do you do when it seems like He isn't doing anything at all about a certain situation? I realized that the way I responded to these questions would determine whether or not I would become bitter. Bitterness is a result of unfulfilled expectations. We become bitter when we focus on that lack of fulfillment. I wanted answers to my questions, and the answer that God began teaching me was to wait on Him.

God uses a number of different Hebrew words in the Bible that are translated into the phrase *wait on the Lord.* Each of the Hebrew words has a different meaning. In Psalm 62, the word *wait* means "to be quiet before God," "to be lost in wonder and astonishment at God's working," and "to be at rest before God."[3] This particular meaning of wait is what I call *purposeful rest.* This rest represents the quietness and confidence of trusting the Lord to fulfill His purpose.

Waiting on the Lord demonstrates our love of God as we trust Him and obey Him with a joyful, confident, patient expectation and awe because we know He will act in His best timing.

Waiting on the Lord is active involvement in living out our personal relationship with Jesus Christ. In Philippians 2:12 and 13, God states through the Apostle Paul that the Philippians obeyed God's commands even when Paul was not present. Paul advised them to *work out* their salvation with fear and trembling because God was working in them *"both to will and to do of his good pleasure."*

Waiting on the Lord is a true, sincere act of worship. Worship demonstrates love. It shows that we value God and esteem our Heavenly Father as worthy of our worship.

3 Adapted from Strong's # 01747 and the Complete Biblical Library # 1800

Waiting on the Lord is based on our commitment to trust God. According to Psalm 62, our trust is to be in God alone. He is our rock, our salvation, and our defense. Because of Him, I cannot be *greatly moved*.

For six months, I continued stretching and rotating my foot whenever I wasn't walking or asleep. As the scar matured, the bubble finally disappeared, the vibration went away, and I stopped having to stretch my foot. During this time, Mary, my physical therapist at Christian Hospital Northeast, evaluated my burns to determine their approach for my therapy.

She adamantly declared, "You can't possibly move your foot like that, Ken!"

"But I am moving it like that," I responded.

"You can't. Your foot was burnt too badly for you to have that much movement. Those therapists at St. John's Mercy Hospital did an awesome job with you."

I agreed with her assessment. The therapists did do an awesome job. But only God could have allowed the scar to mature as it did, causing me to move and rotate my foot for relief. Unknowingly, I had performed additional therapy on my foot, giving the ankle a greater range of movement and making it possible for me to walk without a limp. The best therapy was truly God's doing—not man's. Mary also explained that because of my being able to walk without a limp, I would have healthier legs, no varicose veins, and fewer back problems.

One day while at the burn clinic at St. John's Mercy Medical Center after the bubble healed, I talked with my doctor about how God had used that bubble to make me do the therapy needed for my ankle to have full function.

"No," he teased, "we actually put a battery-powered vibrator in your foot, and the batteries have just finally lost their power."

I laughed. "Sure. I know better than that."

"You're right. God did this for your healing."

What an awesome God we serve! He is worthy of our waiting on Him.

Power and strength belong to God alone. I have learned that God gives us His strength as we wait on Him. He gave me His strength and power to do the required therapy in order to have usable limbs that function correctly. God will share His glory with no one. He alone receives all the glory for my miraculous recovery. I have full function in my legs. I don't limp. Even though I have only parts of fingers, I have the dexterity to pick up small items with both hands. To God be the glory! God worked in my heart, giving me a desire to do my therapy and to follow the instructions of my caregivers. I praise Him for all He did to reclaim my body to full function. Along with God's grace and the care of the medical professionals, God threw in His own special miracles to make my recovery His work.

Just like God used the bubble in the scar tissue on my foot for me to do more therapy, He used the struggles in my life to teach me to wait upon Him. These struggles were annoying, but they led me each day to wait on the Lord, and they still do. For me, waiting on the Lord is the spiritual therapy I need to live each day in Christ's victory. Truly, as I wait on the Lord, He renews my strength. He helps me to mount up with wings as eagles. He enables me to run and not be weary, and to walk and not faint (Isaiah 40:31).

Consider Our Foe

Before the plane crash, I had been struggling with feelings of inadequacy, bitterness, and distrust. By entertaining this bitterness, I learned that I was giving Satan an opportunity to inflict more of his lies and confusion. I still had not learned that my only hope was to wait on the Lord. Only as I waited on the Lord would I be able to acknowledge the part the evil one, Satan, was playing in my inward struggle, and only then would I be able to resist him. During the pastors conference, instruction was presented on spiritual warfare—a relatively new concept to me. As I listened, I realized that through my personal struggles God was wanting to teach me these vital truths.

In Psalm 62, the Psalmist first acknowledged God's place in His life. *"Truly my soul waiteth upon God: from him cometh my salvation. ²He only is my rock and my salvation; he is my defense; I shall not be greatly moved."* We also must acknowledge the place God has in our lives by being saved and surrendering ourselves to Jesus Christ. Only then can we deal with Satan. The Psalmist recognized the fact that the enemy was devising evil against him by speaking lies and by seeking to destroy him. *"How long will ye imagine mischief against a man? ye shall be slain all of you: as a bowing wall shall ye be, and as a tottering fence. ⁴They only consult to cast him down from his excellency: they delight in lies: they bless with their mouth, but they curse inwardly."* The Psalmist was talking about actual people, but as I learned in this conference, the force behind these people was demonic. God tells us in Ephesians 6:12 that we do not wrestle against flesh and blood but against Satan's evil forces.

Just as God had (and has) a purpose for my life, so did (and does) Satan. His plan was evil against me, my family, our ministry, the other three pastors, their families, and their ministries. Satan wanted us to be discouraged. He wanted us to believe his lies about God and what God was doing in all of us through this severe trial. He planted doubts and fears about the future and whether or not God would care for us. Would God be able to provide for our huge medical bills? Would I be able to become a part of the real world again? How would our family adjust to my handicaps? Satan wanted to create distrust, to take advantage of our weaknesses, and to destroy us.

But God was faithful to sustain us. God's plan was for good—not evil. We were plagued with a plethora of questions, but we understood that Satan is the father of lies and that God gives us the freeing truth of His Word to dispel the bondage of those lies. Even as we struggled with hopelessness, God was with us, giving us hope. He is the God of all hope (Romans 15:13), and He wanted us to know that He is our strength and power. God wanted us to know He was working out His divine purpose in our life.

As God had protected me by keeping me alive, He also protected my family and helped them through the many trials they faced while I was in the hospital.

One night shortly after I entered the hospital, my wife heard a loud crash and felt a jolt to the house. She looked out the bedroom window to see a car attempting to back out of our neighbor's yard.

The boxed cedar the young man hit with his car

She saw our neighbor, who was only wearing boxers, running out of his front door. His wife followed close behind him, carrying a pair of trousers in her hands.

"Stop!" our neighbor yelled, stooping to pick up a rock. "Stop! Or I'll throw this rock through your window."

"Put your pants on!" The man's wife was yelling, holding out the trousers she carried.

The Crash Site

The remains of the plane after it had burned
The remains were hauled off in the back of a pick-up truck.

The propeller and engine resting on tree roots over the top of a deep washout

Pulling Ken up in a litter from the muddy shelf

The Crash Site on Day After

Tree top the plane hit

The limb broken off by the plane

Washouts and steep terrain of the field

The Crash Site 2015

The splice is still in the wires.

A wood fence runs along the edge of the pasture by the deep washouts. Most of the trees are gone. This photo shows the steep grade of the field.

Behind the fence at the bottom of the field
The deep washouts are still there.

Ken's Burns

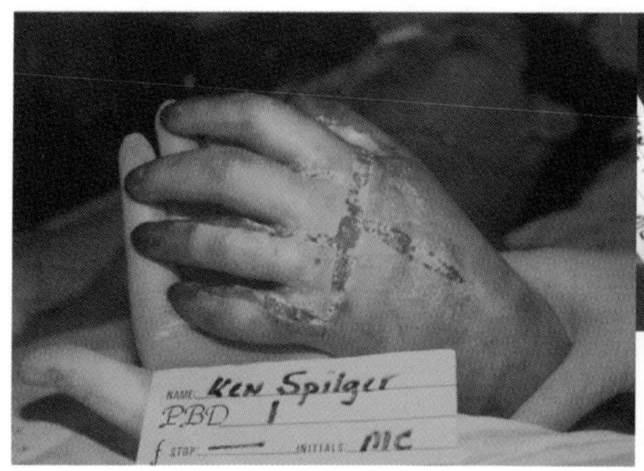

Escharotomies on left hand

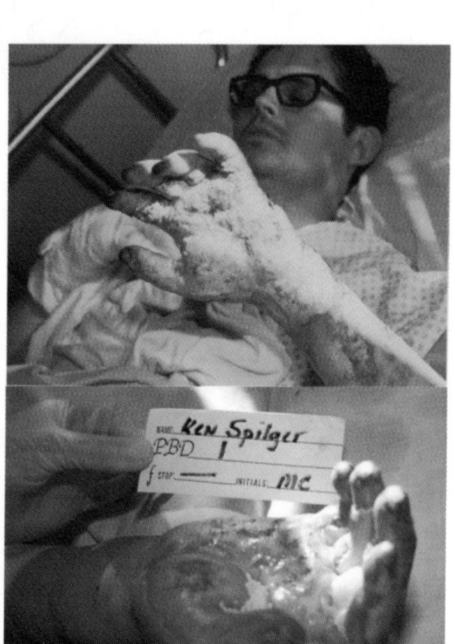

Right hand - day 1

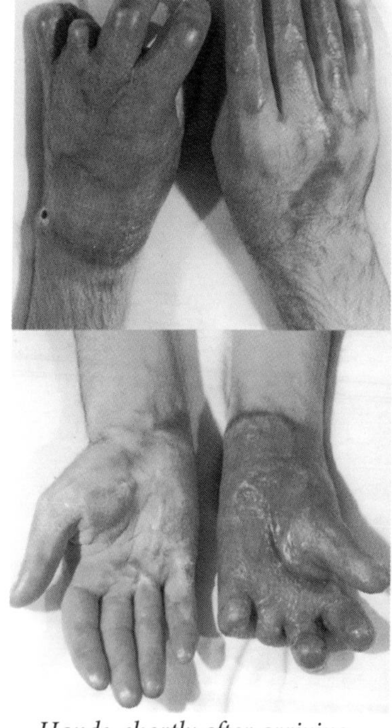

Hands, shortly after arriving home from the hospital

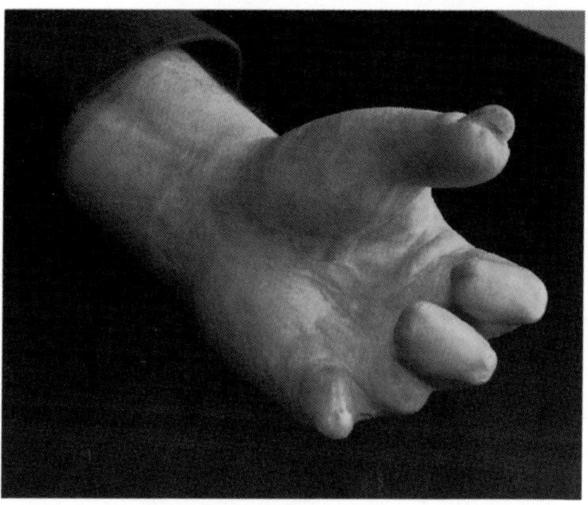

Left hand - today

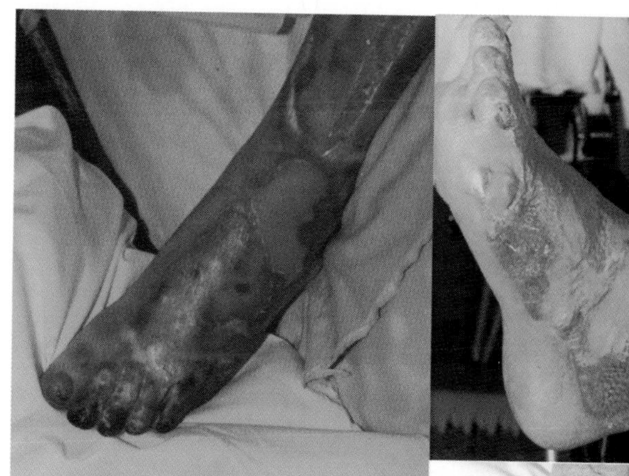

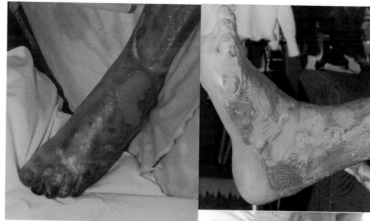

Left foot - before and after grafts

First photo of right leg

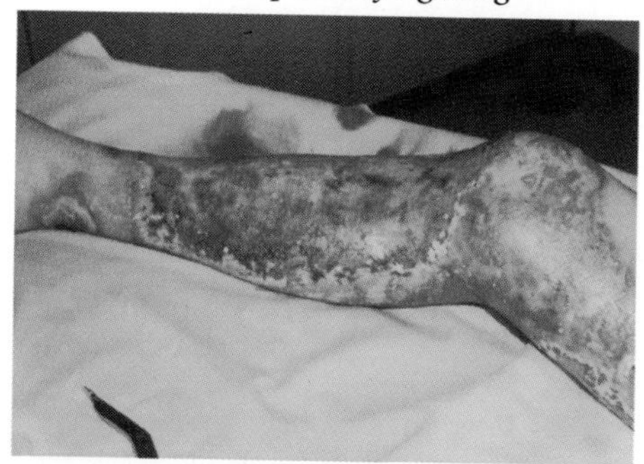

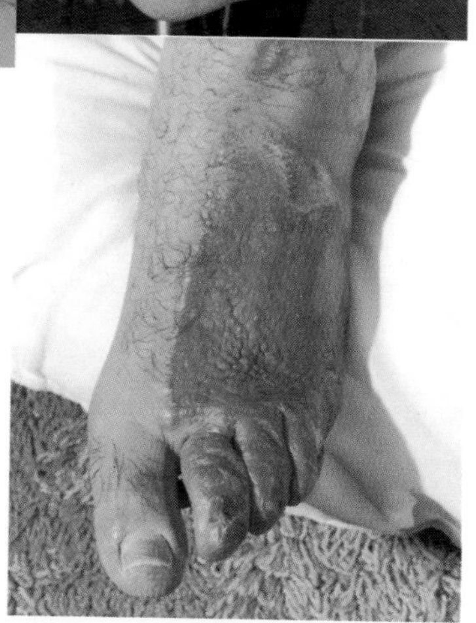

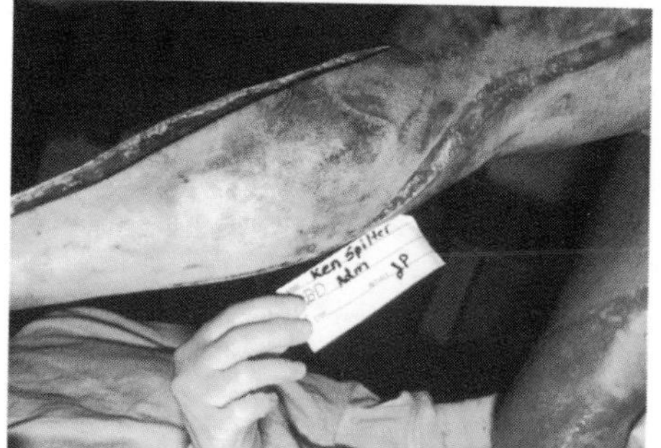

Left leg escharotomies

Donor site

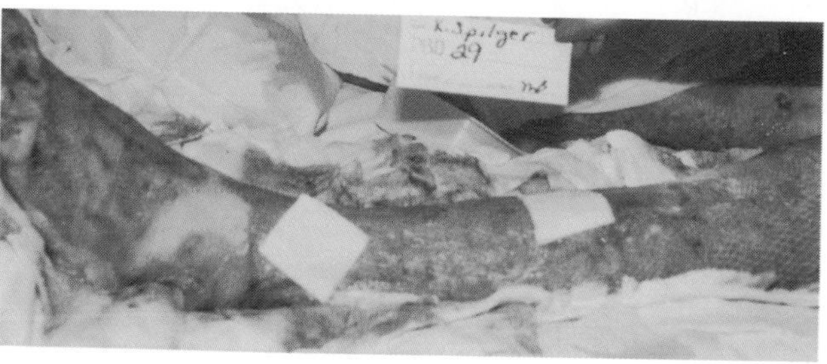

Pseudonymous infection on the graft of the left leg

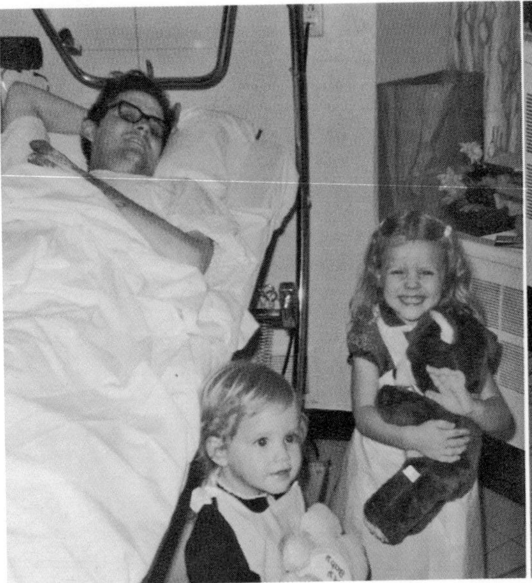

Girls with their birthday gifts

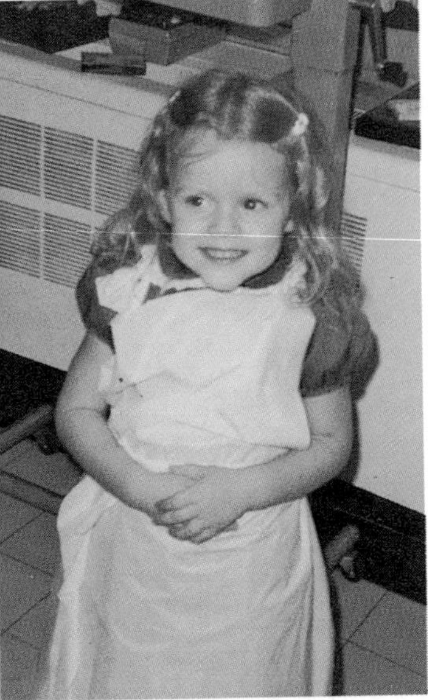

Anna in her make-shift isolation robe

Birthday Party

Giraffe cake

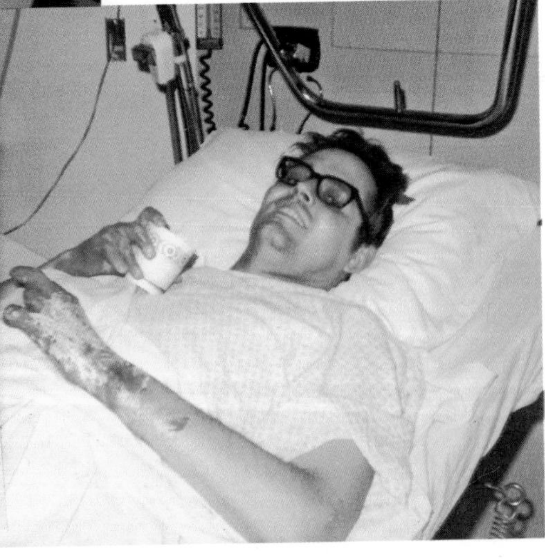

Ken celebrating from his Styker Frame Circle bed

NOTE: This was the first time Ken saw the girls since before the accident occurred.

Miscellaneous Pictures

Christmas Ornaments Ken painted for therapy while in the hospital
Most expensive tree ornaments our girls have

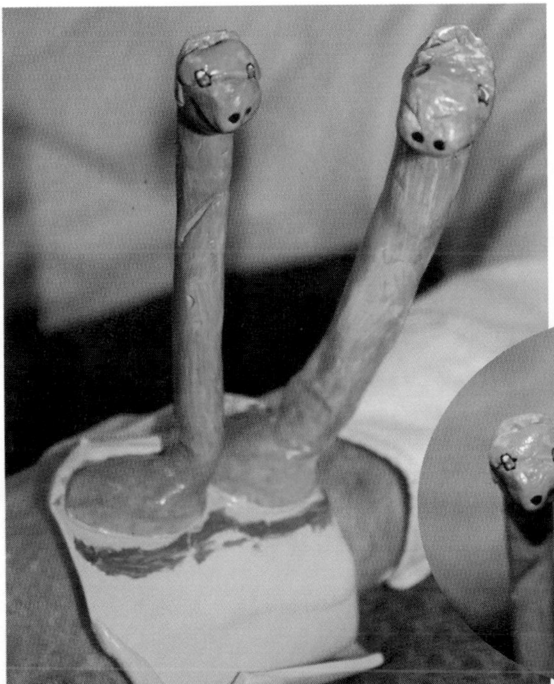

Arnie & Agnes

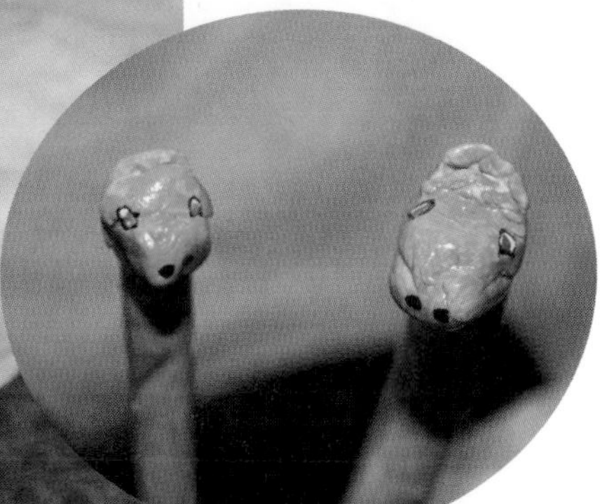

Family 1980

Family - January 2014

Beth chuckled at the sight. Though perhaps a bit embarrassing, things were under control, so she settled back down in bed, hoping to find the sleep that had been evading her. Within seconds, however, she heard a knock at the front door. She got up, went to the door, and cautiously peered through the peephole. She saw her nocturnal visitor was her neighbor's wife. As she opened the door, she discovered that the car she had seen trying to back through the neighbor's yard had actually struck a tall cedar bush in front of our house—just inches from the room where my parents were sleeping. Had the bush not been there, the car would have driven right into their room. God had protected my family from further harm and grief.

The young man who had driven the car agreed to work off the damage to our property. He removed the battered cedar bush and two other bushes and planted grass in their place. Years later, we saw him at a restaurant. He thanked us for helping him see Christianity at work and for helping him see that he needed to turn his life around and head in the right direction. He was now attending college and hoping for a bright future.

That night Satan had tried one more attack, one more point of confusion, one more *roar* to bring fear. In 1 Peter 5: 8 God describes Satan as a *roaring lion* who seeks to destroy God's people. But God gave the victory.

As I have already mentioned, in Ephesians 6 God gives us vital instruction in how to stand victoriously in His whole armor. He taught us how to take our place in the blessing of His great salvation (Ephesians 1-3), how to walk wisely (Ephesians 4-5), and how to be Spirit-filled (Ephesians 5:18). By taking our place in these truths, we can be strong in the Lord (Ephesians 6:10). This strength enables us to identify the true enemy (Ephesians 6:12) and to stand in God's complete armor (Ephesians 6:14–18).

Satan wants to destroy our personal integrity and the integrity of our relationship with Jesus Christ. We must remember that, although our battle is a spiritual warfare, people are often unwittingly involved. Therefore, we must know and recognize our real enemy—Satan.

During my hospital stay, our integrity was brought into question. Someone began making an accusation, saying that the plane crash was God's judgment on a specified sin in my life. This accusation was of their own making and in their own mind. God was dealing with my pride and selfishness, and He was using the plane crash, burns, and recovery to refine the work He began with my prayer of surrender at the conference. This was not God's judgment but His refining to bring glory to Himself. Thankfully, God protected my family and me in this situation, and brought His complete resolution concerning this accusation.

In the book of Job God details the accusations of Job's *friends* concerning sin in his life. Yet we know from the beginning chapters of this book some things that they did not know at the time of their discussion. The trials came because God wanted Satan to see Job's strong integrity. Like Job, my responsibility was and is to wait on the Lord—and rest in His purpose.

Our church deacons were gracious to destroy any malicious mail that came to the church. (I have been told that only one or two pieces of this kind of mail came.) God used these faithful men to shield my family from these unfounded accusations.

Satan is a hypocrite and desires to lead us into the same trap. But when we are following God, He gives and protects our integrity. During this time, our family coined the phrase "Life is real" to help us through the struggle. Not only is life real, but God wants our life to be real. He wants our life to be sincere, without hypocrisy, with true integrity.

Two friends came to visit me toward the end of my hospital stay and were a great encouragement in this matter. God used them to confirm that this trial was to bring glory to Himself—not to bring His judgment on me. I knew I had to focus on God—not on the gossip or the gossips. I learned that I needed to focus on the truth of the situation, on the truth of God's Word, and the truth of Jesus Christ. I was engaged in a spiritual battle, not one that was with flesh and blood. I had to take on the full armor of God in order to stand in the battle (Ephesians 6:10-18). As I availed myself of His armor, I demonstrated a willingness to wait on Him to work and to make right the wrong, and He graciously did.

Count on Our Friend

The severity of my injuries put my emotions into waves of differing highs and lows. The pages of this book document the many ways that my Lord was and continues to be my Friend. He gave me salvation and strength at the crash site. He gave me hope and confidence in the ambulance. He gave me healing and protection with each surgery. He gave me the comfort of His presence with the pain. He gave me determination and perseverance with the therapy. As my Friend, His joy is my strength, His grace is sufficient, and He is enough.

When the whole world walks out, Jesus will always walk in! We can wait on Him. We can always count on Him. He will always do what is best for us—even if the best involves plane crashes, death, injuries, or illness. He wants us to speak the truth in our own hearts about our relationship with Him because our *expectation* is from Him—not man or things. Our Heavenly Father is the only One in whom we can truly hope. He is our best Friend.

The *purposeful rest* in Psalm 62 is commanded in the midst of adversity. The Psalmist bases that rest on the foundation of a life whose expectations (i.e., cords, attachments, hopes) are in God alone: "*My soul, wait thou only upon God; for my expectation is from him*" (Psalm 62:5). God boldly makes this command because He has called me to Himself as Christ said in Matthew 11:28–30, "*Come unto me, all ye that labour and are heavy laden, and I will give you rest.* [29]*Take my yoke upon you, and learn of me; for I am meek and lowly in heart: and ye shall find rest unto your souls.* [30]*For my yoke is easy, and my burden is light."* When I am bound to Him in His yoke, I have exchanged my weak strength for His great power. My expectation is in Him. Truly, He is enough.

God used this purposeful waiting in my life during the time surrounding the crash to bring me to a deeper knowledge of Who He is. He taught me that He is committed to all of His children. He alone is my salvation, my glory, my rock of strength; I can trust Him at all times. I can pour my heart out before Him, and I can run to Him for refuge (Psalm 62:6–8).

I am grateful for that Friend Who *"sticketh closer than a brother"* (Proverbs 18:24). He gave me hope, and He also sent tangible help from my human friends. Help came in the form of many meals prepared by the loving hands of church families and neighbors. One of our neighbors knew our financial need was huge and worked with an amateur magician to put on a magic show benefit for us. They also knew I had been told to avoid extreme heat, extreme cold, and anything that would make me sweat. Even now, I must be careful because a third of my body's ability to perspire was destroyed by the burns, and my sensory feeling is limited. This neighbor's sons shoveled snow and mowed our lawn. When we offered to pay them, they responded, "My parents said

Mr. Vogelsang and Assistant at the Magic Show

I couldn't take any money. Besides, I just wanted to do it." Their work in our yard was a great help.

Others came to help in so many additional ways:

- Our church family helped with the girls and with responsibilities around the church.
- A pastor-friend put together a tricycle and wagon for our girls at Christmas.
- A Sunday school class from an area church brought gifts and played games at our house one evening around Christmas.
- One brother-in-law taught me how to tie a tie one-handed.
- Churches and individuals gave financially to help us in our need.
- One friend drove from Denver, Colorado, several times while I was in the hospital to lend his support and encouragement.
- Family and friends wrote letters and sent cards telling us of their prayers.

This short list does not begin to tell the story of the loving kindness of many people. God was a faithful Friend who ministered to us in our need through the many friends we have here on earth.

Conquer by Faith

We cannot put our trust in man. God often uses people as His instruments of healing, provision, giving of strength, and encouragement, but we must never forget that it is the work of God and not the work of man. And, as we have already seen, Satan can also use men. Psalm 62:9 states that no matter the status of man, whether upper or lower class, all are *"altogether lighter than vanity."* If vanity is emptiness, then according to this verse, men are lighter than nothing. In other words, man is quite unimportant in the works of God. What an excellent reason to *"wait on the Lord!"*

The enemy only gives oppression, and God instructs us not to place our trust in his perverted, oppressive schemes (Psalm 62:10). He is a robber. But praise God, we always have security in the Lord. True blessing comes when we wait on Him. In His timing, He will bring what we ask for if, and only if, it falls into His purposes for our lives. Throughout the process of asking, seeking, and knocking, there is also the waiting. Each action requires waiting on God's timing, but God promises that we will receive, we will find, and He will open the door for us (Luke 11:9, 10).

God boldly states in Psalm 62:11 that power belongs to Him alone, *"God hath spoken once; twice have I heard this; that power belongeth unto God."* Then in verse 12, He confidently assures us that mercy belongs to Him exclusively and why this is true, *"Also unto thee, O Lord, belongeth mercy: for thou renderest to every man according to his work."* These two truths have become the basis for me to wait on the Lord with *purposeful rest.*

Satan likes to accuse God of not giving us what he makes us think we need. His strategy worked very well with Adam and Eve and often works very effectively with us as well. Throughout my life, God has assured me that I can trust Him to give me what is my just reward and that I can trust Him to carry out any necessary revenge. Thus, he has freed me from bitterness that has at times threatened to take over in my life because of unfulfilled expectations. I have learned that I must put my expectation in the Lord because He knows the end from the beginning, and He knows how He wants me to get there.

God alone is our strength. He wants our obedience, our faith demonstrated by our works, and our full trust in His faithful promises. In all of these areas, we demonstrate that we are waiting on Him to fulfill His purpose. Waiting on the Lord is the spiritual therapy that we must practice in this life to exchange our weakness for God's strength, our bitterness for His mercy, and our turmoil for His rest.

God's blessing—true happiness—comes to those who desire God's strength. This strength comes as we receive God's challenge, exchange our weakness for His strength, and wait on the Lord. When our fellowship with God is in place and we are receiving God's strength, we are able to truly trust our gracious Heavenly Father.

Trust

We resemble God's Son
as we trust His Father.

"O LORD of hosts, blessed is the man that trusteth in thee."
– Psalm 84:12

God's blessing—true happiness—comes to those who desire to trust in Him. This trust comes as we pray to God, engraft His Word, and focus on the Lord.

*"Seeing then that we have a great high priest,
that is passed into the heavens, Jesus the Son of God, let
us hold fast our profession. 15 For we have not an high
priest which cannot be touched with the feeling of our
infirmities; but was in all points tempted like as we are,
yet without sin. 16 Let us therefore come boldly unto the
throne of grace, that we may obtain mercy, and find
grace to help in time of need."*

– Hebrews 4:14–16

CHAPTER FIFTEEN

Prayer

"Dear Kenny,

Was real sorry to hear of your accident. Truly the Lord was with you anyway.

We would like to tell you, all night the night of your accident we couldn't sleep and God showed us we should pray for someone in your family but didn't seem to know why. How gracious He has been to both of us to answer our prayers for you on that terrible night. We truly know your suffering must be beyond imagination. Our minds and prayers are for you every day for a fast recovery to health. Read Psalm 91."

(*Note on card from Ken's cousin*)

How many other people were praying for me the night of the plane crash? I will never know. I know my wife was awake in the wee hours of the morning praying for me because of her deep concern over the stormy weather around St. Louis. I do know that my mother-in-law, my brother, my twin sister, my cousin, and at least one of our deacons were all awakened by God to pray for me. These represent only the ones who have shared their stories. God burdened their hearts to pray, they responded to His call to pray, and God answered their prayers for my protection.

As I traveled to the hospital in the ambulance, I took a deep breath. My thought was, "I can breath! I'm going to be alright. God has heard my prayer." I felt a great confidence that God was answering the cry of my heart when I surrendered to Him at the end of that conference. I had no knowledge that God had called people to pray for my protection. Even without understanding the magnitude of my injuries, and the fragile position of my life, because people were praying, God placed His confidence in my heart that all was well. I had hope.

Hope

Once the news of the plane crash became more widespread, people from all over the world began praying for me. Many sent cards and letters to assure me of their prayers. In fact, the literally hundreds of cards lining the walls of my room in the Burn Unit reminded me that I was not suffering alone. I was being remembered in prayer at all hours of the day and night. In the midst of the pain or at times when I was afraid, one look at that wall of cards brought tears. Each card was an overwhelming reminder of the confident assurance that God loved me. I could hold tight to my profession of faith in Christ. I was assured of His ability to heal my burns. I knew God's people were praying because I sensed God's presence and peace. He gave me hope.

Hebrews 4:14, 16 says, "*Seeing then that we have a great high priest, that is passed into the heavens, Jesus the Son of God, let us hold fast our profession...Let us therefore come boldly unto the throne of grace, that we may obtain mercy, and find grace to help in time of need.*" Trust in God produces effective prayer. Jesus has finished His earthly work for us and passed into the heavens. His position with the Father encourages us to pray, and because of His finished work on Calvary, we can have hope and trust in God.

Help

Long before the plane crash, God had already used my left hand to teach my wife and me much about prayer. In January of 1975, after Beth and I were engaged to be married, we became aware that I would have a problem wearing a wedding band on my left ring finger. I had so many warts on my ring finger that it would have been very difficult to slip a wedding ring onto my hand during the ceremony.

The secretary where I worked while attending Bible college and seminary kindly made an appointment for me at a dermatologist's office. I went to see this doctor only to find that the price for treatment was more than I could afford. On top of that, he could offer no guarantee that the warts would not reappear.

I tried to remove some of the warts using a wart remover, but those futile attempts left scars. Beth and I decided to pray, and we claimed the promise of Matthew 18:19: *"Again I say unto you, That if two of you shall agree on earth as touching any thing that they shall ask, it shall be done for them of my Father which is in heaven."* Next to this verse we wrote "Ken's warts— 1-25-75" in the margin of my Bible. Almost three months later, we wrote "4-14-75" next to the day we had claimed the promise, recording the date God removed all of the warts, without leaving any scars! We were married later that spring, and my ring easily slipped onto my ring finger. Praise the Lord!

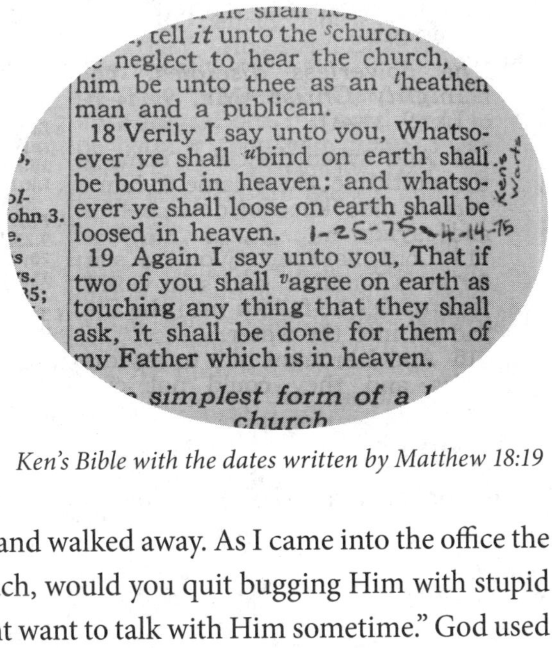

Ken's Bible with the dates written by Matthew 18:19

Shortly after the warts were gone, the secretary where I worked asked me about my visit to the dermatologist. When I showed her my hand, she stated emphatically, "Don't even tell me!" and walked away. As I came into the office the next day, she said, "Preach, would you quit bugging Him with stupid things like warts? I might want to talk with Him sometime." God used my warts to give me an opportunity to share the plan of salvation with her as well as preparing us to trust Him for help in the future.

After the crash, the truth that Jesus knew the trial I was facing was a source of great help and strength to me. I knew I could trust Him. He understood and helped me because *"we have not an high priest which cannot be touched with the feeling of our infirmities; but was in all points tempted like as we are, yet without sin"* (Hebrews 4:15).

Each of my grafting surgeries was scheduled to take place early in the morning. Before each surgery, our church family prayed throughout the night for me as well as for the doctors and the staff, and for the grafts to *take*.

On the morning of the first graft, Beth greeted the doctors as they entered my room to take me to surgery. "Our church members prayed all night for you, for Ken, and for this surgery," she informed them.

"Okay," one of them responded nonchalantly.

The grafting of my left hand included an amputation of fingers because of the deep burns I had sustained to them. During this surgery, the doctors also grafted the third-degree burns on my right leg and right hand. Neither area was as badly burned as the left side of my body.

Skin grafts are not always successful the first time. Often a graft has to be done a second time, or even several times, before the grafted skin successfully adheres. Several years after the plane crash, this fact became very real to me when I greeted a missionary we had invited to our missions conference. When he saw my left hand he asked me about my burns and shared that he had been burned as a teenager. He then asked, "How many grafts did you have?"

I replied, "Three."

He looked at me and said, "I had three grafts before any took." We stood there and wept. We both understood that he had experienced all that pain only to have to go through it again. That my first graft was 100 percent successful was truly a miracle of God.

The morning of my second surgery, Beth again met the doctors as they came to my room and said, "Our church members prayed all night for you, for Ken, and for this surgery. We prayed that God would guide you as you place the grafts, and that they will take—like the first graft."

This time their "thank you" was somewhat more enthusiastic.

For this surgery, my chest was the donor site. My little toe and the tips of my second, third, and fourth toes on my left foot were amputated, and then my left foot and leg were grafted. Most of the muscle in my left calf was removed because of the deep burns in the muscle.

When the bandages were removed three days later, my body had turned a bright green from just under my arms to the tips of my toes. This type of infection, called a pseudomonas infection, will often completely strip the grafts from the body, requiring the area to be grafted again. In spite of this infection, this second skin graft was still 97 percent successful—another miracle of God indeed!

The morning of the third surgery, Beth once again met the grafting team and said, "Our church members prayed all night for you, for Ken, and for this surgery. Thank you for the specialized care you are giving Ken."

She expected the same response she'd had before. Instead, she was met with an even more enthusiastic, "Thank you."

"What you are doing for Ken with your prayers and encouragement is more important than what we are doing," one doctor added. "All we can do is put the grafts down; God has to make the grafts take. Please keep up the prayers."

In spite of yet another pseudomonas infection, which required treatment with strong antibiotic creams, this grafting also adhered 100 percent. To us, we had received a definite indication that God was answering the prayers of His people.

My left hand was so severely burned that parts of the fingers had to be removed. My ring finger, the finger God had healed of the warts, was amputated. Before that surgery, I had already asked the doctor to remove the parts of my fingers that would not be useful to me. I especially did not want unsightly stubs that could easily be bumped or cause pain.

The doctors chose to leave more of my little finger than I felt I would be able to use effectively. As it healed, the end of my finger bent down into the palm of my hand. Skin grew over it, attaching to the inside of my finger. This did not present a problem until I was home and began wearing my JOBST gloves, which put steady pressure on my whole hand. The pressure on that little finger became so unbearable that I called Dr. Ayvazian to ask him what to do.

"Cut the finger off of the glove to relieve the pain," he said.

"I asked you to remove everything that I wouldn't be able to use," I reminded him at the end of the call. "I won't be able to use that small part of my finger."

"Ken, I took an oath to save life when I became a doctor. There was life in that part of your finger. If you want it removed, you can have a plastic surgeon remove it."

At my next burn clinic appointment, when the doctor had finished his exam, he began to lightly touch my left hand in several places. "Can you feel this?" he asked.

"Yes."

"If it was a hook, you wouldn't. If I had not been in the burn unit making that news broadcast when you were brought in, your left hand would be a hook."

Through that short conversation, I saw again that God's promise to answer prayer in Isaiah 65:24 is true: *"And it shall come to pass, that before they call, I will answer; and while they are yet speaking, I will hear."* God had guided the surgeons. He had caused the grafts to take. He had spared my hand.

Even our grandchildren are fascinated by my left hand. When they were little, they would sit in my lap and study it. When they were old enough to comprehend, they would ask questions like, "Why didn't God grow more fingers on your hand?"

"Because God obviously had other plans for my hand!" I would respond.

In 2007–08, our oldest daughter and son-in-law attended Baptist Bible Translators Institute (BBTI) in Bowie, Texas, before going to Uganda as missionaries. Our church members graciously arranged for Beth and me to be at their graduation. We were thrilled to meet various classmates and teachers. The first person we met after arriving at BBTI exclaimed, "Oh! So you're the grandpa! We've been praying that God would grow fingers on your hand!"

Our grandchildren were so convinced that God would grow fingers on my hand, they asked everyone to pray that God would do it! I think God could if He wanted to, but God's purpose and plan for me is to live without those fingers. Their absence is a constant reminder to me that God protected me during that crash in which others died. He is in control of my life. He has a plan and a purpose for my life. And that reminder has become a God-given tool to use in witnessing about salvation to many!

What precious faith those children have! Through their prayer for me to grow fingers, they have also learned that their Heavenly Father sometimes says, "No, I have something better for you."

God is our help. As we seek Him in prayer, He helps us to focus on Himself and to seek His purpose.

Comfort

My last graft was on the back side of my legs, my buttocks, my lateral and medial thighs, and the medial areas of my left calf, left foot and leg. I had to lie on my stomach every second of every day for a week to protect those tender grafts. I have already shared about the discouragement I faced at the prospect of having to walk the following Monday after such prolonged immobility. I did not realize at the time the impact this whole experience would have on me. Another lesson I learned was how important prayer is to receiving God's comfort.

That Sunday night, one of our deacons called me at the hospital after the service.

"Hi, Pastor Spilger," he said. "I am calling to let you to know that the church will be praying all night. We're praying that you'll be able to walk tomorrow."

"Thank you," I said.

"We're also praying that you'll progress well enough to be able to attend the conference with Dr. Roberson in a week."

My heart sank. I thanked him again, but I was inwardly disappointed at the news he had shared. What they thought would be a morale booster for me was simply one more source of frustration to me. My annoyance wasn't because of his call or their prayers; rather, I was frustrated because I now knew I would have to do my best to be there. Though I offered him my words of gratitude, my head was screaming, "No! Now I have to try, and I don't want to!"

Thankfully, while the church people prayed, God did a work in my heart. I went to sleep that night troubled, frustrated, and distressed. I woke up Monday morning with new hope. When Beth arrived at the hospital the nurses greeted her at the door with a message.

"You have a new husband this morning," they said.

Indeed, she did! God's people had gone to the throne of grace, and God had heard their heartfelt prayers. They had begged for His mercy and grace in my time of need, and God gave it—not simply for me to take that first step but also to face the struggles ahead (Hebrews 4:16). As a result of their prayers, God had influenced my heart, and His influence was being reflected in my life.

God was at work burning off the dross—my façade of hypocrisy—so He could build His character in my life and help me focus on His purpose. I realized anew that the pain and suffering I was experiencing was to bring me to the point of depending only upon His strength—after all, I had no strength of my own.

Often as I lay convalescing in my hospital bed, I wondered how anyone could experience the pain I felt and live. During those moments, my mind went back to my Lord Jesus Christ, who knew and understood my pain. *"Great is our Lord, and of great power: his understanding is infinite"* (Psalm 147:5). Jesus my Saviour had come with His limitless power and immeasurable understanding to bear my human misery. He had experienced my pain. My hope was in Jesus Christ—not in my circumstances. I could personally go boldly to His throne of grace and obtain His mercy and supernatural help in my time of need. I found great comfort in this truth. I could trust Jesus because He understood me, loved me, and was caring for me.

During my days of convalescing, my mind often visited the past. Thinking about my maternal grandmother's testimony also became a great comfort to me. She had been burned in a house fire long before I was born. The medical professionals of her day had none of today's procedures to reduce the length of a burn survivor's suffering. In fact, more pain was inflicted upon her because of their old-fashioned procedures. Through it all, she thought on the truth of Christ's sufferings. Like He knew my pain, He also knew her pain for He

Ken's Grandmother

had experienced it. As God worked out His mercy and grace in her life and helped her through the suffering, I knew I could depend on Him to do the same for me. Someday, I will see my grandmother in Heaven, and we will rejoice together over the fact that God cannot fail to fulfill His promises!

The burning off of dross did not end with the plane crash. I have learned that God continues His work of grace in each of us until we reach Heaven. Only then will His work be complete in His children. God used this trial in my life to teach many people much about prayer and God's comfort.

In May of 2011, Beth and I were in England with two single missionary ladies whom our church supports financially. One of them, Marcia Kittleson, had been staying with us when the plane crashed. I was given the opportunity to speak to a group of people about the plane crash and my extensive injuries. When the time came for questions, a lady in the audience cautiously asked me, "Was there ever a time that you lost your faith in God or doubted Him?"

Most of the people attending this meeting would not have claimed to be Christians. I was so glad for the opportunity this woman's question gave me to share Christ's comfort with them.

God allowed me to share the following answer:

> *As I lay there in my bed, overwhelmed by the pain of the burns, I thought, "How can I feel this much pain after receiving all of the pain medicine they could possibly give me and still be conscious and alive?" I have no way, humanly speaking, to describe the pain I felt. You have to experience it yourself to understand it. Only burn survivors understand the pain of which I speak. Yet as I lay there weeping, I kept thinking, "Jesus understands. He was tempted even in this point of pain and suffering. His suffering was even greater than what I am experiencing. He understands."*

The lady was visibly moved by my answer. Tears began to well up in her eyes. She could not speak, though she tried. I am so grateful to God for His work in my life. He prepared an answer for this woman more than thirty years before she asked the question.

Not only did we see His answers to our prayers then, but He also helped us grow in our understanding of how vital prayer is in our everyday life. We learned that we can trust God to give His unbounded mercy, grace, and strength in times of need.

*"Wherefore lay apart all filthiness and superfluity
of naughtiness, and receive with meekness the engrafted
word, which is able to save your souls. [22]But be ye doers of
the word, and not hearers only, deceiving your own selves.
[23]For if any be a hearer of the word, and not a doer, he is
like unto a man beholding his natural face in a glass: [24]For
he beholdeth himself, and goeth his way, and straight-
way forgetteth what manner of man he was. [25]But whoso looketh into the perfect law of liberty, and continueth
therein, he being not a forgetful hearer, but a doer of the
work, this man shall be blessed in his deed."*

– James 1:21–25

CHAPTER SIXTEEN

Scripture

"*Dr. Ayvazian, how* much is each day in this hospital costing me?"

The doctor patted my shoulder. "Ken, don't worry about that. Just get better."

I had already been in the hospital for several days, so I knew our indebtedness to the hospital was steadily rising higher. Though Beth and I had not talked about this matter, I knew she had to be facing the same concerns—perhaps more so because she would be the one dealing with the hospital regarding their fees.

When the first bill came, Beth stared at the sum written at the bottom of the page. Overwhelmed and in tears, she knew the only thing she could do was to take it to the Lord and ask Him for direction and help. God gave peace from His Word that night as she read Isaiah 26:3, "*Thou wilt keep him in perfect peace, whose mind is stayed on thee: because he trusteth in thee.*"

The next day she left for the hospital early, trusting in God's promise to supply all of our needs (Philippians 4:19). She went straight to the business office and was ushered to the desk of one of the officers.

"I'm not sure what we can work out to pay this bill," she explained. "Our insurance coverage is only a drop in the bucket. I know it won't cover the costs of such a huge bill, and we're only a few days into Ken's treatment. He will have to be here for several months. Do you have any idea how much his hospitalization will cost? I'm not sure how we'll be able to pay for such a huge bill."

"Well, let's get some information about you and your family," the financial officer began, "What is your husband's profession?"

The woman went on asking questions about our insurance and our family. She jotted down notes on a separate sheet of paper. Then she took the bill from Beth and stapled it to the sheet of information she had just recorded.

"Why don't you come back in a few days after we have had time to look into all of this."

Several days later, Beth went back to the business office.

"Because your husband is a minister," they told her, "we've decided to adjust your bill by giving you a 10-percent discount. And we will wait for payment until the liability insurance settles with you. I am sure that because of the nature of the accident, there will be liability to cover the hospitalization costs."

Relief flooded over Beth's troubled soul. Our already stretched income simply could not be stretched any further. God's promise was true! God would give peace, and He would supply our needs. Through the writings of the Apostle Paul, God said, *"my God shall supply all your need according to his riches in glory by Christ Jesus"* (Philippians 4:19). And that's exactly what God did! He used churches, individuals, and the eventual settlement from the liability insurance to meet every need, including the Exercycle, the JOBSTS garments, the physical and occupational therapy, and more than I could possibly list.

Some people have asked if we became rich from the liability settlement. Allow me to answer that question with a resounding, "No!" God used the trial process to build our relationship with the three widows and to give us much understanding about the crash itself. This was more valuable than money. Every need was met. Every single bill was paid, and that is all that mattered. God's Word held true!

Faced with many decisions, and without my input, Beth daily went to the Lord in her quiet time. She sought God's help to face the day by begging for strength, for direction, and for a promise that would help guide her. Shortly before the plane crashed, Beth began reading the book of Isaiah in her quiet time. As she read, God gave her the peace, direction, and help she requested. Often, as she read through this precious book of the Bible, God reminded her not to be afraid, that He was leading her, that He was God, and that nothing was too hard for Him because He is the Creator. As she focused on God, He would give her *"beauty for ashes"* as well as *"the oil of joy for mourning."* (Isaiah 61:3) He would also supply her needs, give His confident, undisturbed strength, and His ultimate peace—even before she asked. My wife learned to totally depend on God and to take His Word as her guide. Her relationship with God was not dependent upon my relationship with God. As His child, she would be accountable for herself when she stood before the Judgment Seat of Christ.

He Giveth More Grace

by Annie Johnson Flint

He giveth more grace when the burdens grow greater;
He sendeth more strength when the labors increase.
To added affliction He addeth His mercy;
To multiplied trials, His multiplied peace.

When we have exhausted our store of endurance,
When our strength has failed ere the day is half done,
When we reach the end of our hoarded resources
Our Father's full giving is only begun.

Fear not that thy need shall exceed His provision,
Our God ever yearns His resources to share;
Lean hard on the arm everlasting, availing;
The Father both thee and thy load will upbear.

Chorus:

His love has no limit, His grace has no measure,
His power has no boundary known unto men;
For out of His infinite riches in Jesus,
He giveth, and giveth, and giveth again.

~ *Song that ministered to Beth*

Many times throughout that long, hard experience, we went to God's Word to get direction and to ask for a promise concerning each dilemma. God was faithful! As Romans 15:4, 13 tell us, He is our hope and His

Word gives us hope: *"For whatsoever things were written aforetime were written for our learning, that we through patience and comfort of the scriptures might have hope...Now the God of hope fill you with all joy and peace in believing, that ye may abound in hope, through the power of the Holy Ghost."* Everything we need for life and godliness is found in God's Word (2 Peter 1:3).

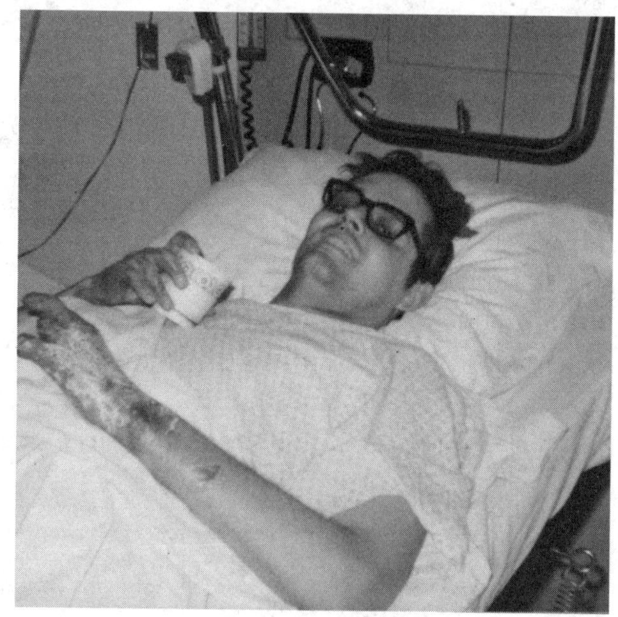

Ken in his Striker Frame Circle bed

As I lay in my Stryker frame circle bed, especially after I began to feel better, God flooded my soul with the verses I had committed to memory. The one promise I held onto from the beginning was Romans 8:28: *"And we know that all things work together for good to them that love God, to them who are the called according to his purpose."* I had memorized that verse many years before, and God brought it to my mind many times as I faced daily pain and difficulty.

In James 1:21-25, God says engrafting His Word into our life is the key to growing in His purpose. As I recovered from my burns and was able to study God's Word again, I began to see the correlation of the skin grafts to engrafting Scripture into our lives. The term *engrafted* in James 1:21 means *to implant or graft,* just as the doctors did with the skin on the severely burned areas of my body. God wants the truths of His Word to become a living part of our souls. He works to make His Word alive and powerful in us.

Preparation

I have already alluded to the fact that before any skin grafts can be placed on burn wounds much preparation must take place. For me, this preparation began with cleaning off the mud that was caked to my body when I fell into the ravine and onto that muddy ledge at the crash site. I was covered in so much mud that when Beth swabbed my ears two months later, we still found a good deal of good ol' Missouri clay!

Firefighters pulling Ken up from the muddy shelf

The next step of preparation was the doctors' performing escharotomies to relieve the pressure from the swelling and constriction caused by the burns.

Once the burns had been cleansed and the constrictions relieved, I went through a waiting period. The burned surfaces needed to become *ripe* to the point that the grafted skin could be received and sustain life in the new skin. Otherwise, the new skin would not grow, thrive, and become an integral part of my body.

The bed of the wound site will not accept a skin graft if debris, infections, or scabs are present. To prepare my wound bed for the grafts, the medical technicians put me into a large sterile soaking tub. After a long soak, the technicians used gauze and special tools to carefully go

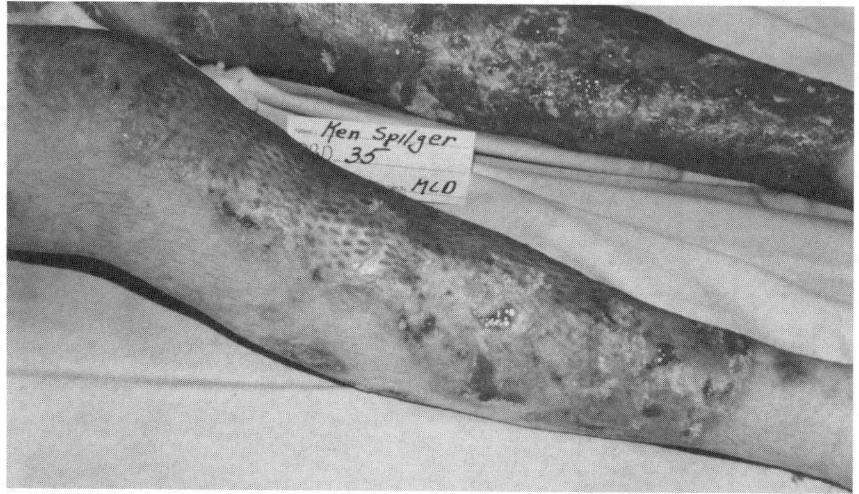

Ken's grafted skin

over my wounds and remove the loosened dead tissue, foreign bodies, and dirt. This procedure, called *debridement*, helps the healing process by removing anything that would hinder healing or allow infection to set in. Once the painful debridement was complete, the doctors could clearly see the depth of my wounds and could then determine the proper treatment for the area. I can personally attest to the fact that this process is quite painful. I also understood it was very necessary for my recovery. Debridement, which takes days and even weeks to complete, was not a process to which I looked forward. Even after my grafts had been placed, the technicians continued to debride the areas in order for proper healing to take place.

If my wounds had not been cleansed properly before the grafts, my body would not have received the new skin. If the grafts were not properly debrided, they would not stay on and thrive as a part of the larger body of skin.

Reception

Once my wound beds were completely debrided, surgery was scheduled. The surgeons explained that during surgery, the debrided area would be *roughed up*, causing bleeding. The new skin graft would then be laid on these bleeding beds and held tightly in place by bandages.

Very careful attention was given to my grafts every day. The dressings had to be changed, and the wounds had to be cleaned. If any infection was noted, antibiotics were immediately started as treatment. This process was painful for me to endure, but I understood the procedure had to be followed for the grafts to thrive.

Like the wounded physical body must go through a series of preparations to receive grafts, so the spiritual body must be prepared to receive God's Word. My heart, like my body, has to be made tender, or *ripe*—ready to receive God's Word into my soul. I must receive it with meekness, not telling God what I am going to do but listening to Him. No Christian can grow spiritually in his own power, demanding his own way, and God's Word makes the difference in every Christian's life.

Application

With preparation made and hearts ready to receive God's Word, we can, with meekness, make personal application. Just like the new skin had to be applied to the wound, God's Word must be applied to our life.

Hear

Hearing the Word of God, an important first step in receiving God's Word, results in the growth of our faith, which is pleasing to God. Romans 10:17 says, *"So then faith cometh by hearing, and hearing by the word of God."* Hebrews 11:6 says that faith is the foundation of our relationship with God: *"But without faith it is impossible to please him: for he that cometh to God must believe that he is, and that he is a rewarder of them that diligently seek him.*" My surrender to God, by faith, was necessary for my reception of God 's Word in order to apply it.

God often brings circumstances into our lives to deepen our understanding of His Word so that we will apply it into our lives. In the same way God used the financial pressure from the plane crash, He has used other trials to prepare our hearts to receive His Word so that we can trust Him and live by faith.

Not long after we were married, God worked to teach us that we could trust Him to meet all of our needs. When we were living in Hartington, Nebraska, a missionary was staying with our family over the Memorial Day weekend. At that time, all of the stores in Hartington were closed on Sundays and holidays. We had food for the weekend but no meat. We were also supposed to take potato salad to a lunch after a funeral on Monday, but we had no potatoes nor eggs. Neither did we have the money to buy fuel to drive to another town where the stores would be open.

As Beth was serving in the nursery that Sunday evening, she prayed, "Father, we need meat, potatoes, and eggs. You will have to give them to us because we have no way to get them."

That night a family came to church who didn't normally attend on Sunday nights. "Who is keeping the missionary?" the wife asked me.

"We are," I replied.

"I have something for you." She gave us two dressed chickens from her freezer to serve to the missionary.

After we arrived home, someone called and said, "Our refrigerator isn't working. Could you possibly use some eggs before they spoil?"

When we went to pick up the eggs, they said, "Oh, and could you use some potatoes? We were given 100 pounds today, and we can't possibly use that many before they go bad."

Without saying a word to anyone but God, all of our needs for that weekend were met. God was teaching us the truth of Philippians

4:19: *"But my God shall supply all your need according to his riches in glory by Christ Jesus."* God was engrafting this verse into our souls, so He could use it in us to teach us to trust Him for the rest of our lives. He used the reminders of His earlier provision to remind us to trust Him as we faced the huge medical expenses from the plane crash.

Hear
Read
Study
Memorize
Meditate on
God's Word

God wants us to move beyond being *hearers* of His Word. In James 1:25, He promises blessings for doers of His Word: *"But whoso looketh into the perfect law of liberty, and continueth therein, he being not a forgetful hearer, but a doer of the work, this man shall be blessed in his deed."*

Read

In order to apply God's Word to our lives, we must not only hear God's Word but also read it. God has promised rewards for those who read His word: *"Blessed is he that readeth, and they that hear the words of this prophecy, and keep those things which are written therein: for the time is at hand"* (Revelation 1:3). In this verse, God included all three of these aspects in His promised blessing: hearing, reading, and doing. In Deuteronomy 17:18, 19 God is even more specific about the blessings of reading His law: *"He* [the king] *shall write him a copy of this law in a book out of that which is before the priests the Levites:* [19]*And it shall be with him, and he shall read therein all the days of his life: that he may learn to fear the* LORD *his God, to keep all the words of this law and these statutes, to do them."* Reading God's Word would result in blessings in the king's life. He would learn to fear God and to be obedient to Him.

Study

Notice that God did not simply want the king to hear and read His law; He also wanted him to write it. As the king was writing out God's law, I am sure he had questions about what he was writing. I am reasonably sure he studied these in order to apply them to life situations. This brings us to another important aspect of engrafting the Word into our souls: study. In 2 Timothy 2:15 God says, *"Study to shew thyself approved unto God, a workman that needeth not to be ashamed, rightly dividing the word of truth."* This verse means that the student of God's Word will compare Scripture with Scripture, do word studies, study the verses in the context of the passage, and seek God for a greater understanding of that truth.

As the doctors had to approve the timing of the skin grafts, likewise God approves the heart that has been prepared by the study of His Word. A doer of the Word who has carefully studied the Scripture will be discerning and have no need to be ashamed.

As anything hindering the healing process of grafted skin must be discarded, so must we discard anything that would hinder the Word of God from becoming a viable part of our life. Sin in a Christian's life must be confronted continually. We daily need to examine ourselves in the light of the Word of God to see if something is present that does not please Him or that would allow Satan to build a stronghold.

"Lay apart all filthiness and superfluity of naughtiness" means that all the debris of sin, deceit, pretense, envy, evil speaking, moral defilement, and even good works must be laid aside—as a piece of clothing is removed and laid aside. We must each take responsibility for that which displeases the Lord and move on to the healing that comes from knowing and applying God's Word to our life. Is this process painful? Yes! As the debridement of my burns was a very painful process, the process of confessing sin can be quite painful. But for the grafts to *take*, debriding must be done, and for the Word of God to *take* in our hearts, confession (agreeing with God about how bad our sin is) must also take place.

Sin that has not been confessed allows Satan to take up residence in parts of a Christian's heart where that sin is harbored.

Ephesians 4:27 says, *"Neither give place* [or a piece of our heart—our mind, our emotions, and our will] *to the devil."* Not only has God commanded us to deal with each area so He can take His rightful place, but He has also given us *mighty weapons* to tear down the strongholds (2 Corinthians 10:4).

The cares of this world and the deceitfulness of riches can and will choke out and destroy the fruit of God's Word in our life (Matthew 13:22). Our attention must be directed to remove the distractions, keep short accounts with our sins, and cleanse our lives of all evil.

Memorize

Memorizing Scripture brings with it the blessing of having personal victory over sin. In Psalm 119:11, the Psalmist says, *"Thy word have I hid in mine heart, that I might not sin against thee."* When we memorize the Word of God, a guide is placed in our heart to measure our words, attitudes, and actions. What are we thinking about? What captures our attention and becomes our focus? Do these areas of attention please God and make the Gospel of Christ beautiful? Do our activities bring honor to the Lord? We should not be asking, "What is wrong with this? Why can't I do this, or why can't I have that?" Rather, we should filter each decision through the Scripture and ask, "What is right with this? Would God be pleased with this?" Examining ourselves in this way is applying God's Word to our lives. Our spiritual growth will only come with the application of God's Word.

Like the grafted skin produces more skin on our bodies and grafting a fruit tree produces more fruit, God uses His engrafted Word in our lives to produce His fruit in us. This fruit is the result of receiving His grace. Jesus said in John 15:8 that God is glorified when Christians bear much fruit: *"Herein is my Father glorified, that ye bear much fruit; so shall ye be my disciples."* Bearing fruit enables us to reflect God's glory because producing His fruit causes us to resemble His Son. If we could produce our own fruit, we

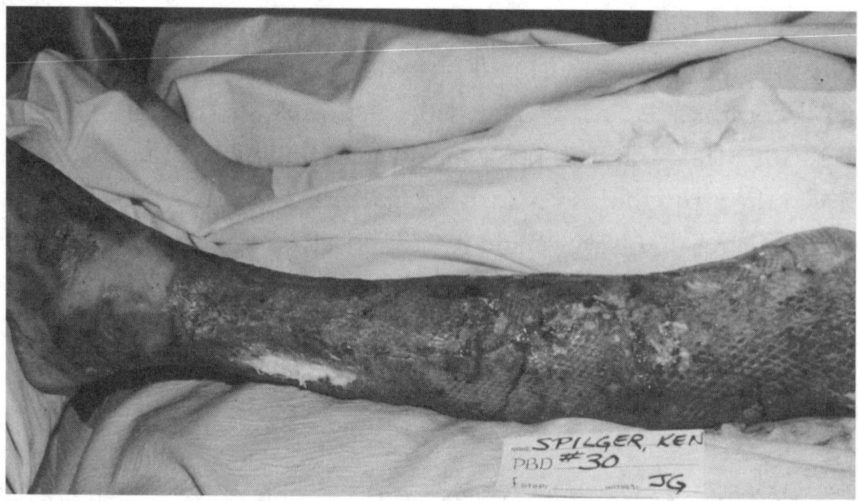

Grafting on Ken's left leg

would receive the glory and would not resemble Christ; therefore, we cannot produce our own fruit.

Meditate

As my wound beds had to be *roughed up*—humbled, we often need the humbling work of God in our lives to help us receive the Word of God in a way that will allow us to bring forth fruit. The financial pressures Beth and I felt resulting from the plane crash softened our hearts to cry out to God and receive His promises. God mixes trials with His Word to enable us to trust Him with all our needs.

The Scripture tells the Christian to *"receive with meekness the engrafted word, which is able to save your souls."* In other words, believers are to humbly receive the Word of God. Meekness is *power or strength under God's control.* Meekness is not and never has been about being wimpy nor being able to obtain my desires in my own power. Meekness is simply allowing God to bring about His fruit in my life as I read, memorize, and meditate on God's Word every day.

Meditation on God's Word is the final step of engrafting Scripture into our lives. The Bible tells us in Joshua 1:8 that meditating on God's Word will help us to have *good success. "This book of the law shall not depart out of thy mouth; but thou shalt meditate therein day and night, that thou mayest observe to do according to all that is written therein: for then thou shalt make thy way prosperous, and then thou shalt have good success."*

As I have already mentioned, all of my grafts were successful. I believe this blessing was, first of all, due to the prayers of God's people but was also because of the careful attention given to each graft by my caregivers. In the same way, we must give careful attention to the grafting of God's Word into our souls. Then sufficient time must be allowed for healing in those areas of our *wounds*.

Beth and I have candidly shared our struggles from both before and after the plane crash. These struggles were very real and painful. We have shared how God used the trials of the plane crash to lead us to His victory in Christ. We both agree that a vital ingredient in this journey to embrace God's purpose has been His engrafted Word in our souls. Our daily goals include giving ourselves to God to hear, read, study, memorize, and meditate on His Word. Doing so has enabled us to do what God teaches in His Word and to receive His blessing.

Trust in God is possible when we receive His Word, which becomes the protection for our very being—our mind, our emotions, and our will. The Word of God will "*...save your souls*" as James 1:21 states. As we faced the pain, decisions, struggles of finances, and all of our other needs, God, through His Word and the working of His Spirit, gave peace, confidence, direction, and much more than we could have dreamed. His fruit was produced in us. We learned to trust Him.

*"In the LORD put I my trust: how say ye to my soul,
Flee as a bird to your mountain? 2For, lo, the wicked bend
their bow, they make ready their arrow upon the string,
that they may privily shoot at the upright in heart. 3If the
foundations be destroyed, what can the righteous do? 4The
LORD is in his holy temple, the LORD's throne is in heaven:
his eyes behold, his eyelids try, the children of men. 5The
LORD trieth the righteous: but the wicked and him that
loveth violence his soul hateth. 6Upon the wicked he shall
rain snares, fire and brimstone, and an horrible tempest:
this shall be the portion of their cup. 7For the righteous
LORD loveth righteousness; his countenance doth behold
the upright."*

– Psalm 11

CHAPTER SEVENTEEN

Focus

I was being moved in my Stryker frame circle bed from one room to another in the burn unit. My trip down the hall was a simple procedure, but in my mind, I was being pushed down Interstate 70 to Kansas City. I liked being in my room in the burn unit where the cards on the wall reminded me of all the people who were praying for me.

"Why are they moving me?" I wondered. "Why is it taking forever? Will this journey ever end?"

We kept going and going. I was so tired. "Nothing makes sense," I thought.

These cards and letters "wallpapered" the hospital room

My confusion with being moved perfectly pictured the confusion I had allowed to control the focus of my life, my family, and my ministry—pre-crash. I knew God had begun moving me out of the confusion created by my pride. Now with the plane crash, I found myself wondering, "Why is all this happening to me—to us? How can I do this? Can I still trust God?"

The only certainty I had been feeling in my life was hopelessness. But that feeling of hopelessness was as much a lie as my confusing *trip* to Kansas City. I am thankful that I knew my only hope was to focus on God and trust in Him.

Choose to Trust God

George Mueller was once asked the best way to have strong faith. He replied, "The only way to learn strong faith is to endure great trials. I have learned my faith by standing firm amid severe testings."[4]

Through the crash, God was giving us a great trial to endure, so we could learn to keep our focus on Him and trust Him with strong faith. In the midst of my confusion and hopelessness, God was revealing how much hope we really could have. Based on previous experience, I knew I could trust Him completely because God never changes.

One lesson I learned from the crash was God's abruptly showing me that every moment is precious and that only as I trust Him can I fully live these moments. He gave me comfort, which I could share with others. He poured out His love in my heart, which gives the confidence that He will always demonstrate His love to me in my trials. His strength was made perfect in my weakness. He enabled me to choose to have the mind of Christ, teaching me that I can trust Him for victory in the future.

God taught me to wait upon Him. He taught me to trust Him to be my defense and my salvation. He affirmed that I can access him through His Son in prayer. He gave me promises from His Word and proved His faithfulness to those promises.

Throughout both this trial and my life, my desire has been to focus my trust in God, like David, who wrote in Psalm 11:1, *"In the LORD put I my trust."*

---

[4] *Streams in the Desert*, June 2, page 178.

Recognize the Conflict

When David was a young shepherd boy, he was anointed to be king. But when the time came, he instead found himself running from Saul and his forces. I imagine David wondered at times if he would ever make it to the throne. The confusion of his trials may well have begun to distort his focus. I personally think this questioning may be why David wrote Psalm 11. I imagine his counselors were telling him to quit and run away by saying, *"flee as a bird to your mountain."* Possibly they were counseling him to panic because the enemy planned to murder him. *"For, lo, the wicked bend their bow, they make ready their arrow upon the string, that they may privily shoot at the upright in heart."* And finally, they implied that David should give up because his situation was futile. Since there was nothing he could do, they asked him, *"If the foundations be destroyed, what can the righteous do?"*

In the days following the crash, the *voices* of the enemy suggested that I could not trust God. But as I meditated on this particular psalm, God taught me why I could trust my Heavenly Father.

We were facing a great trial that involved pain, fear, loneliness, weakness, and uncertainty. We knew this trial was not a mistake; rather, it was God's appointment for us to learn great faith. Still, evil voices were also speaking to us, saying, "Just give up. Quit! *'Flee as a bird to your mountain.'*" The voices were subtle at times, but they were very real.

They whispered, "People don't understand. They don't really care. They'll turn on you. *'For, lo, the wicked bend their bow, they make ready their arrow upon the string, that they may privily shoot at the upright in heart.'*"

Sometimes, the voices questioned my Lord, "Does God really care? If He messed up this bad now, how can you trust Him with the rest of your life? *'If the foundations be destroyed, what can the righteous do?'*"

David had to deal with these types of thoughts, and so do Christians today. Though questions in themselves are not wrong, the way these questions are sometimes addressed can bring us to some wicked ways of thinking.

When properly addressed, however, these questions can bring the believer to God's truth. That's why God told us in 2 Corinthians 10:4, 5 that He has given us His *mighty weapons* to tear down wrong ways of thinking. These weapons help us examine our thoughts and make sure they are in agreement with what Christ wants us to think. God's Holy Spirit helps us bring these thoughts under the scrutiny of God's Word. Only then are we able to cast down our evil imaginations and hold up God's Word of truth.

My commitment to Jesus Christ was definitely in place. I had surrendered my life to Him the best I knew how at the pastors conference in Kansas City. But now my life would never be the same. The burns I had suffered left permanent damage to my body. My hands and legs would always be stiff from the scars. At the time of my stay in the burn unit, we did not know for sure the full extent of my recovery.

Beth faithfully stood strong. Statistics show that the divorce rate among those who face a crisis such as ours rises significantly. However, God used the plane crash to strengthen and stabilize our marriage.

My parents and extended family were incredibly supportive. Some families cannot endure the emotional pain of watching a loved one suffer like I was suffering. However, my family and my wife's family used this time to demonstrate their love to me.

My church family stood strong with me. Some churches or places of employment use times like these to let an injured worker go. The employer might not want to face the additional financial obligation required to get the work done. Not my church! My church family used this time to pray, to give of themselves, and to love us in many ways. I cannot begin to share how their loving kindness ministered to our hearts. I remember how Beth wondered what she would do to provide for our family's needs, not only when I was in the hospital but also when I returned home and was still recovering. Imagine her shock when the treasurer gave her my paycheck that first week after the accident and told her that my pay would continue while I was out of the pulpit!

When we entered into this time of suffering, we did not know how anything would work out. We had to walk through it together. Our focus had to be on the Lord. Years earlier, when I was a Bible college student, preparing to preach a message from Psalm 11, God gave me a special grace to focus my trust in Him when foundations seemed to be shaken or even destroyed. Now we knew He would continue to use the truths of this Psalm to give us this needed grace.

Times will come in every Christian's walk when he questions the circumstances of his life. During these times of puzzlement, every Christian has a choice. He can look at God through his circumstances and demonstrate fear, or he can look at his circumstances through God and demonstrate faith. The choice the Christian makes will determine where he places his focus.

Seek to Know God

How big is your God? Is your God the God of the Bible? How you answer these two questions will determine your victory or defeat. God has much to say about Himself in His Word. Psalm 11 is but one passage that contains many characteristics of the true God. Romans 10:17 says, *"faith cometh by hearing, and hearing by the word of God."* We can take God's Word at face value and trust in it. His Word is truth; it is sure. The truths about God contained in Psalm 11 have worked to advance our faith. From them, we can know who God is, so that we can trust in Him.

God Is Holy

In Psalm 11:4 we learn that we can trust God because He is holy. *"The LORD is in his holy temple."* He could not have been in His holy temple if He Himself were not holy. Because God is holy, He can do no wrong. The circumstances of the plane crash were all a part of God's plan for Ken Spilger. That plan included the loss of three lives; months of convalescing in the burn unit; months of therapy and rehabilitation; learning to walk, write, drive, and even to live again. These conditions did not take God by surprise. God didn't say, "Oops! I goofed! I lost track of Ken's plane."

God desires that every believer would be like Christ, including the area of holiness: *"But as he which hath called you is holy, so be ye holy in all manner of conversation* [the way we live]; [16]*Because it is written, Be ye holy; for I am holy"* (1 Peter 1:15, 16). The trials surrounding the plane crash were part of God's work to develop His holiness in my life. Since I knew my Heavenly Father could do no wrong, I understood that even though the circumstances were hard, they were not meant for evil. They had been divinely orchestrated by the hand of my holy, loving Heavenly Father for my good.

God Is Sovereign

Psalm 11:4 says, *"The LORD's throne is in heaven."* As our sovereign God, He rules from His throne in Heaven. Being sovereign, God possesses supreme or ultimate power, as Luke 1:37 declares, *"with God nothing shall be impossible."* Because God is sovereign, He is able to control everything that comes into our lives.

Because God was working in my life to make me more like His Son, He knew every circumstance of the plane crash would be required. God knows exactly what His children need. He knew

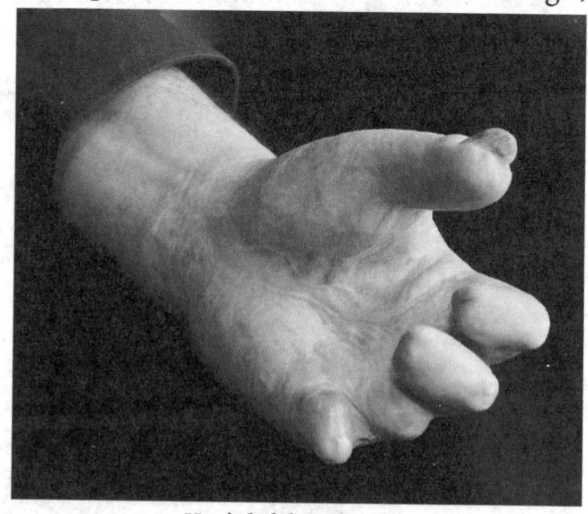

Ken's left hand today
He bears scars all over his body.

exactly what ingredients were needed to evoke a change in my life. Because of this knowledge, in His sovereignty, He allowed the accident to take place. Yes, I bear the scars of burns on my body, but they also constantly remind me that He loves me. He loves me so much that He did not want me to merely live a selfish life. He wants me to have the abundant life—real life. Because I know He never makes mistakes, I can trust Him!

God Is Wise

As God sits on His throne, *"his eyes behold, his eyelids try, the children of men"* (Psalm 11:4). He examines each of His children through the lens of His wisdom as they pass through the trials He allows in their lives.

As I lay in my hospital bed experiencing pain greater than I ever could have imagined, an overpowering sense of God's blessing came over me. I began to ponder the truth of Romans 8:28, *"And we know that all things work together for good to them that love God, to them who are the called according to his purpose."* Several years later, I read a message in *The Sword of the Lord* by the late Dr. Curtis Hutson, which helped me verbalize the following effects this passage had on my life during my days of suffering.

As I meditated on that verse, I knew I could be grateful for the certainty of God's promise: *"And we know."* The assurance contained in the word *know* caused me to weep with joy. I could trust God with confidence. All doubts, fear, and anxiety were removed.

I was comforted by the circumference of God's promise: *"that all things."* This *all* included my suffering. I felt as though God was hugging me as He surrounded me with His promises. This promise included the full impact of His purpose for my life.

I could rest in the cooperation found in God's promise: *"work together for good."* I could not pick and choose to experience only the life events of which I approved. Instead, I was to simply rest in God's choices for me because His end is always good. Like most Christians, I would choose to leave out anything that might be painful or hard, but God needs *all* of these things in order to work out the good His children really do desire.

I was humbled by the condition for receiving this promise: *"to them that love God, to them who are the called according to His purpose."* I knew I was saved. I had received Christ as my personal Savior. I knew I was called according to his purpose. God was working in my life so that I would love Him in the way He desired.

The day after I came home from the hospital, a pastor's wife called to encourage Beth and to ask how I was progressing. Beth shared all that was happening and, along with the struggles, she shared that she was trusting Romans 8:28 to be true. This wise pastor's wife agreed, and then she shared the fact that verse twenty-eight is not the end of the thought. The next verse goes on to tell us that the purpose of our trials is to make us into Christ's image: *"For whom he did foreknow, he also did predestinate to be conformed to the image of his Son, that he might be the firstborn among many brethren"* (Romans 8:29). What a purpose!

How was I to measure the good that came out of our trial? By comparing it to the standard of measure set up in verse twenty-nine. If the results made me more like Christ, it was good.

Because God is wise, He has a definite purpose for our life.

God Is Love

Psalm 11:5 states that, *"The Lord trieth the righteous: but the wicked and him that loveth violence his soul hateth."* The wicked face punishment while the righteous face trials. *"Oh let the wickedness of the wicked come to an end; but establish* [make firm, make stable] *the just: for the righteous God trieth* [examines, investigates, scrutinizes] *the hearts and reins."* (Psalm 7:9) Many Scriptures reveal that trials demonstrate God's great love for the believer. Like Hebrews 12:6, *"For whom the Lord loveth he chaseneth, and scourgeth every son whom he receiveth."* God is love. This means that He tries His children and distinguishes the righteous from the wicked. *"And we* [those who are saved and have Christ's righteousness] *have known and believed the love that God hath to us. God is love; and he that dwelleth in love dwelleth in God, and God in him"* (1 John 4:16).

When parents correctly discipline their children, they discipline out of love and concern for their wellbeing. No parent wants his child to be struck by a car should he run carelessly out into the street. NO! The wise parent instructs and trains his child, so he will not take such an action. That child may not be hit the first time he runs into the street, but the second time may not turn out as well.

When a teen abuses a time limit, a parent may choose to take away the keys to the family car. This particular action is to remind the teen not to place himself in vulnerable positions, which might bring him harm.

God was indeed putting my family through a very difficult trial, but we also felt His love, comfort, provision, and protection in every step we took. Our struggles were real, but we felt God's loving arms around us. We were confident that our Heavenly Father only wanted the best for us. These trials are evidence of God's distinguishing His children from those who are not His children. Through the choices He made for us, God was helping us to firmly trust Him and His Word and to know His great love.

God Is Just

From Psalm 11:6 we learn that we serve a just God whom we can trust. *"Upon the wicked he shall rain snares, fire and brimstone, and an horrible tempest: this shall be the portion of their cup."*

God is just. He will ultimately right all wrongs. Exacting judgment is not the Christian's place. Romans 12:19 says, *"Dearly beloved, avenge not yourselves, but rather give place unto wrath: for it is written, Vengeance is mine; I will repay, saith the Lord.*" We may not always see what God is doing, but we can trust that He will take care of things.

Being a survivor is wonderful, but not always easy. Some people try to take advantage of a survivor's situation. For whatever personal reasons, seemingly some people are always lurking in the background who want to be close to individuals who have gone through traumatic experiences—especially if it will garner them some desired attention or advancement. Maybe namedropping gives these people a feeling of importance. I don't really know, but we did experience this situation. Sometimes, these people brought as much emotional pain as the plane crash. In those moments, we had to let go and let God do the work. Through His faithfulness, we learned that we could trust God in this area of our life because He is always just.

God Is Righteous

God loves righteousness. "*For the righteous* Lord *loveth righteousness*" (Psalm 11:7). No man is righteous in and of himself. As Christians, our righteousness is Christ's righteousness, which we receive at the time of salvation. 2 Corinthians 5:21 bears out this truth: "*For he hath made him to be sin for us, who knew no sin; that we might be made the righteousness of God in him.*" Before the plane crash, God had begun teaching us that He wanted us—not our performance. Just like all of our righteousness without Christ is like filthy rags, all our performance, as a Christian in the flesh, is worthless (Isaiah 64:6). Our performance was not gaining us any righteousness; we already had Christ's. God simply wanted our fellowship. Though we are righteous in Christ, we are responsible to walk in fellowship with God and to keep our life free from sin. 1 John 1:7 says, "*But if we walk in the light, as he is in the light, we have fellowship one with another, and the blood of Jesus Christ his Son cleanseth us from all sin.*"

God Is Omniscient

The final lesson God taught us through Psalm 11 comes from these precious words, *"his countenance doth behold the upright."* The Psalmist is focusing on God's pleasure in His children as He, in His omniscience, lovingly cares for us. Because of His attribute of omniscience, God knows everything about us. And even though He knows us through and through, He still loves us! Because of this great love, even when we feel like our foundations are being destroyed, we can know that He is looking upon us with great care.

Shortly after I had my first skin graft, Beth and my parents noticed that another Christian family with whom we had been fellowshipping in the burn unit had suddenly become aloof. Their teenage son had been badly injured as the result of an electrical burn. For a reason unknown to us, the parents had obviously stopped taking time to talk or share how their son was doing.

One day while Beth waited in the family waiting area, the young man's grandmother came in to rest. She tried to ignore my wife, but Beth greeted her. "How is your grandson doing? When will he have his first skin graft?"

"Real faith," the grandmother admonished, "is exercised by simply trusting God to heal—not trusting what doctors can do. You've exercised a lack of faith by letting Ken have the skin graft. What a poor testimony! You aren't allowing God to demonstrate His healing power!"

Beth sent up a quick prayer, asking God for direction on how to answer this woman. "In 1927, Ken's grandmother was severely burned in a house fire," she began. "She had to sit under sheet canopies to protect her from infection. Skin grafting was beginning to be developed at that time, so it was not used by the doctors who were caring for her. She experienced pain upon pain because of the medical world's lack of knowledge about treating burns. Their choice of treatment was to burn off her scar tissue with caustics. It took months for his grandmother's open wounds to close because of not doing grafting. She had to be constantly watched for signs of infection.

"Since then, God, who is all-knowing, has given the doctors wisdom as they have developed new treatments for burns. The doctors have learned that putting skin grafts on the ripe wounds cuts down on the possibility of infection and aids in the healing process. Healing will take place more rapidly and reduce the pain level significantly. It was God, the Creator, who gave these doctors the understanding to develop the best treatments for burn patients. We're grateful for that God-given understanding. Every choice we have made will help Ken heal faster."

"Huh!" was the woman's only response—though it was quite an emphatic "Huh!"

A few days later, the young man went through his first skin graft and was soon on the road to recovery. The family also began to renew their relationship with us. Our all-knowing Heavenly Father allowed my grandmother to suffer burns many years earlier to give Beth a platform from which to help this lady and her family. God also used the victory my grandmother experienced as she walked with the Lord through her trial to encourage me.

All of the Right Ingredients

Several years after the plane crash, some of the leaders of a Burns Recovered group in conjunction with the Burn Unit contacted me and invited me to speak at a Burns Recovered Seminar on the subject "Learning to Live with Your New You." In preparation for the talk, I asked our daughter Esther to bake a batch of chocolate chip oatmeal cookies. She accompanied me to the seminar, and while I gave my talk, she passed out the cookies. As I finished, I asked the audience if they had enjoyed the cookies. What could they say when a cute eleven year old girl was watching their response? The listeners enthusiastically responded that they liked the cookies. I offered them another cookie. Many of them accepted another of Esther's homemade cookies. (Incidentally, I was invited to come back and give this talk again, but this time my session was titled "The Chocolate Chip Cookie Talk.")

I don't know a person who doesn't like chocolate chip cookies, and let me testify, chocolate chip oatmeal cookies are even better! Have you ever stopped to consider what all goes into making those delicious cookies? The main in-

Pleasant Valley Chocolate Chip Oatmeal Cookies

Ingredients

2 cups shortening or softened butter
1 1/2 cups brown sugar
1 1/2 cups white sugar
4 eggs - unbeaten
1 tsp hot water
2 tsp vanilla
3 cups sifted flour
2 tsp salt
2 tsp soda
1 cup chopped nuts (optional)
1 pkg chocolate chips
4 cups oatmeal

Instructions

Mix thoroughly:
Sugars, shortening and unbeaten eggs.
Add:
Water, vanilla, and dry ingredients.

Spoon onto baking sheet and bake at 350 degrees for 7 minutes or longer until cookies are golden brown.

If you use butter, add 1 cup extra flour.

gredient happens to be flour. Would you eat a big handful of flour by itself? Not only would it be tasteless and dry, I dare say it would be very hard to get down. What about raw eggs? Most folks do not enjoy eating eggs without first cooking them, but adding cooked eggs to cookie batter certainly would not work well. What about vanilla? The smell is great, but I can testify that the taste is bitter. I can think of many other liquids I would far rather drink than a glass of vanilla! I could continue naming each of the ingredients, which, if eaten alone, would be less than enjoyable, but when they are all combined together, the result is wonderful cookies. If any one of these ingredients is left out, the cookies will be less than enjoyable or not cookies at all. Each ingredient is necessary to make the cookies the best they can be. The same is true of every trial we face in our life.

Once the ingredients have been combined, spoonfuls of that wonderful-tasting batter are dropped onto a cookie sheet and placed into a hot oven. I, for one, would not volunteer to jump into a hot oven in order to be a part of the process of making cookies. I am very glad to stand outside the oven and look through the window to watch the *magical* process of chemistry at work. The proper temperature causes those chemicals to work together for good—resulting in a delicious cookie. I can testify that there is nothing like one of Esther's chocolate chip oatmeal cookies hot out of the oven with a big glass of milk!

The plane crash, with its many ensuing trials, advanced our journey of learning to truly focus on God and trust Him. He was conforming us into the image of His Son, the Lord Jesus Christ. Our trial was like the chemistry that worked in the heat of that oven to conform Esther's dough into delicious cookies.

Did our path to Christlikeness end with this one trial? No! We continue to walk through events—though perhaps not quite as dramatic—which God is using to make us more like the Lord Jesus Christ.

Many times life looked hopeless as we faced the months of healing and recovery. We learned that we didn't have to surrender to the confusion; instead, we could choose to trust God. No matter how massive the hospital bills, the seriousness of any infection, the challenge of the situation in ministry—God was always there. He walked with us through this valley. He was continually working out every situation for our best as He conformed us into the image of His Son.

God's blessing—true happiness—comes to those who desire to trust in Him. This trust comes as we pray to God, engraft His Word, and focus on the Lord.

God has been faithful to lead us to desire to know Him. We are able to satisfy this desire only by our fellowship with Christ, especially our fellowship with Him in our sufferings. From this fellowship we are able to exchange our weakness for His strength, which leads us to be able to focus our trust in Him with all our heart. From this basis, we are able to minister God's comfort and abound in His love.

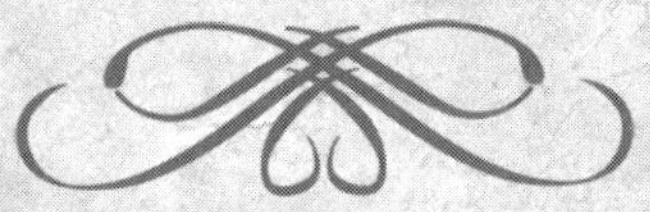

Ministry

Grace is demonstrated by gratitude in our salvation, sanctification, and service.

"Who passing through the valley of Baca make it a well; the rain also filleth the pools."

– Psalm 84:6

Out of our fellowship with God, based on His strength and our trust in Him, we are able to minister His comfort and abound in His love.

*"Blessed be God, even the Father of our Lord Jesus
Christ, the Father of mercies, and the God of all comfort;
4Who comforteth us in all our tribulation, that we may
be able to comfort them which are in any trouble, by the
comfort wherewith we ourselves are comforted of God.
5For as the sufferings of Christ abound in us, so our consolation also aboundeth by Christ. 6And whether we be
afflicted, it is for your consolation and salvation, which
is effectual in the enduring of the same sufferings which
we also suffer: or whether we be comforted, it is for your
consolation and salvation."*

– 2 Corinthians 1:3–6

CHAPTER EIGHTEEN

Comfort

I felt extreme guilt because the other pastors had died, and I had not. Why had God spared my life and not those of Pastor Spurgeon, Pastor Lombard, and Pastor Thompson?

The extreme pain, the loss of my fingers and toes, the many scars, the persistent stiffness, and the changes in my lifestyle left me feeling very lonely. I felt no one could understand the magnitude of the pain I was experiencing and the frustrations of limitations caused by my injuries.

I was totally overwhelmed, but as time went on, God began teaching me about Himself. In my sufferings, He taught me about His mercy, His grace, His love, and His wisdom. I found myself in a unique position in my Lord's care. I learned the truth of the words of the Apostle Paul, *"Blessed be God, even the Father of our Lord Jesus Christ, the Father of mercies, and the God of all comfort"* (2 Corinthians 1:3). I learned that because of who God is, I can trust Him and receive His comfort. In order to sort out my emotions, I had to keep my focus on Christ and my place in Him. I learned that I needed this trial not only to correctly know my Lord but also to effectively minister to others.

God's Comfort

I sat on the edge of the bed, looking at a picture of the three men who had perished in the crash.

"Lord," I prayed, "help me to finish their ministries."

This was not the first time I had prayed this prayer; in fact, I prayed it every night before I went to bed.

That night, however, was different. As I sat there, God spoke to my heart.

"Their work is finished, Ken," came His still, small voice. "Concern yourself only with the work I have for you to do."

3 Baptist ministers killed in plane crash

By ANGELO CONSTANTIN
Globe-Democrat Staff Writer

"It's a miracle anyone survived — I've never seen an airplane so devastated."

That's how Spirit of St. Louis Airport Director Richard E. Hrabko reacted to a light-plane crash that killed three area Baptist ministers and seriously injured another during an attempted landing early Wednesday.

Rev. Spilger survives

The four were returning from a daylong religious seminar in Kansas City when their rented plane crashed about 12:30 a.m., 3½ miles southwest of the airport in West St. Louis County.

The Rev. Kenneth P. Spilger, 30, of the 300 block of Ranavie Drive, Glasgow Village, was reported in serious but stable condition Thursday at the burn unit of St. John's Mercy Medical Center. He is pastor of Grace Baptist Church, 11842 Riverview Drive, Glasgow Village.

THE THREE ministers who died were the pilot, the Rev. Russell B. Spurgeon, 47, pastor of Trinity Free Will Baptist Church, 12143 Old St. Charles Rock Road, Bridgeton; the Rev. Donald W. Lombard, 36, minister at First Free Will Baptist Church, O'Fallon, Mo.; and the Rev. Lawrence D. Thompson, 53, pastor of Oak Hill Free Will Baptist Church, outside St. Clair, Mo.

Hrabko said the airport was in radio contact with the plane shortly before the accident and the pilot reported everything normal.

Weather conditions at the airport at the time of the crash were "changing," Hrabko said, with light rain and fog reported.

THE PLANE apparently clipped the tops of trees and hit a power line before falling into a ravine near Missouri C and Wild Horse Creek Road, police said.

Chesterfield Fire Protection District firefighters first learned of the crash when they were called about 12:35 a.m. with a report of a weed fire.

They found the single-engine plane in the ravine about 300 feet from the road. The victims had been thrown clear of the wreckage and subsequent fire, according to County Police Officer John Samson.

While National Transportation Safety Board and Federal Aviation Administration officials investigated to determine the cause of the crash, people who knew the victims reacted with shock.

FLAGS AT O'FALLON police headquarters, where the Rev. Mr. Lombard was chief chaplain, were ordered flown at half-staff. Police Lt. Michael Henry remembered the chaplain as hard-working and much-admired.

"He dropped in about every other day to see if anyone needed help or counseling," Henry said. "He was very well thought of by everyone that knew him."

Last October the Rev. Mr. Lombard received a department award for talking a man who was quarreling with his girlfriend into giving up a shotgun he had used to threaten police.

The Rev. Mr. Spurgeon also served as on-call minister at DePaul Hospital, Bridgeton. Church members said he had been flying for about three years and occasionally took other ministers on flights to out-of-town conventions and seminars.

HE HAD RENTED the $30,000, four-passenger Grumman Tiger from Arrowhead Airport in West County. Airport owner John W. Bradley said the pastor, a licensed pilot, had flown leased aircraft previously.

"There's no doubt Rev. Spurgeon was a very competent pilot," Bradley said.

The Rev. Mr. Thompson, a father of three who lived in the 500 block of Columbia Avenue, St. Clair, had been pastor of the Oak Hill Church on Missouri 47, three miles from St. Clair, for about a year. Prior to his ministry there, he had been pastor of the Victory Free Will Baptist Church in Kansas City.

He was picked up at a landing site in Washington, Mo., by the Rev. Mr. Spurgeon Tuesday morning.

The Rev. Mr. Lombard lived in the 700 block of Shady Lane, O'Fallon, with his wife, Carolyn.

The Rev. Mr. Spurgeon, also a father of three, lived in the 2800 block of Cherry Point Lane, Maryland Heights.

Rev. Donald Lombard — Rev. Lawrence Thompson — Rev. Russell Spurgeon

Globe-Democrat Photo by John Dengler

The remains of this propeller section were found with other wreckage from the plane near Wild Horse Creek Road in West St. Louis County.

Article Ken looked at each night
You can read the article on page 227.

A peace, which I had not experienced for a long time, flooded over me in that moment. I was solely responsible for what God had called me to do. Awareness of that fact brought a new confidence which only could have come from God. My Heavenly Father's comfort to my hurting soul was overwhelming and gave me a sense of freedom, encouragement, and hope. I could receive God's comfort in that moment because I was embracing God's purpose for my life, not theirs.

Several years later, I was talking with a nationally known speaker about the plane crash.

"Well," he stated seriously, "now you have the ministry of three other pastors to finish."

"No," I told him confidently. "Their work is finished. God will hold me accountable for mine alone."

All of the guilt I had once felt was gone.

Our Trials

Beth was lonely and overwhelmed with the multitude of responsibilities that rested on her. She felt a strong sense of responsibility for my wellbeing, the wellbeing of our children, the wellbeing of the church, and the need to give appreciation to our extended family for their help and care. She neglected her own feelings in order to be strong for everyone else. She was very lonely, and her only place of solace was her quiet time with the Lord. He gave her strength to meet the daily tasks and to comfort those around her. Did she cry? Yes, many a night as she went to bed, or during her time driving to the hospital. She passed the time between our home and the hospital day after day—sometimes singing, sometimes praying, sometimes crying. Choruses and songs like "He Giveth More Grace" and "Rejoice in the Lord" became a comfort.

Several years later as I began to share my testimony with a church in a distant city, Beth began to sob uncontrollably. One of her sisters was sitting next to her in that service and lovingly put her arms around her to give her the comfort she needed. She needed a while to pull herself together, but she did before the testimony was done. When I was done and had gone back to my seat beside her and put my arm around her, her emotions were stayed.

I must hasten to state that she was not always forgotten. Many reached out to help her and to give her encouragement at various times. Sometimes, when we are overwhelmed with so much trauma and so many needs, we easily miss the fact that others are reaching out to help. It is important for those who are seeking to help in such situations to keep reaching out—even if they do not feel appreciated. Beth did not intend to ignore or be unappreciative, but at times her pain obscured their attempts to help. The same can be true for others passing through similar situations.

For example, my mother was so overwhelmed by her own feelings that she did not stop to consider what Beth and our daughters were going through during my hospital stay. The day came, several years after the plane crash, when my mother watched from a distance as a beloved family member walked through a very difficult situation with her husband. Only then did she realize the significance that Beth was my spouse—one flesh with me. Mom had not intended to be self-focused during our trial; she simply had not considered Beth's role. Her own hurt had overwhelmed her thoughts because I was her son. My mother was sincere, desiring to do what was right. Her motives were transparent, but her grief distorted her perspective.

Mom asked Beth's forgiveness, and of course Beth forgave her. She forgave readily because God had already healed those wounds many years earlier through the love He had put in her heart for my mother. Beth realized Mom was dealing with an inordinate amount of hurt and pain while watching me daily endure so much suffering. In fact, because Beth understood a *mother's heart*, she was often able to reach out and be a comfort when she saw my mother grieving.

Walking through this experience with my parents has helped all of us to see that when we walk through pain, our perspective is often distorted. We must receive the comfort others seek to give us, but we must also keep reaching out to comfort others.

We saw similar situations in our church. On the night following the crash, Beth was in her place at church, playing the piano and fulfilling her responsibilities, because she knew she needed the time with her church family. Folks were crying and talking of their concern for their pastor's condition. During the sermon, preached by one of our missionaries, she slipped to the back of the church. At the end of the service, she lowered the thermostats, turned out the lights, and checked the basement of the church, a job I normally did after each service.

Sad and alone, wondering how I was doing at the hospital, she was in a hurry to finish up and get home. My parents were scheduled to arrive soon, and she needed to be there. The church family, seemingly oblivious to Beth, continued to chat with one another. They were overwhelmed with their own pain of learning about my condition and the uncertainty of whether or not I would survive.

As Beth stepped into the foyer, one of the men put his big arms around her. "I know you're hurting," he said. "I want you to know that my family and I care. If there is anything you need, please let us know!"

Suddenly, not feeling quite so alone, Beth dissolved into tears.

A caring church is vital. Our church did indeed care, but the people were also hurting because they were also affected by the accident. They were as overwhelmed as my own family with all of the added responsibility and their concern for me. They needed to receive comfort and care as much as we did. I believe God sent the exact person our church needed to be our interim pastor. Gary Zimmerman, a missionary who lived in St. Louis and who was supported by our church, taught and encouraged our people. He even took full responsibility to make sure the pulpit was filled when he could not be at Grace. Knowing the church was in capable hands was a great comfort to me as a pastor!

A lady in the church cared for our daughters during my surgeries and on a few other days when Beth needed to be at the hospital. Our girls loved spending time at Norma Jewell's house. Her two youngest children who were still in school and living at home, spoiled our girls, and they loved it. Even today they have wonderful memories of their times with this dear lady and her family. What an encouragement to our girls who also needed a little TLC and comfort beyond Mom and their grandparents!

Another lady from the church did some of our laundry on a few occasions. Beth's Aunt Ramona made regular visits to help with the girls and to encourage us. Pastors called and stopped by both the hospital and our home.

In spite of their personal pain and great responsibilities, our deacons, Noel Foster, Don Kress, and Bill Moughton visited me regularly at the hospital. These men along with their wives, Lois,

Karen, and Phyllis, took responsibility for all that took place at the church by working alongside of Gary Zimmerman. These precious people checked on my family and made sure they had what they needed. They even led in continuing my salary so my family's financial needs would be met.

Many others reached out to minister God's comfort to us. They are too numerous to list, but God knows every name. God's people ministered God's comfort to us through acts of kindness, cards, phone calls, and most of all, prayers.

Their Need

I have already mentioned my dear grandmother who was burned in a house fire many years before I was born. Because she successfully walked through her sufferings with the Lord's help, her story brought me great comfort during my convalescence. My grandmother left a strong legacy of trust in God for every trial life brings for her children and grandchildren. Romans 8:18 became her favorite verse because it was a great comfort to her in her time of suffering, *"For I reckon that the sufferings of this present time are not worthy to be compared with the glory which shall be revealed in us."* This same verse also became a source of strength for me during my recovery because of her testimony and example.

Our capacity to meet the needs of others is increased by the trials through which we pass, as God states in 2 Corinthians 1:4, *"that we may be able to comfort them which are in any trouble, by the comfort wherewith we ourselves are comforted of God."* We are able to help others in their need because we have focused on God's comfort and character in our own need.

When a human being experiences trauma with the magnitude of third-degree burns, the suffering is often so intense one easily begins to think no one understands. At this low point, loneliness can take hold. The truth that Jesus was tempted (experienced trials) in every way that man is tempted was a great comfort to me. Jesus suffered without entertaining the sin of feeling sorry for Himself, blaming others, or getting angry. Jesus embraced suffering, so He could comfort us; He truly does understand (Hebrews 4:15).

The necessary medical procedures—every one of them— that I underwent always caused more pain. The medical staff could do nothing about it, and in order for the healing process to be completed properly, they had to continue doing the procedures. On one very difficult day after my second skin graft, I was suffering in great pain. When Dr. Ayvazian, the director of the burn unit, came into my room during his daily rounds, he picked up the medical charts, looked them over, replaced them, and stepped to the head of the bed. He gently placed his hand on my shoulder and simply stood quietly for a several minutes. He patted me and then walked away without saying a word. That simple action on the part of my doctor ministered to me in ways words cannot describe. I later learned he had been burned as a child and had required skin grafts. Because of his personal experience, he chose to become a burn doctor. God had given him a huge capacity to relate to and empathize with a burn patient's suffering.

Dr. Ayvazian

Every nurse and technician who worked on me did a wonderful job—even though the procedures caused me much pain. I realized that their work was essential. Without their ministrations, I would have died from infection. One technician stands out to me in particular because he demonstrated a compassion that could only come from the Lord. During one particularly painful dressing change, I said to him, "You've gone through a lot of suffering, haven't you?"

Startled by my question, he stopped his work. "Yes, I have," he admitted. "Why do you ask?"

"Your dressing changes hurt as much as anyone else's, but you have a unique compassion and tenderness that is very comforting. Your work doesn't feel as intense," I attempted to explain.

He did not offer any more information, and I didn't feel at liberty to ask any more questions. I thanked him for his work and for the compassion he demonstrated.

> *We won a* victory in my life's
> darkest hour,
> with your caring hands and God's
> great power.
>
> "*My grace is* sufficient," Jesus
> whispered to me,
> His light through the darkness I could
> always see.
>
> *With courage — yet* compassion,
> you cared for my burns each day.
> My deepest appreciation to you I
> wish to gratefully convey.
>
> ~ Kathy Spilger Hermsmeyer
>
> (*One year after the plane crash, this poem was written by Ken's twin sister for an appreciation day for all the caregivers Ken had while in the hospital.*)

God is the God of mercy and comfort. When we know the Lord Jesus Christ as our Saviour, we have His Holy Spirit dwelling within us. Because of His indwelling, God's mercy to us is renewed every morning, and His comfort is constant.

God comforts us "*in all our tribulation*"—through all of our trials. However, in that comforting process, He gives us a choice in our responses to the trial. Our Heavenly Father never forces us to rejoice in the trial; rather, He allows us to choose whether or not we will obey. James chapter one says we are to "*count it all joy*" when we go through trials. Why? Because we will develop patience. When we have patience, God can do His perfecting work in us, so we will be mature and sound—lacking nothing.

Christ is our example of focusing on God's purpose for our trials. Hebrews 12:2 tells us that He focused on "*the joy that was set before him.*" Because His eyes were on the final, joyful result, He was able to endure the cross and think little of the shame brought on by His execution. He knew redemption for all mankind would be made complete by His suffering and that because of His obedience, He would be seated at the Father's right hand.

Focusing on God's purposes in our adversity brings rejoicing and gives us the ability to walk through trials because we can see the end result. This focus gives us the hope that through our difficulties we will develop a greater maturity in Christ, a better understanding of the brevity of life, and an increased capacity to comfort others.

In every trial we face, we have a choice. We can choose to become bitter, proud, or doubt God and His purpose. Choosing any of these three will bring doubt, fear and confusion. On the other hand, we can focus on our relationship with Christ and receive God's comfort by praising Him for who He is. When we make this choice, our fellowship with God is deepened. We come to have a greater understanding of His character, which gives us greater confidence and comfort in Him. As a result of having received God's comfort, we will be better equipped to comfort and encourage others to trust Him and His Word.

During each day of my recovery process, I faced clear choices. When the therapist told my wife she could no longer help me dress, I had a choice to make. I could get angry, or I could trust God and give it a try. I have to admit, Beth and I faced some intense moments. One battle in particular was over who would button my shirt. Beth insisted that I button my shirt because she had promised the therapist that she would not help me. She knew she would have to answer to the therapist and that I had to learn to live life independently and not be dependent on others for help in everyday tasks. I wanted her help because I knew the so-called simple task would take me forever. The small buttons were hard for me to manipulate into the button holes. The fight went on until I abruptly realized how absurd I was being. Then we both broke into laughter.

"We can go through a plane crash," I said, "but it's the nitty-gritty of life that gets us down!"

The fight was over. I buttoned my shirt.

God's comfort includes the choices we make in our trials. We can only be comforted and have all of the resources of God at our disposal if we choose to obey Him in the midst of the difficulties through which we are appointed to journey.

As God allows us to go through trials, He gives us the ability to comfort others through their trials. The situations they face will not necessarily be the same type of trial we experienced, but they could be.

While I was recovering, I obviously needed healing and comfort. Beth, who was overwhelmed with her fear and loneliness, desperately needed God's comfort. Our little girls, who were confused and afraid, needed God's comfort. Our extended family, who felt far away, helpless, and did not know what to do, needed God's comfort. Our church family, who was without their undershepherd and was hurting, also needed God's comfort.

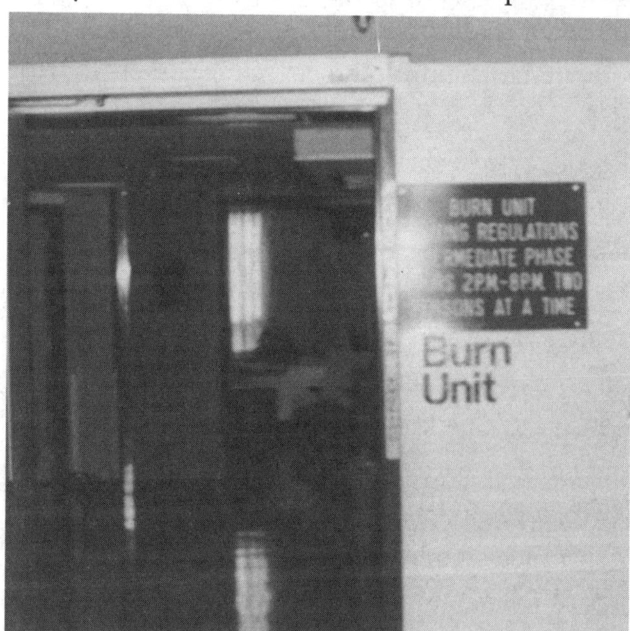

Entrance to Burn Unit at St. Johns Mercy Medical Center in 1980

As a result of my experience, I can now enter any burn unit in the world or talk with any burns-recovered individual and have instant empathy. We know what the other has experienced, and we can relate to one another. My wife can talk with the caregivers of those who have gone through traumatic injuries and recoveries and immediately empathize. Our extended family has a heart for reaching out to those going through severe trials. Our church reaches out to those in need—even beyond our church family. We have this outreach all because we passed through this trial and were ourselves comforted by God. In order to help others walk victoriously through their suffering, God wants us to share what He has taught us in our suffering. God did not say we could comfort others only if we have experienced the same trials they have.

Several years ago, one of our daughters, who walked through a deep trial with us and felt its effects personally, tried to comfort an older lady as she passed through a time of suffering. Our daughter asked questions and tried to offer comfort, but instead of receiving that comfort, the woman railed on her.

"You've never experienced what I'm going through," she said. "Don't think you can ever comfort anyone unless you have experienced that trial yourself."

Our daughter was very hurt by this woman's diatribe. She began asking us a lot of questions about offering Scriptural comfort. We took her to this passage in 2 Corinthians and encouraged her to continue to comfort others with the comfort she has received from the Lord. God did not say we have to experience the same trials. He said, *"that we may be able to comfort them which are in any trouble, by the comfort wherewith we ourselves are comforted of God!"*

Needless and sad to say, that lady lost her opportunity to receive comfort because she was so focused on her own pain.

In February of 2000, Beth and I flew to Alaska to minister in several churches. We flew from St. Louis to Seattle to connect with an Alaska Airlines flight to Fairbanks. Only a few days before our trip, an Alaska Airlines flight went down in the Pacific Ocean, killing everyone on board. As we were checking in for our flight from Seattle, I gave the ticket agent a Gospel tract sharing about our plane crash.

She examined the little pamphlet for a moment and then looked up at me. "I wish you had been here thirty minutes ago. We had a reunion of family members and passengers who were supposed to be on that flight with their families. For whatever reason, they ended up separated and scheduled for a later flight. They all expressed such guilt that they were spared while the others perished."

She paused thoughtfully. "Do you ever struggle with that kind of guilt?"

"Yes," I told her. "God has had to work on my heart regarding that very struggle." We continued to talk, and she eagerly received our ministry of comfort to her, even ignoring other needs around her to get answers to this question. She shared with us that she had already trusted the Lord as her Savior and would rest in the comfort God wanted her both to give and to receive.

Soldiers returning from wars and various conflicts in different parts of our world have shared their struggle of guilt and loneliness over similar issues. Why would God spare their life and take a buddy's life? Why should they have a life to live when others perished in the battle? Could they have done more to help their fallen comrades?

I believe our experience was given to us so that we could better relate to and benefit others going through similar experiences. As God has been faithful to minister to us, we can faithfully minister comfort and encouragement to others.

Article as it appeared in the St. Louis Globe-Democrat on September 18, 1980

"It's a miracle anyone survived—I've never seen an airplane so devastated."

That's how Spirit of St. Louis Airport Director Richard E. Hrabko reacted to a light-plane crash that killed three area Baptist ministers and seriously injured another during an attempted landing early Wednesday.

The four were returning from a daylong religious seminar in Kansas City when their rented plane crashed about 12:30 a.m., 2 1/2 miles southwest of the airport in West St. Louis County.

The Rev. Kenneth P. Spilger, 30, of the 500 block of Banavie Drive, Glasgow Village, was reported in serious but stable condition Thursday at the burn unit of St. John's Mercy Medical Center. He is pastor of Grace Baptist Church, 11642 Riverview Drive, Glasgow Village.

THE THREE ministers who died were the pilot, the Rev. Russell B. Spurgeon, 47, pastor of Trinity Free Will Baptist Church, 12143 Old St. Charles Rock Road, Bridgeton; the Rev. Donald W. Lombard, 36, minister at First Free Will Baptist Church, O'Fallon, Mo.; and the Rev. Lawrence D Thompson, 55, pastor of Oak Hill Free Will Baptist Church, outside St. Clair, Mo.

Hrabko said the airport was in radio contact with the plane shortly before the accident and the pilot reported everything normal.

Weather conditions at the airport at the time of the crash were "changing," Hrabko said, with light rain and fog reported.

THE PLANE apparently clipped the tops of trees and hit a power line before falling into a ravine near Missouri C and Wild Horse Creek Road, police said.

Chesterfield Fire Protection district firefighters first learned of the crash when they were called about 12:35 a.m. with a report of a weed fire.

They found the single-engine plane in the ravine about 300 feet from the road. The victims had been thrown clear of the wreckage and subsequent fire, according to County Police Officer John Samson.

While National Transportation Safety Board and Federal Aviation Administration officials investigated to determine the cause of the crash, people who knew the victims reacted with shock.

FLAGS AT O'FALLON police headquarters, where the Rev. Mr. Lombard was chief chaplain, were ordered flown at half-staff. Police Lt Michael Henry remembered the chaplain as hard-working and much admired.

"He dropped in about every other day to see if anyone needed help or counseling," Henry said. "He was very well thought of by everyone that knew him."

Last October the Rev. Mr. Lombard received a department award for talking a man who was quarreling with his girlfriend into giving up a shotgun he had used to threaten police.

The Rev. Mr. Spurgeon also served as on-call minister at DePaul Hospital, Bridgeton. Church members said he had been flying for about three years and occasionally took other ministers on flights to out-of-town conventions and seminars.

HE HAD RENTED the $50,000 four-passenger Grumman Tiger from Arrowhead Airport in West County. Airport owner John W. Bradley said the pastor, a licensed pilot had flown leased aircraft previously.

"There's no doubt Rev. Spurgeon was a very competent pilot," Bradley said.

The Rev. Mr. Thompson, a father of three who lived in the 500 block of Columbia Avenue, St. Clair, had been pastor of the Oak Hill Church on Missouri 47, three miles from St. Clair, for about a year. Prior to his ministry there, he had been pastor of the Victory Free Will Baptist Church in Kansas City.

He was picked up at a landing site in Washington, Mo., by the Rev. Mr. Surgeon Tuesday morning.

The Rev. Mr. Lombard lived in the 700 block of Shady Lane, O'Fallon, with his wife Carolyn.

The Rev. Mr. Spurgeon, also a father of three lived in the 2800 block of Cherry Point Lane, Maryland Heights.

- used by permission

"And this I pray, that your love may abound yet more and more in knowledge and in all judgment; [10]That ye may approve things that are excellent; that ye may be sincere and without offence till the day of Christ; [11]Being filled with the fruits of righteousness, which are by Jesus Christ, unto the glory and praise of God."

– Philippians 1:9–11

CHAPTER NINETEEN

Love

Phil *was a* burn technician in the burn center—a good one. He demonstrated a huge capacity for the giving kind of love which goes far beyond what is expected.

Three days after my second graft, a pseudomonas infection was found on the grafts and donor sites. The infection turned those areas of my body a bright green color. In fact, I was green from the top of my shoulders to the tips of my toes! The infection also caused a high fever. In order to reduce my fever, I was placed on a hypothermia blanket, designed to lower my body temperature. I was freezing and very uncomfortable. Even though I was not Phil's patient during that shift, he checked on me periodically because he was concerned the fever was not coming down fast enough.

After talking with Beth for a while and looking at the blanket controls, he finally saw the problem: the thermostat had not been set properly. He adjusted the controls and lowered the thermostat, making me even more uncomfortable despite the blankets piled on top of me. Phil's adjustments attained the desired result, and my fever began to decrease.

The discomfort of the situation made such an impression on me that, after arriving home from the hospital, whenever any one of our children was sick with a high fever, I would pray and weep over them as I held them. I will never forget Phil and his ministrations during that difficult experience. When Phil lowered that thermostat, causing me even greater discomfort, he demonstrated the genuine love spoken of by the Apostle Paul in Philippians 1:9-11. Because of his careful attention, my fever was broken, and quite possibly, my life was again spared.

God's great love often overwhelmed me during the events after the plane crash. Because God is my Father, at times He must inflict pain so I will experience greater good. In Hebrews 12:6, God assures us of His great love, especially in times of trial: *"For whom the Lord loveth he chasteneth, and scourgeth every son whom he receiveth."* God does what is best for His children—even if it makes them uncomfortable.

I can personally attest that life isn't always easy, but through selected trials God molds and chisels His children to make them like His Son. He cleanses His children and removes that which hinders them from becoming more like Himself and from drawing closer to Him. Just as my fever had to be brought down to save my life, so sin must be removed in order for the Christian to walk in victory.

After the third graft, I had to lie on my stomach for seven days because the graft was on my buttocks and the back side of my legs. The donor sites were under my arms, my sides, and any available areas on the backs of my thighs. Once again, I developed a very serious pseudomonas infection. And this time I was Phil's patient.

Phil worked carefully, placing a waterproof blanket under my body and pouring a liquid saline solution on my dressings to help with removing them. He cleaned the grafted areas and donor sites, and applied Sulfamylon (antibiotic) cream on all the infected areas. Then he rewrapped the injured sites.

Before all of these steps even began, I had been administered all of the pain medication the law allowed, but it did not stop the pain. The application of the antibiotic cream was especially painful since it was designed to kill bacteria deeper than the surface. Often this cream causes a burning sensation, and that sensation causes even more pain.

The donor sites under my arms included a small part of my chest. When I placed any weight on that fresh cream, the pain was so excruciating that I became nauseous. Memories of those painful dressing changes, which I endured twice each day in the hospital and for a while after I went home, still move me to tears—thirty-five years later.

When I saw that Phil was noticeably moved by my pain and discomfort, I tried to encourage him.

"I know you do what you do so I will heal properly," I said. "Don't feel bad for me. I would die if you didn't do this. "

"I know you understand," Phil nodded. "But after I finish with you, I have to do a dressing change on a baby who does not understand."

I believe Phil's actions demonstrated real love. He was willing to do what needed to be done for the good of his patients, even though it caused them physical suffering and brought him emotional pain. Phil was not alone. Every doctor, nurse, technician, and therapist who cared for me demonstrated this love. Both the fellowship and the chastening we have with Christ in our trials enables us to abound in His love.

A Love-Directed Life

The therapists at St. John's Mercy Hospital and Christian Northeast Hospital worked resolutely on the areas where I was burned. They worked with my limbs every day until my hands bled and my legs ached. Because of our labors together, I can now walk without a limp. I have very good use of my hands because the therapists loved me enough to push me, encourage me, and hold me accountable—even if it caused great pain. Love motivated them to work toward the greatest possible progression in mobility and dexterity. The love that directed them beautifully illustrates the love God wants His children to abound in and to channel to others.

God was using this trial to build that love into my life through my fellowship with Him. He wanted me to live a life that was motivated by His love instead of my selfishness. His desire is for every Christian to possess this love.

Philippians 1:9 says, "*And this I pray that your love may abound yet more and more in knowledge and in all judgment.*" In this verse, the Bible uses the Greek word *agape* to speak of love. This unselfish *agape* love, which only comes from God, values and esteems others by giving and serving. God wants His *agape* love to be so prevalent in us that it guides our decisions. Having that love abound in us helps us to make wise choices based on love, which is directed by discernment (priorities), good moral judgment (sincerity), and ethical tact (discretion). Allowing God's love to direct us will help us form priorities that line up with God's priorities as well as guide us to choose that which is worthwhile, excellent, and vital for our life.

Love-Directed Priorities

When my parents first faced the decision of whether or not to stay with my wife and children and to help them through the difficult time while I was in the hospital, God led them to make the decision to stay. Their decision was based on their great love for our family. This "*love* [that abounded] *yet more and more in knowledge and in all judgment*" was especially needed at that particular time.

When a missionary friend heard about the plane crash on the radio, he immediately pulled off to the side of the road to pray for me. He knew my life depended upon God and the prayers of His people. His decision to pray was a priority based on love.

When a friend living in Memphis, Tennessee, heard the news, he immediately traveled to St. Louis. He knew God wanted him here. The friendship we shared was a priority because of his love for us.

News of my injuries and hospitalization mobilized our church leaders and their families to come to our aid. Many sacrificed time and energy to help Beth, our children, and with the needs of the church. My siblings purchased a Bible to replace the one that had been destroyed in the crash. The one they gave me was even nicer than the one I had lost. A man from the church purchased a briefcase because mine had burned in the crash. When my siblings learned that my skin grafts might require grafts from donors, they made plans to donate their skin if the necessity arose—love motivated them to do so.

Ken's siblings replaced his burned Bible.

All of these people gave sacrificially out of a heart of love, going far beyond what was expected or even needed. As we watched their actions, God used them and His fellowship with us to train us to choose His love-directed priorities.

Beth and I were so grateful for all that Phil, the burn technician, did to demonstrate love and care not only for me but for all of the patients in the burn unit. He always did the hard things—the things that greatly aided in my healing. When we learned he was leaving the St. Louis area for employment elsewhere, we wanted to do something to say "thank you." When my hands received their grafts, the idea for Phil's gift came to us.

After the procedure, my hands had to be elevated, so a pillow was placed on my stomach under the sheet. Phil invariably teased me about the pillow.

"So," he would jokingly greet me. "When's the baby due?"

I always had a comeback.

As a result of this continuous bantering, Beth decided to make a rag doll to commemorate the day when the pillow was removed. She worked hard to finish the doll before Phil's last day of work

Rag doll for Phil's little girl

and to coincide with the time of my *release* from the pillow. Her efforts paid off. When Phil removed the pillow, he found the doll. The baby had been born! I am still not sure if Phil was as thrilled with the birth of the doll as was his little girl!

The love Phil had shown prompted us toward our own set of love-driven actions and priorities. Creating the doll and looking forward to the occasion also gave Beth a much-needed diversion from all of the pressure she had been enduring. That act of love ended up blessing all of the parties involved! We could fill a book with so many stories of people who *abounded in love* as they included our needs in their own personal priorities. As God showed us these examples of abounding love, He was also teaching us to abound in love toward others in need.

Love–Directed Sincerity

Each example we have shared demonstrates not only a love-directed life and priorities but also a love-directed sincerity. God desires that our life be marked by this sincerity. In Philippians 1:10 He says, *"that ye may be sincere and without offense till the day of Christ."*

Hypocrisy (the opposite of sincerity) troubles the Christian's soul and creates offenses in his soul. These offenses and guilt will cloud our view of the purpose God has given us. Our fellowship with God is broken when we are not walking in sincerity.

Abounding in God's love helps us guard against these sources of trouble. The transparency of sincerity helps us to clarify God's purpose and to walk victoriously because God's plan is no longer muddled by self-centered agendas. As I discovered in the days after the crash, walking sincerely restores our fellowship and builds in us godly discretion.

Love-Directed Discretion

"Ken, why did this plane crash happen to you?" asked the sons of an area pastor who came to visit me at the hospital.

As I have already shared, a man in the area had felt the need to declare his opinion that the crash was God's judgment on my life. These two men were aware of this accusation. They, on the other hand, spoke to me with tact and discretion, about what I believed to be the reason for the crash.

"It would have only been for one of three reasons," one of them continued. "First, for your death. But you're still alive, and I don't think God would have messed up that bad. Second, because of sin in your life. Has God convicted you of any sin?"

"Not that I'm aware of," I answered.

"Well, then, it must not be for sin, or He would have convicted you of it. So it must be for the third reason—to bring glory to Him."

I smiled. God was revealing that He was in control of everything pertaining to my life and that I was simply to trust Him. I realized that I needed to follow Jesus' example on the cross and say, *"Father, forgive them; for they know not what they do."* (Luke 23:34) God could take care of righting the misconception surrounding the purpose of the plane crash.

Christians in whom love abounds are not very easily offended. Traumatic events like the plane crash can cause all kinds of offenses to take place. In our case, some people did not like the way they were informed of the situation or that others had been told before they were. Those who stepped into places of leadership were sometimes stretched so far that misunderstandings took place. I praise God that those situations were resolved quickly! I can say with the Psalmist in Psalm 119:165, *"Great peace have they which love thy law: and nothing shall offend them."*

Only God can love perfectly, but walking in His abounding love makes dealing with offenses and being without offense possible. Abounding love makes forgiveness a reality.

Love-Directed Fruit Bearing

Beth and I attended an all day pastors meeting the year after the plane crash. We were invited to join the main speaker and a few other pastors for the noon meal. The speaker asked me to share briefly what God had done in my life through the plane crash. As I stood to speak, my first thought was of my left hand with all its missing and misshapen fingers. I held up my hand.

"God gave me a witnessing tool! People often ask what happened to my hand, and I have the opportunity to share what God has done in my life as a result of the plane crash. Often, I am able to share my salvation experience and how it affected my outlook during this trial."

I further explained that I could not have endured the trial of the plane crash without having first known Christ as my personal Savior. With His abounding love shed abroad in my heart, I have been able to view life from His perspective and to walk through many challenges. I know I could not have done it without Him.

God used this trial to pour His love upon me, so that He could bear fruit in and through me. My purpose in life is to glorify God. My Heavenly Father gives me love that abounds in order to accomplish that purpose. With that abounding love, He gives me direction, He focuses my priorities, He clarifies my sincerity, He directs my discretion, and He produces the fruit that He has for my life.

Through each of these people and events surrounding the crash, God was deepening our fellowship with Him, increasing our strength in Him, and building our trust in Him. As we have grown in our walk with Him, He has taught us more about Himself and has enlarged our capacity to minister His comfort and His love. A deep desire to know God and to abound in His love does not require a traumatic event for its inception. God has made it simple—*"Draw nigh to God, and he will draw nigh to you"* (James 4:8). Crises, however, give us the opportunity to examine our relationship and walk with the Lord. These crises reveal the depth of our sincerity and peel back the layers of self that have built up in our hearts. They debride the wounds we have left untended, leaving us with nothing between ourselves and God, giving us the chance to heal properly so that God is able to pour out His love in our hearts (Romans 5:3–5).

God was faithful to teach us to keep our focus on Him so that we could trust Him. He gave us His strength. What an opportunity we have to walk in fellowship with Him! What an opportunity you have to walk in fellowship with Him! You have read our story—the details of our struggle to embrace God's purpose for our life and ministry. You have seen that He was faithful to us. Will you let Him work in your life? Will you join us as we seek to embrace God's purpose?

Let Him reveal your selfishness. Let Him give you the desire to live in fellowship with Him, to exchange your weakness for His strength, and to trust in Him alone. We will be forever grateful that God has patiently worked in us so that we would receive His grace, and that He has placed us in a position to reflect His glory as we seek to resemble His Son.

Russell (R.B.) & Elaine Spurgeon and Mark

Don & Carolyn Lombard

Lawrence & Ruth Thompson

The Widows
Embraced God's Purpose

Russell Bea ("R. B.") Spurgeon

The Pilot of the Plane

Born September 23, 1932, in Mountain Grove, Missouri, Russell married his high school sweetheart, Elaine Shorter, soon after graduation in 1951. In December of that same year, at the age of nineteen, he was born again. In 1954, at the age of twenty-one, he surrendered and announced his call to preach the Gospel.

R. B. and Elaine had two daughters and one son: Jean Ann, Carol, and Mark.

Elaine Spurgeon Caskey's Story

The weekend before the plane crash was a very eventful time. On Friday, I left to attend the "Active for Christ" women's retreat held at our state campgrounds at Niangua, Missouri. Meanwhile, on Friday evening at our church, a special choir practice was scheduled to prepare for the "I Love America" cantata.

One young mother arrived at the practice and, unbeknownst to her, after she pulled into the parking lot and was talking to someone through the window, her eighteen-month old baby crawled out of his car seat, out the open car door, and under the car tire. As this young mother was attempting to straighten her car in the parking place, she accidentally ran over the child. The baby was rushed to the hospital. R.B. went to the hospital, providing what comfort he could to the distraught mother and father throughout the weekend until the report came back that after being kept overnight for observation, miraculously, the baby was totally unharmed.

On the Saturday of that weekend, our oldest daughter, Jean Ann, her husband Mike, and their toddler Timmy were leaving for a vacation in Florida that included a visit to Disneyworld. R.B. had an uneasy feeling, a premonition that came to him in a dream, about a crash. Presentiments of this sort were not typical and totally out of character for him.

However, because of that uneasy feeling, he went to see the young couple before they left, fearing he would never see them again. He asked them to reconsider about leaving to go on this trip because of the dream. They told him that they had reservations and tickets, which they would lose. Because rescheduling the vacation would have been very costly, they decided to leave as planned, promising to be very careful along the way. His uneasy feeling persisted and, as circumstances unfolded, he was correct—only not in the way he was thinking.

That Saturday was full for R. B. In the midst of hospital care, other pastoral duties and preparing his sermon, he noticed that Mark, our son, was having trouble with his bicycle. He stopped everything else to fix the bike and for the two of them to spend some time with each other. Of course, he had no idea how meaningful that extra time would be to his thirteen-year-old son in the days to come.

On the following Tuesday morning, R. B. prepared to fly to a seminar for ministers in Kansas City with fellow pastors, Don Lombard, Lawrence Thompson, and Ken Spilger. He was up early checking the weather, flight plans, etc. for a single-day round trip. That evening I went to Mark's junior high school to attend a parent-teacher meeting. R. B.'s arrival home was delayed. It was raining, but I did not worry because I knew he was a cautious pilot. I simply thought he had waited for the weather to clear.

The following morning, Wednesday, at about 5:30, I received a call from Carolyn Lombard, asking if any of the men had arrived at our house or if I had heard from them. While we were on the phone, she said that someone was at her door, so we hung up. By this time I had a sense of dread. I think I even went into a form of shock. I remember feeling numb while waiting to hear something.

It was about 6:30 a.m. when our associate pastor, Daryl Ellis, and his wife Linda knocked on my door. As soon as they came in, I simply said, "You have bad news for me, don't you?" Then they told me about the plane crash and that R.B. had been killed along with Don Lombard and Lawrence Thompson. Nothing was said about Ken Spilger. Perhaps the Ellises had not known at the time that he had survived. I learned later that the medical examiner had contacted Jerry Norris, the pastor of the Fenton Free Will Baptist Church and he, in turn, had called Daryl.

Our son Mark was a sound sleeper, so I decided not to wake him until my daughter, Carol, and her husband, Rick, were with me. I also faced the problem of how to tell R.B.'s father, Flint, who had a bad heart and lived 180 miles away. I knew my brother-in-law, Bert, would soon be leaving for work, so my first call was to him. He agreed to give their father the news. My next call was to Carol. She and Rick and their toddler Luke came right over. We then woke Mark and told him about the crash. He burst into tears as we tried to comfort him.

In the meantime, while Daryl and Linda were helping us locate Jean Ann in Florida, Jim Mounts, a church member, came walking in with a large coffee maker, a can of coffee, and some sweet rolls. His family had heard the bad news on the radio and came to lend us support as part of our church family.

In the midst of my own grieving, my thoughts were with Carolyn Lombard, Ruth Thompson, and, of course, Ken Spilger and his family. I went to visit with Ruth and Carolyn soon after the accident to express my sorrow for them. Carolyn had grown up on the farm next to the Spurgeon family, and she had been close to R. B. throughout his life.

On Thursday, we still had not located Jean Ann and Mike, who had left only a sketchy and tentative schedule. We contacted Disneyworld, but by the time Disney officials attempted to reach them, they had left the park. My nephew, Larry, a truck driver living in Florida, contacted other drivers on the CB network and broadcast their license number. One of the drivers spotted their car on a beach parking lot and contacted the local authorities, who sent a deputy to find them on the beach. Once contacted, another church member, Paul Burtis, made arrangements for them to fly home Friday morning while he flew to Florida to drive their car back to St. Louis.

R. B. had left a letter in his desk, expressing his wishes in case of his death. While we were still looking for Jean Ann, the rest of the family gathered to make funeral arrangements. Friday, we followed his wishes and had visitation at Trinity Church with many people, who had been touched by his life and ministry, coming to pay their respects throughout the day. These included children and families from the church, personal friends, business and professional leaders from the community, and denominational leaders.

On Saturday, we traveled to Mountain Grove, our hometown, to have a joint funeral for R. B. and Don Lombard along with graveside services. Reverend O. T. Dixon, who was the officiant at R.B.'s ordination service in 1954, conducted the funeral. On Sunday, a memorial service was held at Trinity Church with Reverend Reford Wilson, Director of Foreign Missions for the Free Will Baptists, leading the service. Several people from the congregation shared moving testimonies and memories.

In addition to the natural grieving that comes to a widow who has lost the love of her life, her high school sweetheart, and husband of twenty-nine years, I was deeply troubled in a vague and uncertain way. Perhaps it was during the memorial service, perhaps through a pastoral visitation, or likely both, I came to understand that, as a part of our union, I was feeling some of the responsibility R. B. had known as a pilot. There is no question he would have been deeply hurt had he lived to see the pain and loss the crash has caused. Herein lay the source of my own trouble.

When I visited Ken Spilger in the hospital, he was such a comforter and encourager to me. Even while he was lying there in terrible pain and shock with burns covering much of his body, he reached out to me. He said, "During the flight, I did not have any anxiety or fear. The flight was smooth. If R.B. Spurgeon were to have lived and come to me saying, 'Let's go for a flight,' I would have no hesitation in going." Ken's words were such a comfort to me. I thank him for his sensitivity, consolation, and assurances that have stayed with me to this day.

Lawsuits were filed against R. B.'s estate, not out of greed or malice, but to secure rightfully owed funds. During all of the publicity and time in court resulting from these legal proceedings, there were no bad feelings among any of us. It was simply the process required in the state of Missouri to force the Avemco Insurance Company to pay what they owed. After all, we carried the liability insurance for this very purpose. I also really appreciate the assistance of a dear, long-time friend, Leonard Crewse. He obtained excellent legal counsel for me that I could never have afforded otherwise.

During the time after the accident, I felt it was very important for me to be in all of the church services playing the organ as usual. I remember one instance when a friend said something kind to me, and I burst into tears. "I wonder if you have been pushing yourself a little too much," she kindly offered.

I replied, "I feel I need to be here for myself and for Mark."

At home, Mark and I would pray together and cry together, day after day.

R. B. had once told me he thought I would be all right financially by continuing to teach piano and drawing social security for Mark and myself. The church very generously helped me for two months, and then the Lord sent me five new piano students beginning the first of January. I had my piano studio on the lower floor of our home. Mark would sometimes be outside and would come in the front door. My first thoughts were "R. B. is home!" But it was not so.

One month before the accident, R.B. was instrumental, along with the St. Louis area Free Will Baptist church pastors, in organizing a singles group for divorced and widowed people of all ages. This group, which met at our church, was a big help and blessing to me. We would occasionally meet in homes during the week as well as having a Sunday School class all our own on Sunday mornings. Stuart Simpson, a single, ordained minister from Australia who had been a missionary to New Zealand and a fellow pilot friend of R. B.'s, was our very able teacher. R. B. had met him at the Spirit of St. Louis Airport. Being single with an education in both theology and psychology, he was the perfect leader for this group. The social times associated with these classes were special for us all. This ministry was a big help and blessing. My daughter, Jean Ann, and my son-in-law Mike, who lived near me, entertained Mark during these meetings and other times as well.

After a few months, Bob Caskey, a widower in our church, told me about a non-denominational group for singles called Theos which met monthly in West County. His wife, a sister of O. T. Dixon, who had ordained R. B., had died several years earlier of cancer. Bob offered to take me to the first meeting so I wouldn't have to walk in alone. There I found they had a group meeting closer to me which met on Sunday afternoons. I enjoyed this group and found the discussion of problems encountered by singles to be helpful.

My family was so wonderfully supportive. I don't know how I could have survived without Jean Ann, Mike, Carol, Rick, and Mark. The grandkids, Timmy and Luke, brought joy to all of our lives. The joy was bittersweet, of course, knowing how much R. B. loved the children and would have enjoyed watching them grow. Also, my brother-in-law, Bert, his wife, Jewell, R. B.'s father, Flint, and step-mother, Leta, as well as my brothers and sisters-in-law, Harland and Jerry, Lyle and Mildred, Wayne and Ruth, were available whenever I needed them.

My church family could not have been closer and more wonderful. Bea Colby, the church secretary for many years and a dear family friend was especially helpful. Special friends would call me checking to see if I needed anything and if I was all right during the lonely, hard times that followed the initial months. I especially think of Sharon Ruble and Bob Sponsler in this regard.

God used all of these and others to minister to us. One woman, whom I didn't know, wrote me a letter telling me how R. B. had met and ministered to her when her husband was in the hospital dying. Her words were very comforting because she had been where I was. In her letter, she suggested several books to read. When I would awake in the early morning hours, I would read these works, and it seemed to me as if I was being counseled with the Lord at my side. The messages expressed in these writings helped me to understand what I was going through. All of this was a part of God's help and care, expressed through His people.

Now, at the age of 80, as I think on my life, I thank God for all of the people who have touched me. They have helped me and inspired me to be the person I am today. Oh, by the way, Bob Caskey became a very important person in my life. We have now been married for 30 years. Another gift from God.

Donald W. Lombard

Passenger - Flew in seat by the pilot.

Born January 14, 1944, in Monett, Missouri, Donald was saved as a child and surrendered to the call to preach the Gospel in June 1968. Donald married Carolyn in 1966, and though they had no children of their own, Carolyn adopted a son, Chip, after Don's death.

Carolyn Lombard's Story

While in college, I had gone on a missions trip to Mexico and was sharing about it in a service at Grant Avenue Baptist Church in Springfield, Missouri. As I walked up a side aisle, I noticed a young man walking down another aisle. We met and talked at that meeting, but I never dreamed I would ever meet him again. Was I ever surprised when Don Lombard transferred to the college I was attending! We began to date in 1965 and were married the next year. Life with Don was always an adventure. He loved life, art, the ministry—everything.

After college, Don and I served a church in Bryan, Texas, for three years. Then God moved us to O'Fallon, Missouri, to a little church that was just starting. It was exciting as we helped the church grow and go from meeting in the basement of a house to building their own beautiful building. Don was always busy helping others. He was involved with the local police department as their chaplain and later became the chaplain in charge of their entire chaplaincy program.

That fateful event in the early morning of September 17, 1980, was a total shock to me, but as I look back, I can see that God had been giving us warning signals that something was going to take place.

- Six months before the accident, I dreamed that I lived all alone in a house in Harvester, Missouri. Don was not in that dream.

- In August, Don and I spent three days visiting our parents. While in the home of his parents, his sister, Marilyn Hull, overheard a conversation between Don and his father. Don was saying, "I feel like my work in O'Fallon is over, but I don't know where God wants me to go." His father assured him, "God will let you know."
- On the Monday before the accident, Don officiated at a funeral. While at the funeral home, he noticed a certain casket and commented to the funeral director that he really liked it. When he came home from the funeral, he was showing me his pin-striped suit and mentioned that he looked good in that suit and wanted to be buried in it. I wonder now if these were thoughts in his mind because he had just been at that funeral or did he have a premonition that something was soon going to happen to him?
- In the wee hours of the morning as he was preparing to leave for Kansas City to attend a one-day pastors seminar, he awakened me three times, set me up, and told me how much he loved me and how happy he was. He was to meet R. B. Spurgeon and two other pastors to travel to the seminar. As I look back on his conduct that morning, I can see that it was as though he knew he was saying his last goodbye.

After returning from the visit with our parents in August, we continued our regular routine, waiting for God to show us the next step. Don was busy with his ministry at the church and his job as chaplain of the O'Fallon police force. School had started, and I was again teaching at Lincoln County R-IV in the O'Fallon, Missouri, area. It never entered my thoughts that life would change so drastically for me at 12:30 a.m. the morning of September 17.

I was almost ready to leave for school early that morning but struggling with an uneasiness as to where Don was. I thought perhaps he might have stayed with the Spurgeons in St. Louis since their flight home had been delayed to miss a storm during the night. Before I walked out the door to leave for school, I called Elaine Spurgeon. She was wondering the same thing—where were our husbands? While still on the phone with Elaine, my doorbell rang, and I laid down the phone to check the door. As I opened the door, I saw people and cars everywhere—lining the street and packed into the church parking lot across the street from our home. A pastor-friend stepped inside, and his countenance told me something was terribly wrong. Somehow, I felt that it had to do with Don. "Don is dead, isn't he?" I asked.

"Yes," he replied and then proceeded to tell me what had happened to all four men.

I immediately went into shock and felt totally numb. The rest of the day is a blur. I remember only that people came and went throughout the day. I have no idea who put the phone back on its receiver.

I do remember that sometime during the day, I went to the church study and sat down at Don's desk. On the desk was an index card with the song "Over the Next Hill We'll be Home." I knew then that Don knew he was going Home. He had told me what suit he wanted and what casket he wanted and now I held in my hand the song he wanted for his funeral.

Somehow, my family in southwestern Missouri was contacted, and they came to me immediately. I still remember my two nieces and a nephew as they came to hug me, bursting into tears and blurting out, "We'll never have fun again." They would miss their fun-loving uncle. With my family there to help, we went to the funeral home to make funeral arrangements. The overriding feeling I carried those first days after Don's death was total shock. I actually don't remember a lot of what happened but know that somehow God carried me through that time.

Days later, after having attended two funerals and three memorial services, I was deep in grief. It is only natural to grieve over the loss of someone very close to us, but if we allow it to help us grow spiritually and emotionally, we can come through the experience a stronger person.

In the days following the services, I was still in shock, but people were very kind and did their best to comfort me. Even those who had not gone through the same kind of loss that I was suffering could still show comfort and give assurance that God is our real Comforter. He has promised that He will not give us more than we can bear (1 Corinthians 10:13).

When going through my loss of Don, I knew that others might not wholly understand how I felt, but God did. I was grateful for all the support and comfort I received from those around me, but I also realized that God was the One to whom I had to go with every need I experienced. He became my only true Comforter and Help. We may wonder why God allows us to go through these hard times, but we have not been promised a life of ease.

The next phase of my life involved some difficult decisions that I would have to make. The church in O'Fallon meant the world to Don and me, but they would have to find another pastor and would need the parsonage where we had been living. I would have to find another place to live. A house in Harvester, Missouri, was offered to me free of charge but, after the dream I had had before Don's death, I could not face living there. I found another house and moved into it.

Since I loved teaching, I decided that it would be good to return to my teaching job quickly. Teaching would give me something to keep me busy and also something other than my grief on which to focus. My principal was very supportive and kind and gave me time to get my life back in a sustainable order before returning to the classroom. I wanted, and needed, to be back with my children.

Those first days back at school were very difficult. When my fellow teachers met me in the hall, they obviously were desperate to know what to say to me. The greatest difficulty I experienced was when my students entered my classroom that first morning. Each took his seat without saying a word. Normally, the students would hug me and never stop talking. They continued to be very quiet even while I filled out the attendance sheet. Finally, I took a stool and sat in front of the class. "You were told not to upset me or make me cry," I said as a matter of fact. They all nodded their heads in agreement. "I want to answer your questions, and if I cry that will be okay," I told them. I wanted them to feel free to talk about the situation.

My fellow workers were very considerate of me. One of my closest friends came by my room and said, "I am covering all your playground duty for you." The principal often came to my room and would say, "Go take a break. I'm covering your class for you." However, I soon realized that people do not know how to genuinely comfort others in their time of a loss such as this. I wanted to talk about Don, but they were afraid it would upset me. Parents had cautioned their children not to bring it up in the classroom. I am so glad I encouraged my class to ask questions. Yes, I cried, but there was healing in the fact that I could talk about my loss.

I remember going to the hospital to visit Ken and Beth thinking I would try to encourage them. Although they were going through a very difficult time in their life, as soon as I entered the room, Ken became an unbelievable inspiration to me. Conversation with Beth also helped me greatly. I found it amazing that, in spite of all that they were going through, they could be such an encouragement in that they were concerned about my wellbeing.

I tried to be strong for my church family, my own extended family, and friends, but several years later I was still struggling. No one wanted to talk with me about Don because they were afraid of increasing my grief. Finally, I asked Ken and Beth if they knew of a counselor where I could get help, and they gave me a name. The counselor thought it would take several sessions, but in one session I found the help I needed to move on with my life. During that session, we looked at pictures, talked about my beloved husband, and cried together. I felt God's healing touch. Later, I went to a restaurant that Don and I had frequented and felt a freedom from the grief that had had such a clutch on my life. I thank God for the help and direction the Spilgers gave to me.

In the Scriptures, God tells us to expect tribulations, and James 1:2 even says to consider it all joy when we encounter various trials. God has a purpose for these trials. As we go through them, He demonstrates His ability to sustain us through great pressure. He walks with us every step of the way, controls the intensity of the trials, and enables us, through His Holy Spirit, to come out of them victoriously.

Since Don's death, I have felt like I have been in shock most of the time. I spent a lot of time teaching and used anything I could think of to help me keep going. However, God has been with me and put up with me during the rough times. During these times I have found myself drawing closer to the Lord and coming to the realization that He must rule in my life.

In 1987 I took classes at the welfare department in St. Charles to adopt a child. While taking this class, I was told to go to the hospital to see a seven-year-old boy who had been *damaged* badly. I fell in love with him. He only weighed 27 pounds at that time. Until the mother lost her privileges as a parent, I was only able to get custody of him. As soon as the opportunity was available, I adopted him. Chip is a very talented artist and now has three boys of his own. One of his sons has a rare disease known as VGM (brain malfunction of the vein of galen). A whole vein is missing. Cylas is the only living person of his age with VGM. God has allowed this miracle for some reason that only He knows.

I retired from teaching at Lincoln County R-IV in 2005. After that, I suffered a stroke. Since Chip was with me, he was able to get me to the hospital quickly. As a result of quick treatment, my speech came back. Three days after the stroke, I was transferred to a rehabilitation center where I spent only one month. It was difficult, but I worked very hard at therapy.

While I was in rehab, my sister and several of my close friends took on the task of selling my house and making preparations to move me to Springfield. I now live at an independent living facility in Springfield. Though the move was difficult, I am adjusting and get out a little. I am so grateful to still be able to walk some.

I know the Lord is coming soon, and all will be well. An old song that we used to sing rings out in my heart, "God Will Take Care of You," and I am reminded that God will take care of me. I have found His grace to exceed all my guilt and sin. I have found Him to be faithful in everything—even when my heart was broken. I did not really lose Don. I just gave him back to God. We shall meet again. I do not understand everything, but I know Jesus is my Saviour, and His grace is sufficient in all things.

Lawrence Delmon Thompson

Passenger - Flew in seat by Ken

Born May 16, 1925, in Salem, Missouri, Lawrence married Ruth when they were both 18 years old. Lawrence served in the United States Navy during World War II. In 1951, he received Christ as His Savior, and the following year, he surrendered to the call to preach the Gospel.

The Thompsons had two sons and a daughter: Danny, Michael, and Pam.

Ruth Thompson Atkinson's Story

I met Lawrence Delmon Thompson when we were both sixteen years old. Our birthdays were exactly six months apart. Lawrence was "larger than life" and always the center of attention. He loved people, and they loved him. His sense of humor kept everyone around him in stitches, and he was the life of any gathering he attended. We fell in love and were married in 1944 when we were both only eighteen years old. After we were married, Lawrence served in the Navy during World War II for two years. He accepted Christ as his Savior in 1951 and felt that God was calling him to preach the Gospel. In 1952, he started the Salem Free Will Baptist Church, in Salem, Missouri, which he pastored for eight years. From there, he moved on to pastor Bear Point Free Will Baptist Church in Sesser, Illinois, for three and one-half years; Riverview Free Will Baptist Church in Bettendorf, Iowa, for five years; Victory Free Will Baptist Church in Kansas City, Missouri, for twelve years; and then Oak Hills Free Will Baptist Church, between St. Clair and Union, Missouri, for one year until his death.

The twelve-year long ministry in Kansas City was a very active, busy, and somewhat hectic ministry. The phone was always ringing. Lawrence was very good with people and loved ministering to their needs, so he was gone on visitation almost every night. When he returned from visitation, I would put on the coffeepot, and we would sit together and discuss the day. With so many responsibilities, sometimes trying to get everything done became overwhelming for me. On Saturdays, I did my hair and went shopping. But the most challenging Saturday job was to put together the church bulletin. This task involved choosing the songs, typing everything in perfectly formatted order, obtaining Lawrence's approval, and then having it ready in a timely manner so Lawrence could print them out on an old mimeograph machine. I remember many times when the burdens of the ministry seemed too great, and I would say, "I can't do it."

Lawrence would calmly lay a comforting hand on my shoulder and say with conviction and a bit of humor in his voice, "You can do it. I have confidence in you." These words would come back to minister to me later when I desperately needed the calm reassurance they offered.

We moved to St. Clair, Missouri, on August 17, 1979, where Lawrence pastored the Oak Hills Free Will Baptist Church. This thirteen-month period before Lawrence's death was like the "honeymoon" that we had never had. It was as a gift from God. We were able to purchase a little four-year-old home of our own instead of living in a parsonage. We even got to choose our own paint and carpet colors! The ministry was a mission church full of young families, and for several reasons, it was less hectic and easier on us. We still continued the post-visitation coffee times and grew even closer to each other. By this time, we had been married for thirty-six years and were more in love than ever. Lawrence wrote a short poem for me on our thirty-sixth anniversary, only three months before his death: "Roses are red, violets are blue. If I live another 36 years, I want to live them with you."

In September, 1980, an exciting opportunity came when an annual one-day pastors seminar came to Kansas City. We made plans for Lawrence to attend the seminar, and I would accompany him to Kansas City to spend the time with our daughter and grandsons there. By this time I was 54, and Lawrence was 55. Our children were Danny

(35) living in St. Louis, Michael (31) living in California, and Pamela (28) living in Kansas City. Our original plan was for the two of us to accompany two other pastors to the seminar, but unknown to us, Pastor Spurgeon contacted a fourth pastor, Ken Spilger, who took my place, and I stayed home. R. B. Spurgeon, a dear pastor friend and pilot, made plans to fly the group from St. Louis to the seminar in Kansas City on September 16. Several friends remember that during the noon meal shared by the group at the seminar, those at the table with Lawrence were entertained by his humor, and they all shared a precious time of fellowship. The group had a wonderful day together and then headed home to their families.

Lawrence called me before 10:30 p.m. from Kansas City to let me know that their return was being delayed because of weather. Three times they were given clearance to fly but were again detained. Finally on their way, when they came to Columbia, Missouri, the reports said that flying conditions in St. Louis had cleared. As the group neared the airport, they did not realize they were flying too low. The plane hit the treetops and crashed at approximately 12:30 a.m. September 17.

Meanwhile, back at home, I anxiously awaited an update call from Lawrence, but to no avail. My panic grew, and I called my brother, Bill Harrison, who happened to live next door. He and his wife came to sit with me while we waited for news. Sometime during those hours, Bill went back to his house to call the airport. Very little news was available, but he did find out that a plane was down. Details were sketchy at first, but by 4:00 or 5:00 a.m., he had learned that three were known dead with one survivor. Only later did we find out that Ken Spilger was that lone survivor.

The days and weeks immediately after the crash were a blur of deep grief for me. Two days after the crash, two representatives from the organization sponsoring the one-day ministers seminar came to my home to bring their condolences. I later learned that each of the widows as well as Pastor and Mrs. Spilger had all received visits. The visitors sat with each widow, talking with each lady about her loved one, and then praying with them before they left. These visits ministered to each of us in a special way.

I recall one very vivid memory of a time about two weeks after the crash. I was feeling so alone and was so fearful of where life would take me. The panic and hysteria built up in me until I felt I was most likely having a full-blown panic attack. I remember mentally saying to myself, "I can't do it!" Then I felt a physical sensation of a hand on my shoulder, and I could hear Lawrence's voice telling me, "You can do it. I have confidence in you." I laughed out loud and cried, thinking my sweet husband was a rascal who even ministered to me after his death. His words of assurance brought me comfort for many years to come when I faced seemingly overwhelming circumstances.

Through the continued grief, I soon realized that the crash had forced me to cling harder to the Lord since He was literally all I had. In retrospect, I feel that before the crash, I had perhaps clung to and depended more on Lawrence, my rock, than I did on the Lord. In the days and weeks following the crash, I remember singing, "My Lord knows the way through the wilderness, all I have to do is follow," over and over again. It especially helped me at night when I had difficulty sleeping. Through this tragedy, Jesus had truly become my Shepherd.

Emotionally, I was forced to become a stronger person than I had been when Lawrence was my strength. My children and friends continued to minister to me. One of the supernatural circumstances God brought my way came in the form of a friend from a former church. Linda had done my hair every Saturday for years while we lived in Kansas City. Because she had grown up in a home with little parental influence, she quickly grew to think of Lawrence and me as her mom and dad. Now divorced, Linda, who was a nurse, got a night job in Washington, Missouri, to be close to me. As it turned out, she and her girls ended up moving in with me. Since Linda worked nights, I would get the girls up in the morning, fix their breakfast, and prepare them for school. That necessity gave me a reason to get up in the morning. The two young girls would snuggle and cuddle with me during our times together, and the four of us shared an evening meal together each day. Linda and the girls lived with me until the end of that school year, filling a void and offering purpose, love, and companionship. Eventually, Linda moved back to Kansas City and is now happily married. Now that I have also moved back to Kansas City, Linda and her husband Frank faithfully visit me each week, often bringing me special treats and taking me out to lunch.

My brother, Bill, and his wife also offered much precious help and counsel during the months after the crash. Bill also filled in as pastor of Oak Hills Free Will Baptist Church in Lawrence's place until they called a permanent pastor several months later.

Another long-time friend and neighbor, Frieda, was also a great encouragement during the time following Lawrence's death. She continues to be a dear friend to this day.

Sadly, I have lost both of my sons to illness in the last three years. However, I still have my daughter and son-in-law. I am especially close to them both emotionally and physically—living only one and a half blocks from their home. Visiting with their four grown children, their spouses, and their twelve children (my great-grandchildren) gives me much joy.

My advice to others facing similar challenges is to trust in and draw closer to the Lord. I encourage you to get as close to Him as possible as He is the greatest source of comfort during dark times. Although I still had my family, including sisters and brothers, they could not take the place of my husband. The day of that crash, I not only lost my husband, but also my soul-mate, pastor, best friend, position, and purpose in life. Having lost all this, I had only God as my strength and sustainer.

Several years after the crash, I remarried. Bill Atkinson also was a pastor and pastored in Georgia. Recently, he also was taken to Heaven.

Now, I can clearly see the hand of God, not only in the circumstances that led up to the crash, but in His care for me since that day. I am grateful for the deep relationship I have with my Savior, and I am trusting in His care every step of the way through this life. The same words that helped me through those first dark days still carry me through each and every day. "My Lord KNOWS the way through the wilderness; all I have to do is FOLLOW!"

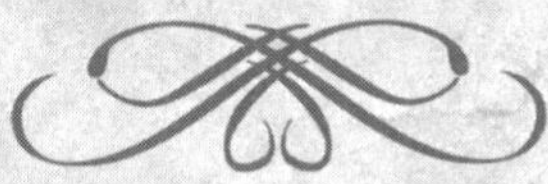

Our Children

Embraced God's Purpose

"Lo, children are an heritage of the L*ORD: and the fruit of the womb is his reward.* [4]*As arrows are in the hand of a mighty man; so are children of the youth.* [5]*Happy is the man that hath his quiver full of them: they shall not be ashamed, but they shall speak with the enemies in the gate."*

– Psalm 127:3-5

Anna Spilger Huckabee

The plane crash happened when I was so young that I don't really remember it. The aftermath was so much a part of our lives that it almost seemed ordinary. We quickly adapted to having a dad with fingers missing, who couldn't do a lot of strenuous activity in the summer, who had to be careful not to bump or injure his delicate skin. What had happened became matter-of-course, normal, a statement of fact about myself and our family.

The other children from that same plane crash could not say the same thing. Their dads were gone forever because of that one horrible event.

How did God use the plane crash in my life? He used it to help me appreciate what other children might have taken for granted. My dad was there to take me to my first day of school, listen to me learn to read, and agonize with me through long division. He took me to my first teen summer camp and my first youth activities. He was there when I had my first crush on a boy and provided me with vivid nicknames that helped me immediately get over it. He was there when I graduated from high school and college.

Dad took us on family vacations and helped us get to know our extended family in a way that we never would have if he hadn't been spared. We went to national parks and gained an appreciation for beauty in places most people would not have called beautiful. He taught me how to ride a horse and not be afraid—even when I got bucked off.

He prayed with me when God called me to be a missionary and helped me plan my life so I could stay on target for that calling. I went with him on visitation and heard him counseling people with struggles. I learned to seek his wisdom and counsel. When God called me to lay aside my dream of missions, Dad helped me work through that struggle.

Dad was there as my husband-to-be and I courted and fell in love. He knew almost as soon as I did that James was the man for me. He gave me away at my wedding. He held his first grandsons the next year—the first twins to be born in the family since my dad and his twin sister. He baptized each of my children who have been saved (all but the youngest). He sent my husband and me to the mission field with those grandchildren, offering support and encouragement along the way.

My dad was there. God gave me that. Because of the plane crash, I have been able to hold those moments dear. I'm grateful for how God chose to work in my life by letting my father live.

– Anna Spilger Huckabee

Esther Spilger

As a sixth grader, I was still struggling with learning.

"Why am I so different from others?" I wondered.

Learning was the hardest task I faced each day until my parents found the cause—dyslexia and dysgraphia. Once that discovery was made, I felt relief. My struggle had a name. I could deal with it!

That is when the work really started! I had to work with this "problem." Dad would come alongside of me and say, "Don't give up, Esther! You CAN do this!" I knew he knew what he was talking about because I had watched him relearn how to do everything after the plane crash. He never gave up.

He would remind me of Grandpa Spilger's words to him as he left to return to Nebraska the day Dad came home from the hospital: "You can lie there and feel sorry for yourself, or you can get up and do something about it." He would say, "Esther, you have the same choice." I did have a choice. I could either feel sorry for myself and not do anything, or I could do something about it. I chose to follow Dad's example. I would DO something about it! If he could relearn to do everything, I could learn to learn. Dad reminded me that nothing was impossible with Christ because He will give me strength in my choice to overcome my limitations. God didn't ride the Exercycle for Dad. God didn't do my school assignments for me. But Jesus was with us both through every bit of it.

I have purposed to live my life by this philosophy.

– Esther Spilger

Naomi Spilger Walsh

"*I can't do* this anymore!" "I'm too tired!" "I just have to quit!" Life brings challenges that test our endurance. While training for races, I frequently hear myself say these words in my head. Running takes endurance and patience to keep putting one foot forward in order to get to the finish line.

I was born about four years after the plane crash. By the time I came along, my parents had already settled into the post-plane-crash "new normal." I saw my dad handle his disabilities with daily strength and determination. To this day, he rarely lets his disabilities stop him from anything. For example, when we were remodeling the basement of our house, Dad needed help because he couldn't hold the screw and use the drill at the same time. So he recruited my sister, Esther, to hold the screw for him. His solution, unfortunately, did not turn out so well for Esther, who had to nurse a damaged thumbnail!

Life can be full of crises and traumatic times, but with God's grace, we can move on to the next day and eventually settle into a new routine. Running a marathon takes patience and determination. My parents are an excellent example of turning a crisis into something good by running the race set before them. Hebrews 12:1 and 2 says, "*Wherefore seeing we also are compassed about with so great a cloud of witnesses, let us lay aside every weight, and the sin which doth so easily beset us, and let us run with patience the race that is set before us, [2]Looking unto Jesus the author and finisher of our faith; who for the joy that was set before him endured the cross, despising the shame, and is set down at the right hand of the throne of God.*"

– Naomi Spilger Walsh

P. S. Because of my Dad's difficult recovery from the plane crash, I have a boldness, as a nurse, to speak to my patients about their need to make the right choices for their own recovery.

Paul Spilger

Life! Most people don't seem to give much thought to the idea of life! Today is December 24, 2014, and I am now 25 years of age. Approximately nine and a half years before I was born, my dad was the only survivor of a plane crash.

Life! Most people take this not-so-simple gift from God for granted! Life is so special, precious, beautiful, and my dad was gifted with his a second time! Just think, if my dad had not survived: five special, precious and beautiful blessings would have never been born. Because Dad was given this gift of life, I was given a gift called life.

This makes me think. In 1 Samuel 1, we see Hannah, who was unable to have children, praying and asking the Lord for a son, and then promising to give back what was given to her. To me, Hannah's story parallels the story of my dad; he was given life, and the life he was given on September 17, 1980, he has since given back to God.

Life! He was given life—a simple gift for God to give, yet so complicated for us to understand fully. My life has had a great example to learn from, and being like my dad would be a great accomplishment!

My dad has taken this gift of life and used it to glorify and praise the One who gave it to him! I strive for the day when my own kids will say this about me! Life is indeed such a wonderful gift!

– *Paul Spilger*

Jonathan Spilger

I walked through the house standing as tall as my approximately three and one-half foot tall body would let me. My left hand hung at my side with my fingers curled in as far as I could make them. In my right hand I carried a "tract" that I had scribbled and folded myself. I walked up to my mom and said, "Hi. I'm Jonathan Spilger, and I'm the only survivor of a plane crash." I had heard my dad say those words maybe thousands of times when he gave out his plane crash tracts, and I couldn't come up with another way to witness to people.

Even at that young age, I knew that the story God had worked in my dad's life had changed both his life and ministry. I thought, at that time, that I needed the same change, and that only a plane crash would give me a way to minister to people. My parents chuckled at my wanting so much to be like my dad. They would then explain that God would give me my own stories.

I can remember throughout my life having many conversations with my parents in which the phrase, "God is giving you your life story" was a means of comfort. As God has worked His plan and story into my parents' lives, He will do the same for me. He will also do the same for you.

Most of us, thankfully, will never go through a plane crash. But all of us have a story—a plan and a purpose that God is weaving into our lives. As you read this account of one couple's story, allow God to show you the greatness of His purpose and plan in your own life.

– Jonathan Spilger

Stephen Spilger

When I think of September 17, I first think of my birthday, but something far bigger that happened on that day has changed my family and my life in a significant way. Thirteen years before I was born, my father was in a plane crash with three other men, and Dad was the only one to survive.

You might think that because I grew up with a dad who had a deformed, fragile left hand, that we never played sports with him. That's simply not the case. He always figured out ways to play sports with us—even when that meant he had to both catch and throw the ball with his right hand when playing baseball. Because my dad never acted handicapped, I never thought of him as handicapped. Generally I forgot that he had been severely burned and did not have all of his fingers.

The way the plane crash changed our family has been amazing. The accident taught us that when you trust God, He can show you great and mighty things and that He works in mysterious ways. What I have learned the most from the plane crash is that no matter what you're going through, God will help you through it and show you how to overcome the problem.

"I can do all things through Christ which strengtheneth me." (Philippians 4:13)

– *Stephen Spilger*

Joanna Spilger

My dad calls us "the runt and the cripple." I am the youngest of my parents' children, and it just so happens that I am also the smallest—but not by much. I was born 15½ years after my dad's plane crash, so hearing about the plane crash and the effects it had on my dad's body, like fingers missing and stiff legs, has been a normal part of my life. When my dad started calling us "the runt and the cripple," I would wonder who he was talking about because I never considered him crippled, and I never considered myself a runt! Whenever our family would have work days around our house, it seemed like my dad and I would always get teamed together and would be assigned the hard jobs—like having to do intense landscaping in our front yard. Dad would say, "Here they go again—giving the hard job to the runt and the cripple!"

That characterization has turned into a fun nickname for Dad and me. Even though he may have some fingers missing and I may be the smallest of their kids, we are still able to "move mountains together"! *"And he said unto me, My grace is sufficient for thee: for my strength is made perfect in weakness. Most gladly therefore will I rather glory in my infirmities, that the power of Christ may rest upon me*" (2 Corinthians 12:9). My siblings and I have tried to live by my parents' example that in spite of any "weaknesses" we may have in our lives, God can still use us to do amazing things.

– *Joanna Spilger*

Epilogue

The crash site along Wild Horse Creek Road in west St. Louis County, Missouri, has changed significantly since September 17, 1980. Only the splice in the electrical wires remains as a reminder—the solitary evidence that a plane crashed on that spot. The field has been leveled, and large new homes have been built on the land. The farmhouse has been enlarged, and alongside of it, a new road leads down the ridge to a stable. The firehouse is still in its place, but many of the other landmarks are different or gone.

Our family has also changed. At the writing of this book, God has blessed us with five more children (a total of seven), two sons-in-law, and eight grandchildren. Praise the Lord, all of them are serving God!

In our ministry, God has enabled us to move forward in the purpose He gave us to raise up the foundations of godly generations. Many souls have been saved. Through it all, God has called our church family to a higher level of commitment. Out of Grace Baptist Church, God has called several missionaries to go to the mission field. He has led other missionaries to make Grace their home church. Through the ministries of these missionaries, souls are being saved, churches are being established, and our church is being reproduced both at home and abroad.

The temptation to pick up my own agenda knocks at my life's door, but by God's grace, I remember that He has plucked me from that life of selfish goals. I am able to come to Christ, take His yoke upon me, learn of Him, and enter into His rest. I am so grateful for God's refining fires. Truly our unchanging God is faithful. His mercy is renewed every morning and endures forever. His grace is always sufficient. Nothing can separate us from His love.

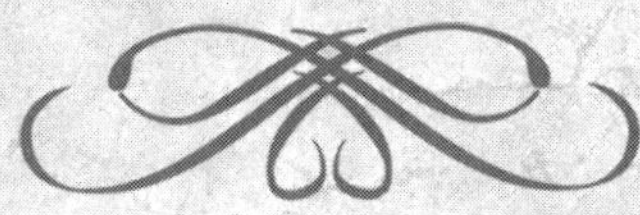

Appendices

"For the LORD God is a sun and shield:
the LORD will give grace and glory:
no good thing will he withhold
from them that walk uprightly."
– Psalm 84:11

Appendix A ~ Glossary
Appendix B ~ Burn Information
Appendix C ~ Sequence of Events
Appendix D ~ Surgery Notes
Appendix E ~ Biographical Sketch

Appendix A
Glossary

Burns: See Appendix B for a complete description.

Debridement: The removal of dead tissue or foreign objects from around a wound. To debride is the verb for going through that process.

Escharotomy: A cut made through the surface of the skin that has been charred to release the pressure caused by the burns and to allow the blood to flow freely to that area of the body. The dead skin is called eschar.

Hypothermia Blanket: A pad or blanket with cooled water running through tubes sealed inside the blanket. It is used to lower the body temperature by placing it either under the patient or on top of the patient. It is also designed to absorb the heat from the body. For Ken, the pad was placed under his body to bring down his extremely high fever.

Hypovolemia: A decrease in the amount of circulating blood in the body. This is due to loss of blood plasma in burn patients.

Hypovolemic Shock: A life-threatening condition in which fluid leaking out of the bloodstream causes a low blood volume, which in turn causes low blood pressure and can potentially lead to the failure of vital organs. To give more fluids to a person in hypovolemic shock would only cause additional problems or even death.

JOBST garments: Custom made pressure garments made for both of Ken's hands and legs by the JOBST company. These garments were worn to cut down on grotesque scar tissue that occurs due to major wounds by putting even pressure on those areas of concern. His hands and legs were measured and custom garments were made to fit him. The gloves and leggings also aided in circulation of the blood due to the fact that his skin was so thin after the grafting process. These were not worn until the wounds were almost completely closed. He continues to wear these pressure garments today on his lower legs for better blood circulation. The type he wears now look like and act as socks.

Lactated Ringers: A type of intravenous fluid administered to a patient through his/her IV used for correcting fluid levels after extreme blood loss brought on by the grafting surgeries. This solution contains sodium lactate, calcium chloride, sodium chloride, and potassium chloride.

Pseudomonas Infection: A serious bacterial infection which can turn the donor site and the grafted site green. It can be deadly. It can be effectively treated with Sulfamylon Cream.

Shock: A critical medical condition that is brought on by a fall in blood pressure due to loss of blood, severe burns and other medical conditions. Evidences of shock in a person are: skin that is cold and pale, irregular breathing, rapid pulse, dilated pupils, and a change in level of consciousness.

Skin Graft: A layer of healthy skin tissue, the dermis and epidermis, placed on the burned area after that area has been prepared to receive the healthy skin.

Stryker Frame Circle Bed: A bed built by Stryker Co. The frame is circular and is operated by a motor allowing the medical personnel to turn a patient that is to be immobile from lying on his/her back to his/her front and vise versa. The bed also helps when a patient has not stood for a long period of time. The patient can be brought to an upright position gradually in order to keep him/her from fainting. [One time the motor went out on Ken's bed. The head side of the bed was gradually sinking to the floor. He was quickly transferred to another circle bed.]

Subluxation: When a joint is totally or partially dislocated.

Sulfamylon (antibiotic) Cream: A strong antibiotic cream used to kill the pseudomonas infections Ken had after two of his surgeries.

Visceromegaly: Enlargement of the abdominal organs - the liver, pancreas, stomach, spleen, and kidneys.

Appendix B
Burn Information

Most burns are classified into three categories:

First-degree Burns: Nearly everyone has experienced this type of burn, which involves the epidermis—the outer layer of skin. Touching a hot iron, a pot on the stove, a mild sunburn, etc. can cause a first-degree burn. These burns usually appear slightly red, possibly form a white plaque at the injury site, and are mildly painful. Most heal in a short time.

Second-degree Burns: This type of burn is more painful because both of the first two layers of skin are involved. The dermis, the second layer, contains the body's blood vessels, lymph vessels, hair follicles, sweat glands, nerves, collagen bundles, and fibroblasts (cells which produce collagen, the protein which helps bind the dermis and heal wounds). The dermis gives the skin its flexibility and the strength it needs to allow the body to move or to give when pressure is exerted on any area of the skin. The dermis also contains the body's pain and touch receptors.

Third-degree Burns: In a third-degree burn, the epidermis is totally destroyed, and the subcutaneous tissue of the deeper parts of the dermis (called the subcutis) is damaged. The subcutis, a network of collagen and fat cells, helps conserve the body's heat and acts as a protective "shock absorber" against injury. When any part of the body is burned to the subcutis, there is no pain in that area because the nerves have been damaged or destroyed; however, every third degree burn is surrounded by very painful first- and second-degree burns. Keratin and hair shafts are also destroyed. Third-degree burns exhibit charring as well as a hard eschar—dead tissue, which cuts off circulation. Most third-degree burns require grafting of skin from another part of the body that has not been burned.

Deep Tissue Burns: These burns involve all three layers of skin but also go deep into the muscle. This type of burn can involve the bone being burned, also.

Appendix C
Sequence of Events

A *chronology of* events around the plane crash and after:

Date of Event **Basic Event**

9/16/80....... Flew out of STL for KC, MO, for pastors conference

Left very early to meet Russell Spurgeon and Don Lombard at Pastor Spurgeon's church on McKelvey to go to Lambert Airport to pick up plane. Then flew to Washington, MO, to pick up Lawrence Thompson.

9/16/80........................Spent the day at the conference

Took taxi to conference

9/16/80..........................Tim took Ken to the airport

Ken spent time with Tim Jensen (our nephew who was attending Calvary Bible College) after the conference. Met the other three men after spending time with Tim. It was late.

9/17/80........................... Plane crashed at12:30 AM

- *Beth was called to come to the hospital at 2:10 AM.*
- *Bill Hoss took Marcia and Beth to hospital and stayed until he had to leave for work.*
- *Dr. Ayvazian and others talked with Beth in the waiting room about Ken's condition and the accident.*
- *Beth was allowed to see Ken for a few minutes before he was taken to the burn unit for escharotomies.*

• Beth was questioned by authorities about who was on plane and for what purpose.

• Called people to let them know about the crash and Ken's condition.

9/17/80.......................................Escharotomy

Early morning; around 5:00 AM. See partial notes from Dr Ayvazian on this procedure and medications in Appendix D.

9/17/80...........................Beth & Marcia returned home

Shortly after lunch; Don & Karen Kress picked us up and drove us to get our car at Russell Spurgeon's church. They graciously followed us home.

Late 9/17/80...........................Ken's folks came to STL

Arrived after the 10 P.M. news on TV was finished.

9/18/80...................................Visited crash site

Police drove Paul, Ann, and Beth to see the site before they went to the hospital to see Ken.

9/17–11/14/80.......Burn Unit at St. John's Mercy Medical Center

59 days

11/17–11/29/80..........................Therapy at St. John's

10/06/80.......................................First Surgery

• Amputation of 4 fingers and part of thumb on left hand. Graft to right leg and right hand.

• Bones in left hand fingers were black from the burns. (Appendix D)

10/13/80.......Burton Brush (Dad) underwent surgery in Omaha

Dad was obviously in distress when they stopped to visit on their way home to Hartington, NE, from Chattanooga, TN. They stopped at the hospital in Omaha, which resulted in Dad having surgery on Monday.

10/14/80.................................Second Surgery

- *Amputation of left little toe and partial amputations of 2nd, 3rd and 4th toes on left foot.*
- *Grafts to left foot and leg. Much of the leg muscle removed because of the depth of the burns. (Appendix D)*

10/17/80..............................Infection discovered

Treatment started for pseudomonas infection. Green from top to bottom. Fever high and placed on a hypothermia blanket (controlled refrigeration) to bring down fever.

10/18/80...........................Grafts okay after infection

All looks good!

10/20/80......................3,600 calories consumed today!

10/23/80......................4,500 calories consumed today!

10/27/80..................................Third Surgery

- *Grafting of the buttocks and perianal area, lateral and medial thighs, and the medial areas of the left calf, left foot and leg. (Appendix D)*
- *Stryker frame circle bed; must lie on stomach for a week.*

10/29/80......................Pseudomonas infection found

Sulfamylon cream administered to wounds.

11/2/80...........................Grafts declared "excellent"

Returning to Silvadene cream instead of Sulfamyon cream!

11/4/80.........................Scheduled to begin walking

Dizzy; had to wait.

11/5/80............................Began walking; made it!

11/7/80.............................Measured for JOBST

To be delivered in two weeks.

11/7/80............................Physical Therapy evaluation

Doing well in all areas. Encouraged to dress himself, brush teeth on his own, and shave himself.

11/11/80............Conference at church with Dr. Lee Roberson

Ken was able to go to the meeting dressed in pajamas and a robe. Sat in an easy chair purchased by his parents.

11/14/80.......................................Discharged

Paul and Ann left for home after eating a late lunch with us.

11/15/80........................First time to bathe Ken at home

Brother Foster "happened" to call when it was about time to get Ken out of the tub. Brother Foster came to show Beth how! It worked until Ken was strong enough to get out on his own.

11/16/80........Attended regular church services for the first time

Wore loose-fitting jogging outfit.

11/17–11/29/80..........................Therapy at St. John's

11/26/80 ....Received JOBST garments

- *Arrived late in the day so no attempt made to put them on.*
- *Beth's family came for Thanksgiving!*

11/27/80...............................Thanksgiving Day

- *Ken wore "real" clothes for the first time*
- *Soaking, debridement, and JOBST took 2½ hours total. Hard time getting on the JOBST gloves because of the pain it caused Ken.*

11/28/80...................Brian Camburn took Ken to therapy

Family still here!

11/29/80..Shoes

Bought shoes that fit over JOBST and still having to wrap areas not yet closed. Instead of 8½ D, we had to buy 9½ EE slip-ons.

11/30/80..........................Tied a tie for the first time

Brad Schaller taught Ken to tie a tie with one hand! It worked!

12/1/80 - 6/6/81..........Therapy at Christian Hospital Northeast

12/2/80...................First haircut since before the accident

12/2/80..............................First time out shopping

At Jamestown Mall with many rest intervals due to weakness and sore toes.

12/3/80...................................First time to drive

Drove home from Christian Hospital NE after therapy.

12/3/80.............................General look of wounds

His right side almost enclosed and looks good. The left side has quite a ways to go. Having trouble with blisters on his toes.

12/4/80.............................Readjustment of JOBST

Took Ken to JOBST office for a refit. Toes cutout of the feet area because of the pain and blisters caused on his big toes. Experiencing tingling sensation in left leg.

12/6/80............................Burn Clinic appointment

Doctor says Ken looks good. If possible, daily therapy prescribed for 1-2 years. With plans to reduce to fewer days a week as necessary. Saw burn unit staff; they're great!

12/7/80.........................First time for Ken to preach

Ken had to sit down to preach at Grace! Television media in attendance with Rick Ame reporting (KTVI, Channel 2 in St. Louis).

12/8/80.....................................General notes

- *Therapy: Ken can slightly bend metacarpophalangeal (MP) joints (third joint up from end of finger) on left hand—a beginning!*
- *His right side is virtually healed closed. His left side still has a 3-inch long opening of about ½ inch at the widest point.*

12/9/80. . . . . .First eye appointment

Eyes checked for new glasses after his were destroyed in the crash. When asked, "Why so long," we explained our 2½ hours each day debriding, dressing, and putting on JOBST; therapy at the hospital and at home; etc.

12/25/80. . . . . .First time to shower

- *Ken's wounds are completely healed, closed, no longer needing debridement.*
- *I learned I could wash his JOBST in the washing machine on gentle and hang them to dry. Saved me hours!*

10/4–6/81. . . . . .Reconstructive Surgery

At St. John's Mercy Medical Center to correct the subluxation of the MP joint on the thumb of Ken's left hand. A pin was put in the MP joint and a full thickness graft was placed in the palm of the hand to release the scar tissue that was causing the joint to pull toward the palm of his hand.

10/17/81. . . . . . .Outpatient Therapy at Christian Hospital Northeast

A splint was made for Ken to wear on his left hand after reconstructive surgery. The surgery was successful and only required the wearing of the splint for therapy.

Appendix D
Surgery Notes

Dr. Ayvasian's Report on September 17, 1980

Examination of the chest at 3:00 a.m. and then at 5:00 a.m. on 9-17-80, shows fractures of the second, third, fourth, fifth and sixth rib on the right posteriorly also possible the seventh rib with no significant displacement. There is definite evidence of increased density in the right upper lobe in the right mid lung which could well represent hemorrhage in the lung parenchyma. There apparently is a small apical pneumothorax. A nasogastric tube is in place at the time of the second examination. The left lung field is well expanded and clear with no evidence of lung contusion. There is not evidence of a pleural effusion.

Examination of the abdomen by means of a KUB at 3:15 a.m. on 9-17-80, shows a normal distribution of air in the gastrointestinal tract. No evidence of fractures of the lumbar spine or pelvis can be identified. There is no evidence of a dynamic ileum or any evidence of mechanical obstruction.

Examination in the Burn Unit at 5:00 - 5:30 a.m. on 9-17-80

30 year old minister was involved in an airplane crash early this morning at Spirit of St. Louis Airport, coming from Kansas City. The patient is the only survivor. Three other passengers did not survive the crash, as a result of electrocution. The patient remembers only the

ambulance, and apparently the airplane hit 7200 volt lines through the trees, following a storm. The patient was found conscious, in mud, and brought to our emergency room after midnight. He was fully alert. On examination, he complained of neck pain, but was oriented times three, had abrasions and contusions of the forehead and scalp. His pulses were good. He had a full rales in the right posterior lung field. Cardiac tones were normal. He was tender over the sternum. Abdomen was…non-tender. The skin showed leathery, brown, tan, whitish burns of the left leg, calf, circumferentially and left posterior thigh and buttocks, left hand and fingers and wrists and on the right hand, drama hands, which were pink and red in color. The left leg was tense in the anterior and posterior compartment. There were no Doppler pulses in the left hand forefingers. Only Doppler pulses were noted in the left foot and ankle.

He was treated with hypotonic lactated saline and Silvadene cream.

Escharotomies—September 17, 1980

September 17, 1980, left leg anterior and posterior compartment escharotomies and left thigh posterior compartment escharotomy and left hand and forefingers escharotomies and debridement of loose nails and eschars.

Procedure: After cleansing the wounds that were heavily contaminated with mud with saline and Betadine prep and usual drapes, the scalpel was used to proceed with an anterior compartment escharotomy on the left leg which started between titular and fibular head, and extended all the way down to ankle through round eschar. There was hardly any bleeding, and the escharotomy was carried all the way down to fascia with good release. A small fasciotomy was done just to inspect the underlying muscle which was pink and viable. Therefore, no fasciotomy was done. The posterior leg escharotomy was then done starting from the ankle and extending across the popliteal space midway up the thigh with good separation. Following the escharotomy, the left dorsalis pedis pulse was palpable initially, it was present and detectable only by doppler. Bleeding points were cauterized, and one ankle vessel was ligated with catgut and Silvadene cream dressing and bandages were then applied. The right leg had no circumferential leathery burns, and therefore, no tight compression, so no escharotomy was done on the right side. In the left hand, a doppler pulse was detected on the thumb only and the four fingers of the left hand had no doppler pulses. Therefore, the escharotomy of the hand dorsum was then done in longitudinal direction, and then this was connected in transverse direction just proximal to the m-p joints, and with extensions on the radial side of each finger including the thumb where escharotomy was extended all the way up to the volar aspect of the wrist where a constricting brown eschar was present. The bleeders were cauterized for hemostasis which was adequate in all fingers and immediately following escharotomy of the hand dorsum which was T-shaped in its five prong extension along the radial aspect of the fingers. Good doppler pulses were present after the escharotomy in all fingers of the left hand and the thumb. The patient received 10 to 15 mg of Demerol IV at hydration during the procedure and 5 mg of Valium was given.

First Scheduled Surgery—October 6, 1980

Tangential excision and split thickness skin autografts to right hand, right foot, leg and posterior thigh and left hand and amputation at the transmedial phalangeal level of left little finger, middle finger, index finger and proximal phalangeal amputation of left ring finger and distal phalanx of left thumb.

Procedure: After Betadine prep and the usual drapes and under satisfactory general anesthesia, dermatome was used to obtain five very long sheets of split thickness auto graphs from the right thigh, and the buttocks area. Donor site was dressed with polyurethane foam and saline dressings. The harvested autografts were meshed to 11/2 times and 3 times expansion ratio with a Zimmer mesher. A Goullian dermatome with #50 guard was used to excise the eschars of the left hand and right hand. Amputation of the thumb tip through the distal phalanx was necessary and transmiddle phalangeal for the index, middle and the little finger and trans proximal phalangeal of the left ring finger, as the bones were necrotic as well and were black in color. A Goullian dermatome was used to tangentially excise the eschars down to tendons, fascia, of both hands, all fingers and thumb, the palm of the hand on the left side and dorsum of the hand and the wrist on the right hand. The right hand was injured to a lesser degree, and all the dorsal aspect of the fingers and hypothenar eminence. The harvested auto grafts were placed to 11/2 expansion ratio, over the entire excised area and then dressed with saline dressings. Subsequently a Gouollian and Brown dermatome were used to tangentially excise the eschars of the right foot, ankle, and leg and posterior thigh, down to bleeding fat. The foot was covered with meshed autografts with 11/2-1 extension ratio and the leg and thigh were covered with 3:1 expansion ratio and right knee was covered with 11/2:1 extension ratio.

The wounds dressed with saline, split thickness bandages and then the knees splinted in extension. The patient tolerated the procedure well, and received three units of packed cells and three liters of saline solution. He returned to the recovery room in satisfactory condition.

Second Scheduled surgery—October 14, 1980

T*angential excision and* split thickness skin autografts to left foot, leg and thigh and amputation of left little toe and partial amputation of distal phalanges of second and third toes of left foot.

Procedure: After alcohol prep and the usual drapes, satisfactory general anesthesia, Brown dermatome was used to obtain split thickness skin autografts from the medial aspect of the left thigh, and the buttocks on the left side, and the entire left flank and chest. The donor sites were dressed with polyurethane foam and the harvested autografts were meshed 3:1 and 11/2:1 with the Zimmer meshed expansion ratio. Then a Brown dermatome and the Goullian dermatome was used to excise the eschars of the left foot, leg, ankle, and thigh, all the way down to muscle and fascia, and muscle and fat were excised in most places of the leg and the foot there were thromboses veins and subcutaneous fat and these were excised, and bleeders were ligated with catgut. Excision was essentially down to fascia, and muscle of the leg, and down to fat and fascia in the thigh, and down to fascia in the foot. The second and third and fourth toes were partially amputated and debrided, distal phalanx level and the left little toe was amputated with proximal interphalangeal joint level and the skin preserved and rotated laterally and the entire harvested autografts were placed over the excised areas and covering the entire tangentially excised area. The patient received four units of packed cells and about two liters of lactated ringers, and tolerated the procedure well, and was returned to the recovery room in satisfactory condition. Grafts were dressed with saline soaked split thickness bandages, and the lower limb was splinted in extension.

Third Scheduled Surgery—October 27, 1980

Tangential excision and split thickness skin autografts to buttocks, posterior, upper thighs and on medial aspect of the left popliteal space and debridement grafting of toes.

Procedure: After alcohol prep and the usual drapes, a Brown dermatome was used to obtain several sheets of split thickness autografts from the right buttocks, flank, and chest. The donor site was dressed with Silvadene cream and the patient was then turned on his side and the hypertrophic granulations of the buttocks and posterior thighs at the buttocks crease and perianal area and lateral thighs and medial thighs was well as popliteal space and on medial areas of the left calf, lateral medial aspect and lateral aspect of the left foot and dorsum of the toes were some necrotic bone was also debrided and a small patch of the right calf where all hypertrophic granulations were excised and some of the peroneus tendons which were necrotic and exposed were excised partially and then the autographs were meshed three to one and one and a half to one expansion ratio and were placed over the entire excised areas of the left foot and leg and this was bandaged to the knee with Kling and split thickness bandages, while the patient was still in supine position, then the patient was turned to the prone position on the circle electric bed and the buttocks and perineal area, posterior thighs, popliteal space were covered after additional tangential excision with a Goullian dermatome #30, of the hypertrophic granulations and the area was then dressed with a layer of dressings. The patient received two units of packed cells during the procedure. He tolerated well and was then sent to the recovery room in satisfactory condition.

Appendix E
Biographical Sketch
Ken and Beth Spilger

Ken graduated from Tennessee Temple University (1973) and Temple Baptist Seminary (1975). Beth also graduated from Tennessee Temple University (1975). Both have done further study with Pioneer Bible Institute. Ken has been the pastor of Grace Baptist Church in the Greater St. Louis area for over thirty-seven years. Before that, Ken pastored in North Georgia and in rural Nebraska.

In 1980, Ken was the only survivor of a small plane crash. He experienced third degree burns on thirty percent of his body which required a lengthy recovery. God is using this tragedy to deepen His work in their life and ministry.

Ken and Beth have been married forty years. They now have seven children and eight grandchildren. God has given them a vision to raise up godly generations who will impact this world for Christ now, and for generations to come.